RAV DOVBER PINSON

awakenings

DRAWING LIFE FROM
THE WEEKLY TORAH READING

Published by IYYUN Publishing
650 Sackett Street
Brooklyn, NY 11217

www.iyyun.com

Iyyun Publishing books may be purchased for educational, business or sales promotional use. For information please email: contact@iyyun.com

Editor: Reb Matisyahu Brown
Proofreading / Editing: Yaakov Gershon
Cover and book design: RP Design and Development

ISBN 978-1-7367026-6-6

Pinson, Dovber 1971-
AWAKENINGS: Drawing Life from the Weekly Torah Reading
1. Judaism 2. Jewish Spirituality 3. General Spirituality

RAV DOVBER PINSON

awakenings
DRAWING LIFE FROM
THE WEEKLY TORAH READING

IYYUN PUBLISHING

DEDICATED TO
ONE WHO DESIRES TO REMAIN

ANONYMOUS

האדם יראה לעינים וה' יראה ללבב

"Man sees only what is visible,
but Hashem sees into the heart"

———————

DEDICATED TO

CHESTON AND LARA MIZEL שיחיו

May Hashem, the Infinite Source of all blessings,
continue to bless them and their families with good health,
prosperity and clarity of vision.

contents

opening

THIS WEEK AND EVERY WEEK, ACROSS EVERY CONTINENT on the globe, communities will gather to chant and contemplate a specific portion of the Torah. Individuals and groups will spend many joyful hours each week studying this portion, decoding and internalizing its messages and *Ko'ach* / power. These practices fill each participant with nourishment and strength; one receives many blessings and infusions of wisdom and guidance in his or her spiritual, intellectual, emotional and physical life. As a result, one's important decisions often become easier, relationships become more whole and stable, the mind and heart become more luminous and clear, and one's service to family, community and nation flows with Divine benefit.

We celebrate each of these weekly readings with the vivid sense that we are receiving the Torah anew. Indeed, our sages teach us that when a community reads from the Torah scroll, it is as if they are actually receiving the Torah at Mount Sinai" (*Zohar* 2, p. 206a). Every individual can experience a miniature *Matan Torah* / Giving of the Torah, a present-moment revelation of the Blessed Creator, the Source of all lives. And just as at Mount Sinai, sick individuals were healed in the tremendous downflow of blessings, when the Torah portion is recited in community, healing, power and blessings are drawn down to meet the changing needs of each individual (We read the Torah 248 times a year, corresponding to the 248 main parts of the body: Rebbe Yehudah HaChasid, *Sefer Gimatriyos*, 5. See note 32. The Torah gives our entire body strength).

Every week, something unique and new is revealed in the world. This revelation streams through the particular stories, laws and moral examples of that week's portion — but also through the inner light of each of its words and letters, and the commentaries of each great Torah sage and teacher throughout history on that text.

Reciting and studying the Torah every week, and imbibing its light and blessings, is a tradition dating back to the times of Moshe, the Exodus from Egypt, the Revelation at Mount Sinai, and the journey through the Desert (*Baba Kama*, 82a). In fact, it was Moshe himself who instituted reading from the Torah every week (*Yerushalmi*, *Megillah*, 4:1. *Meseches Sofrim*, 10:1. Ramban on *Vayikra*, 23:2). Yet, throughout the ages there were various customs on how to divide the Torah into portions. There was a custom of communities living in *Eretz Yisrael* / the Land of Israel to read the Torah over the course of three years (לבני מערבא דמסקי לדאורייתא בתלת שנין: *Megillah*, 29b. Rashi, ad loc).[*] The custom of those living in *Bavel* / Babylon was to read the entire Torah over the course of one year. Today, and for over a thousand years at least, the prevailing custom is to complete the entire Torah in one year (Rambam, *Hilchos Tefilah*, 13:1. The Rambam himself, when he lived in Egypt, wanted to abolish Eretz Yisrael's practice and unify the reading, and have all communities read the Torah on a yearly cycle. The Rambam's son, Rebbe Avraham, writes that other leaders stopped the Rambam's efforts).

---

[*] If the Torah was divided into a three-year (or perhaps three-and-a-half-year) cycle, it is clear why Chazal living in Eretz Yisrael referred to 175 *Parshiyos* / portions of the Torah. Subtracting the weeks that have special *Yom Tov* / holy day readings, every year contains about 50 weekly readings (see also *Zohar* 1, p. 100). Three years would have 150 weekly readings, plus another 25 readings in an additional half year: א"ר יהושע בן לוי אנא מימי לא הסתכלתי גו ספר דאגדתא אלא חד זמן אסתכלת ואשתכחת כתיב מאה ושבעים וחמשה פרשיות שכתוב בתורה דבור ודבור אמירה וציווי כנגד שנותיו של אברהם אבינו. In this way, the number of weekly Parshiyos also corresponds to the 175 years of Avraham's life: *Meseches Sofrim*, 16:19. See *Megaleh Amukos*, Chayei Sarah. Interestingly, the *Sefer HaChinuch* tells us that the Mitzvah of "erasing Amalek" (which is performed by reading *Devarim*, 25:17-19) is to be performed once a year — or once every two or three years. Although the source of this ruling is unknown, it suggests one way that the different customs of dividing the Torah into Parshios may have fulfilled this Mitzvah in the course of their Torah reading cycle: ודי לנו בזה לזכור הענין פעם אחת בשנה או בשתי שנים או שלש. והנה בכל מקומות ישראל קוראים ספר התורה בשנה אחת או בשתים או שלש לכל הפחות, והנה הם יוצאים בכך מצוה זו: *Sefer HaChinuch*, Mitzvah, 603.

In order to read the entire Torah in one year, the Torah is divided into 54 *Parshiyos* / portions (although, as above, *Zohar* 1, p. 100 says there are 50 Parshiyos).* Others write that there are 53 Parshiyos (since Nitzavim and Vayelech are essentially one portion, and they are only divided in order to separate the Parshah of *Ki Savo* from Rosh Hashanah: *Tikkunei Zohar*, Tikkun 13). The number 53 is the numerical value of the word גן / *Gan* / Garden, and indeed, the Torah is associated with the Tree of Life in *Gan Eden* / the Garden of Eden. In any case, none of the subdivisions mentioned are the way the Torah was subdivided originally, nor are they the manner in which the Torah is divided within the actual Torah scroll.

Our printings of the Torah (*Chumash* / 'Five Books' of Moshe) are divided into numbered verses and chapters, as well as Parshiyos (*Berachos*, 12a). However, a 'Parshah' within a Torah scroll is a different matter. There is no punctuation in a scroll, so there is usually no indication of the end of a verse. Addi-

---

* Technically speaking, different factors modulate the number of Shabboses upon which a weekly Parshah is read each year. In a year of 365 days, there are 52 weeks and 1 day; if that extra day happens to be Shabbos, there will be 53 Shabboses that year. However, on a Shabbos that falls during one of the *Shalosh Regalim* / Three Festivals or Rosh Hashanah or Yom Kippur, the weekly Parshah is replaced by a special Yom Tov reading, sometimes decreasing the number of Shabbos Torah readings to 50 on an average year [seeming to support the perspective of the Zohar]. However, the luni-solar Hebrew calendar contains up to 55 weeks when an additional month is inserted to keep it in sync with both 'lunar' months and the 'solar' year. Finally, in some instances, a Shabbos will have a 'double Parshah' — two portions read on a single Shabbos.

tionally, there are no chapter headings or changes in 'font', so neither the Parshiyos designated by our sages, nor the numbered chapters in the printed Chumash are indicated in a Torah scroll. There are, however, clearly indicated groupings of text into very long 'paragraphs' or 'chapters', and these also happen to be called Parshiyos.

There are two types of Parshiyos in the Torah scroll: those that are *Sasum* / closed and those that are *Pesuchah* / open. A *Parshah* that is *Sasum* is divided from the subsequent portion by the space of nine letters. Here, a new Parshah begins on the same line where the Parshah Sasum ended. With very little space between one Parshah and the next, the preceding one is considered 'closed'.

A Parshah Pesuchah is followed by empty space extending to the end of the line, so that the next Parshah begins on the following line; thus it is 'open' at the end. The previous Parshah ends before the end of the column, leaving a space at the end of the line, and the new Parshah begins at the start of the next line, albeit without an indentation.

There are a total of 669 such Parshiyos in the Torah. Obviously, these should not be confused with the 53 Parshiyos that today we call the 'weekly Parshah'.

All *Chumashim* / printed books of the Torah have not only enumerated verses and divisions into weekly Parshiyos, but also divisions into chapters.

These chapters were actually introduced by non-Jews during the early part of the 13ᵗʰ Century. Since Jews were at that time sometimes forced to debate the intent of the Torah with their non-Jewish neighbors, it was necessary for them to learn and employ the chapter-verse system in use by non-Jews. With the publication of the *Mikraos Gedolos* (a printing of the Torah accompanied by various classical commentaries) in the year 1516–1517 by Bomberg Publishing House, and even more so with their publication in 1525, chapters became common and standard in all printed books of the Torah.

Nothing is by mere coincidence, even these 'superimposed' verses and chapters, and even though they did not come from Torah sources, meaning can be drawn from their arrangement within the text and numbering (see *Likutei Sichos*, 16, p. 229, note 40). This is all the more so true of the weekly Parshiyos of the Torah delineated by our sages.

Writing about the 669 Parshiyos within the Torah scroll, the illustrious and famed *Mekubal* / Kabbalist, Rebbe Avraham Azulai (1570–1643) writes (*Chesed l'Avraham*, 2, Nahar 14):

"And know: the secrets of the Torah and her ideas, are branches that emanate from the higher dimensions. For in the Torah there are Parshiyos, and in every Parshah there are spiritual emanations gathered into many packets arranged as Pesukim, and these are gathered together to form a Parshah. Similarly, there is a gathering of words that make a Parshah, and a gathering of letters that make a word. Thus, we find that the letters

are the finest branches, and the threads of their flames spread out from each word, which is a spiritual emanation, and the word is the larger branch from which flow all the fine branches, and the letters 'nurse' from the word, and the word nurses from the Pasuk, and the Pasuk nurses from the Parshah, and the Parshiyos nurse from the Essence of the Torah, and all of it is (one great) spiritual emanation, and all the emanations (within it) emanate from one another...."

"Parshiyos" in this teaching refers to the 'paragraphs' indicated within the Torah scroll, but the teaching is also applicable to the Parshiyos of the week. In fact, we find that centuries ago, *Chazal* / the sages of the Talmud and Zohar, teased out meanings from the number of weekly Parshiyos (whether 50, 53, or 175). This displays their understanding that nothing is mere coincidence, and certainly issues of Torah and the customs of Klal Yisrael.

How the Parshah falls out in relation to the calendar is Divinely orchestrated, as is all of life. The Torah portion that is read each week is intricately connected with the spiritual themes, Divine revelations, and human needs arising in the current week, day, and season, as well as time in history.*

---

* The traditional, known source for reading the Torah on Shabbos is the Gemara in *Baba Kama,* 82a: כיון שהלכו שלשת ימים בלא תורה נלאו עמדו נביאים שביניהם ותיקנו להם שיהו קורין בשבת / "Since (Klal Yisrael) traveled for three days without hearing any Torah, they became weary. Therefore, the Prophets among them arose and instituted that they should read from the Torah each Shabbos." In order to hear Torah at least every three days, we read the Torah on Shabbos, and on Mondays and Thursdays.

The Gemara also says at the end of *Megilah,* 32a: "וידבר משה את מועדי ה' אל

בני ישראל", מצותן שיהיו קורין אותן כל אחד ואחד בזמנו / "And Moshe declared the appointed seasons of Hashem to the Children of Israel.' This indicates that part of the Mitzvah of the *Yomim Tovim* / Festivals is that we should read the portion relating to each Yom Tov in its appointed time." Rashi explains, ללמוד מכאן שמצוה לקרות ביום המועד מעניני מועד של אותו יום המועדות: *Megilah*, 31a. This is a source for reading the Torah on Yom Tov, and specifically reading sections connected to the Yom Tov. For example, on Pesach, we are to read the Torah portions that speak about Pesach.

There is another version of this teaching in Gemara, in *Meseches Sofrim* (10:1): משה הקניא להם לישראל שיהו קורין בתורה בשבתות וימים טובים ובראשי חדשים ובחולו של מועד שנאמר (ויקרא כג:מד) וידבר משה את מועדי ה' אל בני ישראל / "Moshe established for Klal Yisrael that they should read from the Torah on Shabbos and Yomim Tovim…as it is stated, 'And Moshe declared to the children of Israel the appointed seasons of Hashem.'" Here the Gemara suggests that Moshe established that we should read the Torah portions connected to the Yom Tov on that Yom Tov — and on Shabbos we should read about Shabbos.

In this way, there are two different sources for reading the Torah every Shabbos. One source is the old institution of the Prophets to read from the Torah every three days (Shabbos, Monday and Thursday), and the other source is from Moshe, to read every 'season'; on each Yom Tov read about that Yom Tov and on each Shabbos about the subject of Shabbos.

The question regarding the second source is, it's understood that on every Yom Tov we need to read the Torah portions connected to that Yom Tov, but is it true that on every Shabbos we should read Torah portions about Shabbos? Shouldn't we read a different portion each Shabbos and in this way complete the reading of the entire Torah?

To understand this, first we need to explore another idea. There is a teaching in the name of Rebbe Chayim Brisker that suggests that the reading of the Torah on Shabbos has a twofold purpose: 1) Accomplishing the Mitzvah of *Limud HaTorah* / learning Torah, and 2) Reenacting *Kabbalas HaTorah* / receiving the Torah in a miniature way.

There is an argument among the *Poskim* / Codifiers of Halachah: Do we need to stand when listening to the public reading of the Torah? The Mechaber rules that we do not, whereas the Rama writes that there are those who are more stringent upon themselves and do stand (*Orach Chayim*, 146:4).

Many reasons are offered why a person would need to stand when the Torah is read (*Mordechai*, Shabbos, 422. *Shu'T MaHara M'panu*, 91). The *Bach* writes that the reason we should stand is because, as the Zohar writes, when we are listening to the Torah being read it is like "receiving the Torah at Mount Sinai," and since Klal Yisrael stood at Mount Sinai when the Torah was given, the custom is to stand (אכן נראה דלאו מדינא היה נוהג כך אלא כיון דצריך כל אדם להעלות על דעתו כששומע הקריאה מפי הקורא כאילו קיבלה באותה שעה מה"ס וכ"כ בס' הזוהר ומביאו ב"י ובה"ס היו כל ישראל עומדין כדכתיב אנכי עומד בין ה' וביניכם לכך כשם שניתנה בס"ת. See also *Yerushalmi*, 4:1: הגון וראוי שיהיו עומדין בשעה שקורין בס"ת באימה ויראה כך אנו צריכין לנהוג בה באימה ויראה. רבי חגי אמר רבי שמואל בר רב יצחק עאל לכנישתא. חמא חונה קאים מתרגם ולא מקים בר נש תחתוי. אמר ליה. אסיר לך. כשם שנתנה על ידי סרסור כך אנו צריכין לנהוג בה על ידי סרסור).

Now, if the main reason for reading the Torah is to fulfill the obligation of 'learning' Torah, then we do not need to stand, as learning Torah can be done sitting (משמת רבן גמליאל ירד חולי לעולם והיו למדין תורה מיושב: *Megilah*, 21a), but if the main reason is to reenact Kabbalas HaTorah, then we would to stand.

We read the Torah for both reasons, however. On every Shabbos we need to fulfill our obligation to study Torah, and on every Shabbos there is a *Kabbalas HaTorah / Receiving of the Torah from Sinai*. Perhaps these two reasons are connected to the two sources mentioned above, that the source that says we read the Torah as not to go three days without Torah is connected with the purpose of Limud HaTorah. The source that says we read the Torah because "Moshe declared to the Children of Israel the appointed times of Hashem" — and thus we read Parshiyos that are connected with the current day — is connected to the reason of Kabbalas HaTorah. What's more, *Matan Torah* / the Giving of the Torah itself actually occurred on Shabbos.

The reason Moshe instituted reading the Torah on every Yom Tov and Shabbos is that the source of every Yom Tov and Shabbos is the Torah, and that day comes about through the *Ko'ach* / power of the Torah. In this sense, when the Torah tells the story of Pesach, it is not merely 'recording' the events that happened, rather, it is the reverse. The source of *Yetziyas Mitzrayim* / Going out of Egypt is the Torah, the blueprint of reality. The cause of the events of Yetziyas Mitzrayim is their stories in the Torah.

For this reason, there is a relationship between the events of the week and the Parshah. The Shaloh HaKadosh, Rebbe Yeshayahu HaLevi Horowitz (16th Century Prague/Israel) writes that the *Yamim Tovim* / holy days of the year are related to the Torah portions that are read during the week in which the Yom Tov falls out. There are no coincidences, and a certain Torah portion is read on the week of Rosh Hashanah, for example, precisely because that Torah portion has a connection with what Rosh Hashanah is all about.

Similarly, the Torah reading of each Yom Tov speaks about what is occurring on a cosmic, spiritual level on that particular day and season. The Parshiyos that we read on Shabbos are intricately connected to that day, week, and season.

The Year Cycle & the Torah Cycle:
Every season of the year relates to the Parshiyos that are being read at that time. Every month has a particular quality, and each week within that month unfolds part of that quality through its Torah reading.*

This is also true for the events commemorated by each Yom Tov, and it is also seemingly the case with Shabbos. Every week, on Shabbos, there is a small 'Kabbalas HaTorah', and that revelation is the 'cause' of that particular Shabbos. The Ko'ach of the weekly Parshah manifests the qualities of that Shabbos, and this impregnates the week.

---

* The Mishnah (*Megillah*, 31a) says that on each Yom Tov, we need to read the Torah reading related to that Yom Tov. For example, on Pesach we read the portion that speaks about Pesach, and on Sukkos, about Sukkos. This,

When the summer ends and the new year begins, we start reading *Bereishis*, the creation narrative. There is a palpable sensation of the newness of the year that has just begun, and appropriately, we read about the beginning of Creation, the birth of the world and of humanity.

Then, the month of Cheshvan comes along, and with it, autumn, which is the beginning of the rainy season in the Northern Hemisphere. Thus, we read the Torah portion of Noach / Noah, which talks of the Great Flood. By Divine Providence,

---

שנאמר (ויקרא כג, מד) וידבר משה :says the Mishnah, we learn from the Pasuk את מועדי ה' אל בני ישראל. מצותן שיהו קורין כל אחד ואחד בזמנו / "As it is stated: 'And Moshe declared to the children of Israel the appointed seasons of the of Hashem' (*Vayikra*, 23:44), and this indicates that part of the Mitzvah of the Festivals is that the people should read the portion relating to them, each one in its appointed time." The verse quoted is the final verse of Chapter 23, a chapter speaking about all the Yamim Tovim, which are called מועדי ה' / appointed seasons of Hashem. Yet, the beginning of the Parshah and Chapter 23 begins: 'וידבר ה' אל־משה לאמר דבר אל־בני ישראל ואמרת אלהם מועדי ה אשר־תקראו אתם מקראי קדש אלה הם מועדי ששת ימים תעשה מלאכה וביום השביעי שבת שבתון מקרא־קדש כל־מלאכה לא תעשו שבת הוא / Hashem spoke to Moshe saying, "Speak to the Children of Israel and say to them, 'These are My appointed times, the appointed times of Hashem, which you shall proclaim as sacred occasions. Six days you shall do work and on the seventh day shall a complete Shabbos, not work shall be done, it is Shabbos...'" (23:1–3).

Thus, part of the מועדי ה' is Shabbos, and since we know from the Pasuk וידבר משה את מועדי ה' that we have to read on every Yom Tov what is relevant to that Yom Tov, by deduction, we also know that we have to read the Torah every Shabbos (see also Rif from the Yerushalmi, *Kesef Mishnah*, Hilchos Tefilah, 12:1). And thus, by extension, if on Pesach we read about Pesach because that is what is occurring during this season, then we understand that on Shabbos we read a portion of the Torah that is relevant to this time of the year, and this particular Shabbos.

this is also the month in which the Flood began.

As the nights become longer, darker and colder, and thus more 'challenging', we begin to read about the challenging journeys of Avraham and his wife Sarah, the darkness they encounter, and their struggles to have children. We continue with the birth of Yitzchak and his journeys and challenges, and the birth of his children with Rivka — Ya'akov and Eisav, and their strife with each other. Then we continue with the birth of the children of Ya'akov, their quarrels between each other culminating with the sale of Yoseph, and his descent into the darkness of Egypt.

During the longest nights of the year, we read of the great prophetic dreams in the Torah, from the dreams of Ya'akov to those of Yoseph and Paroh / Pharaoh.

Toward the end of the longest nights of the year, after the winter solstice (around the secular New Year), we start reading about the collective exile in Egypt and then the first glimmers of the light of redemption. Gradually, events turn around into the positive. After the long winter of uncertainty, finally Klal Yisrael is being redeemed, spring is approaching, the winter nights are getting shorter and more and more daylight is being revealed.

A renewed sense of possibility is attained and we begin to read the Torah portions that speak of the construction and building of the *Mishkan* / temporary Temple in the Desert.

Finally, the spring bursts forth and we feel pure, empowered, and ready for life. With the positivity of our study of redemption, we are empowered and ready to repair and refine anything that needs our attention. Thus, we start reading the Torah portions that speak of the offerings that refine the world and the atonements and rectifications for past misdeeds.

After the initial excitement of Pesach and the first month, we may feel a little down. This is a perfect time to work on ourselves; thus, we read Torah portions related to purity and holiness.

We are moving along smoothly, reading the Torah portions in which Klal Yisrael is readying themselves to actually enter the Promised Land, and then they encounter setbacks. We read of rebellions, contention, complaining, and national meltdowns. These portions we read as we enter the hotter days of the summer.

When we reach the peak of the heat of summer, we can become lethargic and sluggish, stuck in the heat of the summer. We then listen as Moshe recounts our journey in the hot Desert in the final book of the Torah.

Right before Rosh Hashanah, we read of how 'We are standing, all of us, in front of Hashem.' This prepares us to do exactly that on Rosh Hashanah, as we evaluate our entire past year.

In this way, the cycle of the year seems to bend to the arch of the Torah portions that we are reading. Yet, on a deeper level, the reverse is true: the Torah portion is the root source of the conditions that we are experiencing, and each Torah portion gives us the Ko'ach, energy, and information that we need to deal wisely with what is being served. Indeed, the Tikkun of each week, what is being created in that week, and what needs correction, are all related to the Parshah that is being read that week (*Tikunim Chadashim*, Ramchal, Tikuna 33).

This is true on both a cosmic and microcosmic level. For this reason, the illustrious Chasam Sofer (1762–1839) writes that sometimes a person who is learning Torah (for example, the Torah portion of the week) finds within that material issues related to his own personal life. The Torah reading of the week becomes a guiding light for us, showing us how to act or move forward. Not everyone, and not always, is privy to noticing these connections and experiencing these 'revelations' (as the Chasam Sofer connects this to a form of 'revelation' as in *Chulin*, 95b). Yet, they are always actually there, whether we notice them or not.

Live With the Times:
The Alter Rebbe (1745–1812), the holy and profound first *Rebbe* / leader and teacher of Chabad, declared, "One needs to live with the times." This means we need to live with the portion of the week, demonstrating that each Parshah of the week has an intricate connection with the qualities and events of that week. Every part of the Torah contains life-lessons for all times and all events, yet the current Parshah has a precise relationship with current events and issues, both external and internal.

There is a principle in Chassidic and Kabbalistic teachings: everything in the Torah, from the light of each of its laws, statements, stories, and truths, is contained within every human being and relevant to every person's life throughout all generations (*Ohr HaMeir*, Pinchas). Indeed, "There is no word of Torah that is not connected to each individual soul" (*Beis Ya'akov*, Hakdamah), and "All that is written in the Torah, from the first word to the last, is relevant and connected to every person" (Pirush HaGra, *Sifra Tziniusa*, p. 34. See also *Ohr HaGanuz L'Tzadikim*, Miketz. Every person has within him a Moshe, Aaron, Egypt, and so forth. *Toldos Ya'akov Yoseph*, Bereishis. *Baal Shem Tov al HaTorah*, Shemos, 19).

This means that every letter, every word, every event, and every character in the Torah, carries some guidance, encouragement, or blessing for you at every moment.

The word *Torah* comes from the word *Hora'ah*, meaning teaching or life lessons (Maharal, *Tiferes Yisrael*, Chap. 9. תורה שהיא לשון הוראה: *Nesivos Olam*, Nesiv HaEmunah, 2. Note *Zohar* 3, 53b: אמאי אקרי תורה. בגין דאורי). The Torah is also called *Torah Ohr* / 'Torah of Light' — of illumination and guidance, showing us how to live our lives in the deepest and most meaningful way.

The Torah teaches humanity a path of hope and redemption, for the world was created for a purpose, life has meaning, and justice is the foundation of civility. The Torah reveals to us that every human being is born with the Divine Image, and also that every individual is unique and has a special role. Freedom is every person's right, and progress is inevitable. In these ways, the Torah has given hope to the world and a sense of purpose and destiny. The notion that time moves forward and that we are progressing toward a brighter future is also part of the gift of the Torah. The powerful concepts and energies of faith, adventure, possibility, freedom, future, progress, Infinity, Oneness, Compassion, Generosity, and Forgiveness all irrigate the lives of humanity through the Torah.

"There is no Parshah that is not connected with the Resurrection of the Dead" (*Yalkut Shimoni*, Ha'azinu, 941). The Torah enlightens our awareness and lets us appreciate the fact that nothing can ever really die, and even the dead will be resurrected and live again. There is always hope, even when circumstances look bleak; if we look closely enough and work hard enough, we will find kernels of redemption, possibility, and continuation. The overarching trajectory of Creation is towards redemption; all of history is moving upward and forward. It may sometimes seem that society is descending; however, it is actually crouching down to jump higher. We should never give up on humanity or on ourselves. So long as there is life, there is potential for a positive breakthrough. If things seem hopeless, it only means we are called to get up and struggle to reveal the good, and to fight for trust and hope.

Ways to Decode Meaning in the Text & Find Connection:
   To help us unpack the Wisdom of the Torah and its practical relevance — to understand how each narrative and principle applies to our life and our exact circumstances — we need to delve more deeply into the Torah and learn to sense and

decode its hints. As much as the Torah reveals to us, it conceals even more.

"The Torah, on what was it written? With black fire upon white fire" (*Tanchuma*, Bereishis, 1). "Black fire" is the letters, words, and verses of Torah, while "white fire" is the unspeakable mysteries and secrets that lie in between the letters. There are infinite, limitless expanses of wisdom that surround and encircle the limited structures of the letters. On a deeper level, infinite fountains of wisdom are contained even within the 'black fire' of the Torah; only when one reads the black letters superficially do they appear to convey superficial meanings.

In general, Torah is a revelation in which there is *Megaleh Tefach uMechaseh T'fachayim* / "exposing one handbreadth while concealing two." In other words, there can be a revelation through 'nakedness'; when the depth contained within the text is completely exposed, but the more prevalent type of revelation reveals *through concealment*. This type of disclosure communicates a mystery, a secret, as it is clear that what is being revealed is not the totality of what is present, and the secret thereby remains intact, retaining its mystery or ineffability. For example, Hashem subtly reveals Himself through a story, a law, or even a minor nuance in the spelling of a word, and this is done in such a way that one can indirectly glimpse the fact that there is endless depth and light concealed beneath the surface of the text. Yet, the holy, inner mysteries of the Torah are only freely revealed to those who honor and cling to Her and desire to know Her.

There is a beautiful metaphor from the holy Zohar, the primary text of Kabbalah, on this 'revealing while concealing' nature of the Torah, through which our love for the Revealer drives us to toil, pine, and probe deeper and deeper into the mysteries of the Torah until more and more of the Torah is revealed to us.

These are the words of the holy Zohar: "(The Torah is similar) to a lovely princess, beautiful in every way, but hidden deep within her palace. She has one lover, unknown to anyone, and he is hidden, too. Out of his love for her, this lover passes by her gate constantly, lifting his eyes to every side. She knows that her lover is hovering about her gate constantly. What does she do? She opens a little window in her hidden palace and reveals her face to her lover, then swiftly withdraws, concealing herself. No one near the lover sees her, nor reflects on her beauty — only the lover. And his heart and soul and everything within him flows out to her. And he knows that out of her love for him She revealed herself for that moment to awaken (even more love in him). So are the Divine words of the Torah; (through them She) only reveals Herself to Her lover" (*Zohar* 2, 99a).

Everything in the Torah of our Infinite Beloved has infinite meaning. Every slight or brief gesture in Torah is another revelation meant for us to notice it and awaken. Yet, it is up to us to look deeply and listen attentively to every nuance and subtlety, and to tease out more and more meaning in ways which are

consistent with the explanations of our sages, the most dedicated "lovers."

The Torah is like a flickering light that is revealed and immediately concealed. It drops subtle suggestions which then
seem to fade away, for they are meant to draw us in love to the
word of the Living G-d, to cling to every verse, every word,
every letter, and even to the way the verses are sung, to pull us
into tasting deeper and deeper meanings.

Torah study can also be seen as a code, and we are research
scientists, trying to decode, uncover, and reveal more and more
meaning from every inflection in the Torah. There are various ways to decode and tease out its deeper meaning besides
studying the Kabbalists and mystics of the Oral Tradition. Following are a few examples of how each of us can begin to open
deeper understandings encoded in the text, and discover deeper layers of beauty and guidance for our own life.*

NAME:

We may think of names as just a means of identification
in interpersonal relationships; a word refers to an individual
so we can understand an experience or story. A man alone on
an island would not need a name. Yet, in the Torah, names of
people are profoundly related to their essence. Noach means
'Rest' or respite, as he is the hero of the Flood narrative and

_____

* A more in-depth treatment of these ideas will be, G-d willing, explored in
a future series exploring the Five Books of the Torah.

provided rest for all creatures. On a deeper level, he is not only a real person but also an illustration of issues in embodying 'rest'. Avraham means 'Exalted Father' as he is the father and teacher of the exalted revelation of Monotheism; each of us carry something of his essence and function within ourselves. The 'negative' characters of the Torah also have names which express their roles. Paroh, for example, means *Peh Ra* / 'Evil Mouth', as he speaks to entice Klal Yisrael into slavery. As such, to understand the narratives of the Torah more deeply, we need to pay special attention to the meanings suggested by the names of the characters.

DIVINE NAME:

There are various different Divine names — different expressions or revelations of Hashem — in the Torah. Each time a certain Name of Hashem is used, whether in the context of a law or a narrative, it is highly significant. For example, two of the most predominant names of Hashem in the Torah are *Hashem* / 'the Four Letter Name' (Yud-Hei-Vav-Hei), and *Elokim*. Elokim represents the Divine attribute of 'Creator', 'the G-d of Creation' — in contrast to Hashem, which represents 'G-d of Revelation and Redemption'. HaKadosh Baruch Hu / the Holy One in the attribute of Elokim creates the world, and the Name Hashem redeems the world and takes us out of Egypt, literally and figuratively. *Elokim* is more generic and universal in nature, whereas *Hashem* 'personally' takes us out of Egypt and reveals Torah to us. When seeking deeper meanings and guidance for our lives, we need to take notice of when the Torah uses the Name *Hashem* and when it uses the name *Elokim*, or both, or another name.

PLACE:

Similarly, we need to notice the names of geographical places where events happen in the narratives we are studying. What the Torah calls each place is very precise and significant. If something happens in Chevron, for example, we can begin to decode its deeper meaning by considering the meaning of the root of this word: *Chevron* alludes to 'connection'. *Shechem* comes from a root that means 'rest'. The implications of an event in Shechem would be very different than if the same thing happened in Gerar, which comes from a root that means 'sojourn', or Bavel, from a root that means 'dispersion'.

WHERE FROM & WHERE TO:

It is also very important to take notice, when the Torah is describing one of the many journeys, the name of the place where that journey begins, and the name of its destination. For example, one day Ya'akov leaves Be'er Sheva ('the Well of Seven' or '...of Satisfaction"), and he journeys to Charan (the place of 'Divine Wrath'). This progression suggests a descent into darkness. When *Klal Yisrael* / the Collective of the People of Israel leave Mitzrayim / Egypt, they leave a place of *Meitzar* / restriction, constriction. When, on this journey, they avert passing through Pelishtim, we might consider that the root word of this location means '(negative) openness'; a place of mockery and licentiousness.

HOW:

Also crucial to the narrative of a journey is the mode of transportation. Are they traveling by foot, by camel, donkey, horse, or wagon? Each contains symbolic significance. A donkey is a *Chamor*, connected to the word *Chomer* / materiality. A camel is a *Gamal*, related to the word *Gemul* / giving, as in *Gemilas Chasadim* / bestowal of kindness.

TIME:

When a given event occurs, for example, in the day or at night, is also very significant. 'Day' can allude to clarity or a redemptive experience, while 'night' can allude to unclarity or a sense of exile. Similarly, most Mitzvos of the Torah are to be performed during the day, while few are performed at night. Yet, other Mitzvos do not have a time frame. Some are performed only when there is a Beis haMikdash standing, and some are "applicable for all generations."

Within a single day, does the event or Mitzvah occur in the early morning, the afternoon, or twilight?

Days on the calendar are meaningful, such as "on the fifteenth of the month," or even just "for six days" or "on the eighth day." Units of time, such as the "forty days" of the Great Flood, or "You shall count fifty days," are symbolic of deeper truths. All of these examples and more may modulate our interpretation or trigger insight.

PARALLEL STORIES:

Often, we find two or more similar storylines or twists and turns of events, allowing us to draw parallels between them. For example, the twins in one narrative, Kayin and Hevel, in some way reflect twins in another narrative, Ya'akov and Ei-sav. In this type of comparison, the narrative that happened later often comes to create a *Tikkun* / rectification for what happened in the earlier episode. The strife between Kayin and Hevel also reflects on Yoseph and his brothers, who at the end reach a reconciliation. This multifaceted meta-narrative ultimately resolves with the unity and love between the brothers Aharon and Moshe (The love between Aharon and Moshe always existed between them, and did not need to be reconciled like the Yoseph and his brothers. Note that Kayin was Hevel's older brother, Eisav was Ya'akov's older brother, Yoseph's brothers were all older than him. Aharon was the older brother of Moshe. The Tikkun is for the older brother to express only love and support for the younger brother, as with Aharon and Moshe).

Similarly, the story of one group of people can reflect on another group. When 'the House of Ya'akov goes down to Egypt, it mirrors the earlier story of 'the House of Avraham' when they went down to Egypt.

KEY WORDS:

One of the ways the Torah establishes connections between narratives that may seem unrelated at first glance is by using 'key words' or linguistic motifs. The same words, or expressions of the same etymological root, appear in different contexts, establishing a resonance between them, and this, too, invites a deeper reading of the text.

ROOT WORDS:
Most often, root words are composed of three or more letters; occasionally, they have two letters. Noticing the roots of words can help us decode deeper meanings in a text.

Rav Menachem ibn Saruk (10ᵗʰ Century Spain),* who wrote *The Machberes*, one of the earliest Biblical dictionaries (Rashi often quotes him in his Torah commentary), writes that root letters of words need to appear in all variations of the word. He deduces that it is even possible for the root of a word to be one letter, as in the word והזה / "and he shall sprinkle" (*Vayikra*, 14:26), and ומזה / "he who sprinkled" (*Bamidbar*, 19:21), and ויז / "And he shall sprinkle" (*Vayikra*, 8:11). The letter Vav (ו) here is a prefix meaning 'and', so the only letter shared in all these three words is the letter Zayin (ז), and it is thus a one letter root. (Note, the Gemara in *Kiddushin*, 56b, where the word תקדש is read as תוקד אש/ let it burn. In this way, the Shin / ש of תקדש represents אש /fire. In *Sefer Yetzirah*, 3:3, the letter Shin stands for אש /fire. שלש אמות אמ"ש בעולם אויר מים אש).

---

* Dunash Ibn Labrat, also known as, Rav Adonim HaLevi (a student of the Rasag, who later came back to Spain) wrote a series of responsa against Rav Menachem, and because of this he was removed as secretary of the great Rav Chisdai ibn Shaprut. Many Rishonim took different sides in this controversy, but Rashi quotes them both.

Most later opinions argue that all root words must have at least two letters, although sometimes one of the letters does not appear in the actual word.

HOW WORDS ARE SUNG IN PUBLIC RECITATIONS:

While the Torah is written without vowels*, we do have a *Mesorah* / a living tradition going back to Sinai, regarding not only the pronunciations of words but also their melodies. There are higher notes, lower notes, prolonged notes, and shortened

---

* Since the Torah is written without vowels, the words contain many possibilities of interpretation, as Rabbeinu Bachya writes a tremendous *Yesod* / foundation in understanding the Torah... כי בספר תורה שאינו מנוקד יוכל האדם לקרוא ואם ככה את עושה לי, בקמ"ץ תחת השי"ן, כי האותיות כשאינן מנוקדות סובלות כמה כוונות ומתחלקות לכמה ניצוצות, ומפני זה נצטוינו שלא לנקוד ספר תורה כי משמעות כל מלה ומלה לפי הנקוד ואין משמעותה עם הנקוד כי אם ענין אחד, ובלתי נקוד יוכל האדם להבין בה כמה ענינים נפלאים רבים ונכבדים והבן זה, תצטרך אותו בהרבה מקומות / "Since the Sefer Torah is not vowelized, a person could read *Oseh* / 'does' as *Osah* / 'did', as if it had a Kamatz under the Shin. This is because the letters, when they are not vowelized, can carry a few different intentions (or potential meanings), and are thus divisible into as many different 'sparks' of Divine Light. And it is due to this that we are commanded to refrain from vowelizing a Sefer Torah. If they did have vowels, each word would be limited to one meaning and topic. But when a word does not have vowels, a person can understand in it many different wondrous and honorable topics. And understand this: this ability is needed in many places in the Torah": *Rabbeinu Bachya*, Bamidbar, 11:15. Similarly, he writes, קרי ביה לא תחנם, התי"ו בפת"ח והחי"ת בשו"א ובפת"ח. ועוד דרשו בו לא תחנם לא תתן להם מתנת חנם, קרי ביה לא תחנם החי"ת בפת"ח והנו"ן בדגש. ולמדנו מכאן כמה כמה גדול כח התורה שהיא נדרשת לכמה טעמים עד שאפילו תיבה אחת היא מתפרשת לכמה ענינים לפי הנקוד, ובהתנועע הנקוד תתנועע התיבה, כי האותיות הן הגוף והנקוד הוא הנפש, וכן אמרו דמיין נקודתא באתוותא דאורייתא דמשה כנשמתא דחיי בגופא דאינש, וידוע כי אין לגוף תנועה בלתי הנפש, ובהתנועע הנפש יתנועע הגוף לכל פנים ולכל צד, כן הנקודה באותיות התורה בהשתנות הנקוד ישתנה הענין, ולכך היה הענין מוכרח בספר תורה שיהיה בלתי מנוקד כדי שתתפרש התורה לכמה פנים מבלתי כוונת הפסוק: *Rabbeinu Bachya*, Devarim, 7:2.

notes.* This phenomenon clarifies many grammatical issues since phrases such as "Do not steal" could also be read as a question: 'Do not steal?' Clearly, the Torah has a specific intention that we must understand and follow, and so there needs to be a Mesorah of how such phrases are to be read and understood. Millennia ago, the 'song' of the Torah was perhaps conducted by the helper of the one reading the Torah, and they did not have books with the *Taamei Mikra* / musical notation.** However, it has been over one thousand years since Ben Asher (and some sources tell us even much earlier) that we use Ta'amei Mikra.

The sounds of these musical notes are another way of deciphering the meaning of the text. For example, while the Torah

---

* *Megillah*, 3a. *Nedarim*, 37a. The Ran writes that the *Ta'amei Mikra* of the Torah are not *mi-d'Oraysa* / established by the revelation at Mount Sinai: שמלמדין להם טעמים דלאו מדאורייתא נינהו הלכך לא הוו בכלל חוקים ומשפטים. This is also the opinion of the Rosh: לנגן המקראות כהלכתן ולאו דאורייתא הוא ושרי ליטול שכר עליו. Ezra and the Anshei K'neses HaGedolah introduced the Ta'amei HaMikra: *Even Ezra*, Megilas Esther, 9:27. *Abarbanel*, Hakdamah, Sefer Yirmiyahu. Yet, the *Yerushalmi*, Megillah, 4:1, teaches that the Ta'amei HaMikra are indeed *Halachah l'Moshe miSinai*. See also *Zohar* 2, 205b. *Sefer Chassidim*, Siman 302. *Shu't Chasam Sofer* 6, Siman 86.

** Chazal tell us in *Berachos*, 62a, אין מקנחין בימין / "A person does not wipe himself with his right hand...רב נחמן בר יצחק אמר: מפני שמראה בה טעמי תורה / Rav Nachman bar Yitzchak said the reason is because it is with the right hand that one shows the reader the notes of the Torah." Rashi comments: נגינות טעמי מקרא של תורה נביאים וכתובים בין בניקוד שבספר בין בהגבהת קול ובצלצול נעימות הנגינה של פשטא ודרגא ושופר מהפך מוליך ידו לפי טעם הנגינה ראיתי בקוראים הבאים ארץ ישראל.

does not have a word to describe ambivalence, it has a *Ta'am*, an unusual note called a *Shalsheles* (a zig-zag symbol which is placed above a letter). When placed with a word, the word is sung, up and down, up and down, almost suggesting an inability to move forward due to ambivalence. Rav Yoseph ibn Caspi, one of the *Rishonim* / early commentators, writes that a Shalsheles expresses indecision or uncertainty, a type of existential doubt. When a Shalsheles appears as a Ta'am in the Torah, we should pay attention to it and sense if the character in the narrative is experiencing ambivalence, even if it is not explicitly stated.

These graphic depictions of Ta'amei HaMikra also have names which could give hints to a deeper meaning. For example, the Ta'am of the words העשיר לא־ירבה / "The rich should not give more" (*Shemos*, 30:15), is a *Munach Re'vi'i*. In Hebrew, these words mean "leave a fourth." This is perhaps an allusion to the ruling of the sages in Usha (*Kesuvos*, 50a) that one who dispenses his money to charity should not dispense more than one-fifth. Rather "the rich should not give more (than commanded)" by *Munach Revi'i* / 'leaving a fourth' of their wealth (Gra, *Aderes Eliyahu*, Ki Sisa).

Another example of this idea is that Avraham was told that there would be an exile for 400 years, yet, in fact, because of the tremendous hardship of the exile, when "they (the Egyptians) embittered their lives" (*Shemos*, 1:4), Klal Yisrael left Egypt much earlier. The Ta'amei HaMikra for these words are *Kadma V'azla*, which means in Talmudic language, "earlier, and move".

Thus, there is a connection between the words of the Torah and the meaning of the names of their Ta'amim (*Kol Eliyahu*, Shemos, ad loc).

K'RI / HOW A WORD IS WRITTEN, AND
KESIV / HOW IT IS READ:

Just as there is a Mesorah for the vowels and melody for each word of the Torah, there is a Mesorah for how the pronunciation of certain words differ from how they are spelled (And sometimes, within Tanach (but not in the Torah itself, בכל הני כתיב) :ולא קריין וקריין ולא כתיבן דמייתי תלמודא אין בהם אחד בתורה אלא בנביאים וכתובים *Shu't Radbaz*, 3, Siman 1020), actual words are read even when not written at all, and some are not read even though they are written: .תיבות הנקראות ולא נכתבות תיבות הנקראות ולא נכתבות. Ran, *Nedarim*, 37b). In other words, there are sometimes apparent discrepancies between how the word is written, the כתיב / *Kesiv*, and how we pronounce it, the קרי / *K'ri*. Sometimes, the K'ri is almost a totally different word than the K'siv (ישגלנה / ישכבנה *Devarim*, 28:30: *Megillah*, 25b), and sometimes, it is just a different vowelization. For example, a word can be spelled as הוא / *Hu*, which means 'him', but according to the Mesorah, the same word can be read as if it is spelled היא / *Hee*, which means 'her'.

It is important to understand that both 'versions' are simultaneously true. The written version is actually the higher, more concealed, inner meaning, as it exists in 'Heaven', yet when this idea is reflected into the lower, more revealed outer world here on 'earth', it is verbalized in its K'ri form (Rema miFano, *Kanfei Yonah*, 2, Siman 125. See also Maharal, *Tiferes Yisrael*, 66). We are thus invited to explore the relationship between the written and vocalized forms, as the dichotomy between them reveals a richness of meaning that the Torah wants to convey.

For example, regarding Rivka's childlessness and barrenness, the Torah says that Yitzchak, her husband, prayed for a child כי עקרה הוא / "since she was barren" (*Bereishis*, 25:21). As it is written, it says הוא / Hu, as "he was barren," yet the pronoun is read orally as היא / "for she was barren." In the external world, it was more obvious that she was the barren one, while in the hidden, internal world, he was barren. By combining these two intended meanings, we understand that they were both barren, and indeed, שניהם עקורים היו / "they were both barren" (*Yevamos*, 64a. When a K'ri and a Kesiv contradict each other, both interpretations are valid. See, for example, *Pesachim*, 26b).

NUMEROLOGY, LETTER-SEQUENCING, LETTER-EXCHANGE, & OTHER METHODS:

There are also more suggestive and mystical means for revealing hidden meanings in the text. One is called *Tziruf* / letter sequences, in which we re-sequence the letters of a word to create a new word. Tziruf is mentioned by our sages (*Berachos*, 55a) and was practiced throughout the ages (*Sefer HaPeliah*, 1. p 17a. *Sha'arei Orah*, Sha'ar 5. *Shushan Sodos* (Koretz, 1784) p. 69b. *Chesed LeAvraham*, 2:11. *Kesones Pasim*, p. 47b. *Toldos Ya'akov Yoseph*, Noach, 15d. *Dover Tzedek*, p. 96a).

The concept behind this practice is that all words that share the same letters are interrelated and connected at their source. Letters in general, and more specifically in the Torah, are transmitters of Divine life force. A word composed of two letters contains two 'Divine lights' which refract their particular energies according to their presented sequence. When these two letters are arranged one way, their energies combine to refract a particular 'color', as it were, and when arranged in the reverse order, they refract a different tint of that color. The two sequences would reflect the same general 'color', but different shades or tints of that color. A word with three letters creates six possible combinations, and each combination expresses another tint of this same light. Each added letter in a word multiplies the variety of outcomes.

The Zohar (*Tikkunei Zohar*, p. 71b) comments on the verse, "I went down to the *Ginas Egoz* / grove of nut trees" (*Shir HaShirim*, 6:11, see also *Yalkut*, ad loc). *Ginas* / Garden can be viewed as an acronym for *Gematria* / Numerology, *Nutrikun* / acronyms, and *Temurah* / letter exchanges, three methods of textual interpretation.*

---

* Chazal, our sages, make use of these methods, see for example *Nazir*, 5a. *Shabbos*, 104a. See also Tosefos, *Pesachim* 117b, regarding the source of the 39 main prohibitions for Shabbos. See also Yerushalmi, *Shabbos*, 7:2. The *Geonim*, who were the leaders of Yeshivos in Babylon and Eretz Yisrael over 1,000 years ago, speak about the five forms of acceptable letter manipulation, which are called: *Tikkun, Ma'amar, Tziruf, Michlal*, and *Cheshbon*: Rav Chamai Gaon, *Sha'ar haShamayim* (*Sefer haIyyun*), at the beginning.

Gematria is the symbolic employment of letters as numerals. There are 22 regular letters and five final letters in the Hebrew Aleph-Beis, totaling 27 unique graphic forms. Aleph, the first letter in the Aleph-Beis, equals 1. Beis, the second letter, equals 2. Gimel, the third letter, equals 3, and so on until the 9th letter, Tes, which equals 9. The next nine letters represent the double digits: Yud is 10, Chof is 20, Lamed is 30, and so on until Tzadik, which is 90. The next nine letters represent the triple digits, with Kuf equaling 100 and the final Tzadik equaling 900. Gematria is considered another way to uncover and flesh out hidden or alternative meanings within a particular word or set of words.[*]

Nutrikun is the art of creating or finding acronyms within a single word or set of words. A word with four letters, for

---

[*] The word *Gematria* is believed to be a Greek word constructed from two words *Gai* / number and *Matria* / wisdom. In Hebrew, *Gai* means valley, and in Aramaic, *Matria* means mountain. A mountain exists in relation to surrounding valleys, and in this way, mountains and valleys are mirror images. We can learn from this that the numerical value of a word can serve as a 'mirror' reflecting the Divine wisdom hidden within the object. *Gematria* is, perhaps, also related to the word 'geometry': Rambam, *Hilchos G'neivah v'Aveidah*, 8:1. *Tosefos Yom Tov*, Avos, 3:21. What is significant, however, is not the numerical matching up of words and letters itself. A numerical equivalence does not automatically suggest a cosmological or theological relationship; rather, it is an outward expression of a deeper cosmological truth that already exists: Ramban, *Sefer HaGeulah*, in the beginning. Rabbeinu Bachya, *Kad Kemach*, Tzitzis. *Shomer Emunim HaKadmon*, 1, 20–23. An inspired author who illustrates meanings through Gematria first grasps the profound connection between the two ideas and then may discover a numerological correspondence as well: *Degel Macheneh Ephrayim*, Chukas.

instance, can be interpreted as an acronym for a sentence consisting of four words (for an example, see *Shabbos*, 105a. *Zohar* 3, 73a).

Temurah is the method of substituting one letter for another related letter. There are a few ways that this can be done. One way is according to the phonetic relationship between letters. If two letters sound the same or very similar, such as an Aleph and an Ayin, or a Samech and a Sin, these letters are considered interchangeable in the Temurah method. There are five primary phonetic 'families' of letters according to the place in the mouth where their sound is pronounced. These are: 1) *gutturals*, from the throat, 2) *palatals*, from the palate, 3) *linguals*, from the tongue, 4) *dentals*, from the teeth, and 5) *labials*, from the lips. Any letter from within a particular family can be exchanged with any other letter that comes from that same family.

Another method of Temurah is to substitute letters based on their order within the sequence of the Aleph-Beis. For example, one may exchange the first letter of the Aleph-Beis (Aleph) with the last letter (Tav), and the second letter (Beis) with the second to last letter (Shin). Additionally, one may exchange the first letter of the single digits (Aleph) with the last letter of the single digits (Tes), and the second letter of the single digits (Beis) with the second to last letter of the single digits (Ches); the first letter of the double digits (Yud) with the last letter of the double digits (Tzadik), and so forth. There are many other ways to substitute letters. Although this is a valid form of Torah study and exploration, this particular methodology will not be employed in this book, as the purpose here is to stay close to the actual text and simpler meanings of the Torah.

HEARTFUL NOT-KNOWING:

The Torah ends with death and not knowing; Moshe dies and no one knows where he is buried (On top of Mount Nebo he seems on the bottom, from the bottom he seems on top — הלכו ועמדו להם: למעלה וראו כאלו היא למטה והלכו ועמדו למטה וראו אותה כאלו היא למעלה: Sotah, 14a. Moshe himself does not know — אף משה רבינו אינו יודע היכן קבור: *Ein Ya'akov,* Sotah) As his dream of entering *Eretz Yisrael* / the Land of Israel is unrealized at the end of his journey, the grand narrative of the Torah seems to end with an anti-climax — perhaps even with a heartbreak.

Indeed, if you study the Torah in a 'linear' way, from the beginning to the end, starting with the first letter (Beis) and ending your reading with last letter (Lamed), your study is characterized by the sequence 'Beis-Lamed', spelling *Bal* / 'empty'. In this process, you may come to a subtly heartbreaking feeling of emptiness. Not only are you left hanging with the death of Moshe before he reaches his destination, but neither do you reach a destination or sense of wholeness or illumination in your study. However, when, after the last letter of the Torah, you cycle back to the beginning of the Torah, the Beis, your study is characterized by the sequence Lamed-Beis, spelling *Lev* / 'heart' (which represents higher wisdom, *Kaf HaKetores* (on *Tehilim,* 119) attributed to Rebbe Yoseph Taitatzak, a Rebbe of the Beis Yoseph).

You realize that the whole Torah led you back to a wholeness of heart and hope: "And there was light…and it was good."

Many have wondered why the popular symbol of a 'heart' is a shape with two curves on top and a point on the bottom. Besides the fact that it vaguely resembles a right and left atrium on top, many ancient cultures used it as a symbol for romantic love. Interestingly, Rebbe Abraham Abulafia explains that the two Hebrew letters, Lamed and Beis, that form the word for *Lev* / heart, allude to the physical form of the heart: two face-to-face Lameds ('2' is the value of the letter Beis). In an inner way, the Torah has the 'shape' of a heart — a heart of endless love and hope and aliveness.

When life seems dark and confusing, we don't need 'mind' answers, and we don't need to be lectured; we need the Torah of the heart. A heart pumps in and out: darkness and light, emptiness and fullness, not knowing and knowing. When we end the linear pattern of Torah, we immediately begin the cycle again; we approach it as completely new, as if we have never studied it before. When we connect the last letter to the first letter, when we connect 'endings' to new beginnings, we ourselves are renewed, and we feel the life-blood of Torah pulsing through our veins.

When we approach Torah study solely as an intellectual pursuit or use it to boost our pride in containing a lot of information, we have lost the 'heart of the Torah', and the uncontainable, unlimited nature of its wisdom.

The Baal Shem Tov was searching for a fitting husband for his daughter, who was herself an illumined soul and brilliant in Torah. He walked into the *Yeshivah* / Torah academy and asked the *Rosh* / head of the Yeshivah who was the top student there. An intense-looking young man named Yechiel was indicated, studying alone in the back of the *Zal* / hall. The Baal Shem asked him, "Young man, please tell me about what you're studying."

"Forgive me, Rabbi," the student blushed, "I...don't think I can do that." "Fine, no problem," the Baal Shem nodded, "so tell me something from any of your studies that you feel you know well." The student bent his head in humility: "Rabbi, please, what can I say, I don't know anything!" "Nothing at all?" The student silently shook his head, with a small tear glistening in his eye. The Baal Shem Tov smiled. This was the young man he chose to be his son-in-law — one with a heart so wide open, that he was beyond assuming that Torah could be 'known' at all.

The Baal Shem Tov once said that there is תורת המוח / *Toras HaMoach* / 'Torah of the mind', and there is תורת הלב / *Toras HaLev* / 'Torah of the heart' — and he came to reveal the Torah of the heart (*Igros Kodesh*, Rebbe Rayatz, 924. p. 96). This is an experiential, inwardly transformative, expansive, and heart-opening approach to Torah interpretation. It involves simply opening your inner eyes and soul to the text without assuming anything, even if you have read the same passage hundreds of times.

The great sages of the Torah advise: "One who reviews his studies one hundred times is not comparable to one who reviews his studies one hundred and one times" (*Chagigah*, 9b). This is because every single time we open our minds and hearts and study a passage or lesson with child-like innocence, intuition, passion, and joy, an entirely new meaning can dawn on us, filling our life with new light. Indeed, the Torah of the Infinite One is itself infinite and inexhaustible: הפך בה והפך בה, דכלא בה / "Turn it over, and over, for Everything is within it" (*Avos*, 5:22). This is, of course, the master key to all the other methods of mining Torah insights.

With this intention, let us begin the journey....

BOOK ONE:

Bereishis

Bereishis
Reclaiming Our Greatness

T HE TORAH OPENS WITH THE PARSHAH / READING
of Bereishis. Bereishis describes, albeit in an intentionally hidden way, the emergence of the world and
the birth of human beings.

"In the beginning, Elokim (G-d) created the heavens and
the earth...." Having already created the-heavens-and-the-
earth" as a single unit, the first defined phenomenon to emerge
out of the chaos and void was Light.* "Elokim said, 'Let there
be light,' and there was light."

As the first defined creation, this primordial Light can be
understood as the foundation and source of all further creations. Also, "Light" here means much more than physical
light; it is a light of clarity, vision, illumination, and certainty, a light with which man (once created) would be able to
"see from one end of the world to the other" (*Chagigah*, 12a. *Me-*

---

* It is important to keep in mind that although the Torah uses past tense
terms in the narration of Creation, all of the steps in the process of Creation
are also understood as occurring in the present tense.

drash Rabbah, Bereishis, 13:5). Thus, it is clear that "Light" here also means some extremely deep level of awareness.

After creating this light, the Creator 'hid it away for the righteous of the future' (Ibid. *Zohar* 2, 148b). This raises a couple of questions: why reveal this light and then immediately conceal it? And why create such a light in the beginning of Creation if it is just going to be hidden away for the future; why not just create it later, in "the future"?

A similar pattern of revealing and concealing and later revealing occurs when the 'second' creation of light — the luminaries, the sun and moon. "And Elokim (G-d) fashioned the two great lights, the great light to rule the day, and the lesser light to rule by night." This verse seems to contradict itself. First "two great lights" are created, and then the verse continues: "the great light...and small light."

Regarding this contradiction, our sages tell us that the moon was initially created as a luminary equal in greatness to the sun. The moon said before the Holy One, Blessed be He, "Master of the Universe, is it possible for two kings to serve with one crown? The Master of the Universe responded, "You're right... לכי ומעטי את עצמך / so, go ahead and diminish your light" (*Chullin*, 60b). The moon then became the lesser light and shined less brightly. Yet, in the future, "The light of the moon will be like the light of the sun" (*Yeshayahu*, 30:26. *Sanhedrin*, 91b). In other words, the moon will be once again a "great luminary."

Still, the question persists. If the argument of the moon is valid, why did the Creator first create the moon as a "great light" and then diminish it? Why create the moon first in a posture of greatness, only to be diminished? The Creator is omniscient and knows the future.

Actually, this pattern repeats itself often in the Creation narrative. For example, "Elokim (G-d) created the two (male and female) great sea serpents." Yet, our sages tell us, "What did the Holy One, Blessed be He, do? He castrated the male and killed the female, and salted the female to preserve it for the banquet for the righteous in the future" (*Baba Basra*, 74b). Here, again, there is the creation of something great, only to be put aside for the future, when its greatness can be appreciated. Again, why create it now if it is anyway going to be reserved for the future?

Now let us proceed to the creation and emergence of human beings, the story of Adam and Chavah / Eve. First, the verse says Adam alone was created, and then it says, "male and female He created them." This means they were within Adam, two personalities created simultaneously as a singular, larger or 'greater' unit. Then the Torah tells us that first Adam was created, then Chavah.

Picking up on the allusions in these verses, our sages reveal to us that originally, אדם הראשון מן הארץ עד לרקיע / "(The body of) Adam stretched from the earth to the heavens" (*Sanhedrin*,

38b. *Chagigah*, 12a. *Pirkei D'Rebbe Eliezer*, 11), and from one end of the world to the other. Following the eating from the Tree of Knowledge (which, too, was originally the Divine intention, *Medrash Tanchuma*), Adam shrank in size and stature. כיון שסרח הניח הקדוש ברוך הוא ידיו עליו ומיעטו / "When he made a mess of things, the Holy One, Blessed be He, placed His hand upon him and diminished him."

What occurred on a 'physical' level mirrored what occurred on a meta-physical, spiritual or soul level. The greater soul of Adam was broken into a myriad of sparks, with each spark becoming the individual souls of subsequent human beings. Humanity is created 'great' only to be diminished. On a spiritual level, our collective *Tikkun* / soul purpose is to reintegrate and recreate the great soul of Adam.

All of life seems to follow this pattern, from 'great' and singular to 'diminished' and multiple, with the intention of becoming great and unified again in the future (although the destined greatness is not a singularity that excludes multiplicity, rather, it is one that will include multiplicity and individuality).

Without going into depth here, the Torah is telling us that we, and all Creation, come from primordial Light and a status of greatness — even though now we are generally in a state of diminishment. For example, the vast majority of people are not currently illumined to the point where they can "see from one side of the world to the other."

Greatness is essentially where we came from, and thus who we are. We come from a place of light, clarity, revealed purpose, certainty, and utter connectivity to the Source of Life. And because we are rooted there, we will one day become great and 'illumined' again in the future. The question is, why should there be an intermediate state of diminishment?

If we had been born with a conscious memory of our true self and spiritual 'greatness', this illumined awareness would cancel out our freedom to choose. And so, to allow us to participate in our own development and unfolding, Hashem hid away our greatness; the diminishment of mankind is for the sake of our *Bechirah* / free choice. To rebuild and own our greatness, we need to long for it, desire it, and work to earn it. And we *can* desire and long for it precisely because it is where we come from.

And so, Hashem initially creates us in a state of *Gadlus* / greatness, goodness, and deeper awareness, invested with the Primordial Light of Creation. In our inner world, the moon is at first as bright as the sun, and our bodies and vision encompass all of Creation, "from one end of the world to the next". And then, this Gadlus is diminished, at least to the point that we can experience both good and bad, and build the muscles of choice and desiring Gadlus. This eventually empowers us to reclaim and climb back into our inherent birthright, our original greatness.

Our sages tell us that while we are still in the womb, a candle is lit above our heads, and through it, we gaze from one end of the world to the other. In this light of awareness, we learn the entire Torah. Once the newborn emerges fully into the physical and spiritual space of 'the world', an angel comes and taps it on the lips, causing it to forget the entire Torah (*Nidah*, 30b). Again, we might ask, what is the point of learning the whole Torah if it will just be forgotten? The answer is now clear: it is to remember the Torah we originally knew.

The Torah learned in the womb, and the limitless light, is always found deep within us, on a subconscious level. Thus, the act of learning and praying and transforming ourselves is really rediscovery, a conscious reclaiming of what we already know subconsciously. Life is a journey of recovering our Gadlus in a world of *Katnus* / smallness — rediscovering our soul's light in a world of apparent darkness, and remembering our Torah wisdom and moral clarity in a world of ambiguity and uncertainty. Essentially, it is a process of returning to who we truly are.*

---

* In order to determine a person's 'permanent' status, we can look at the beginning and the end of their life.

Since we all begin with Gadlus and will eventually reach Gadlus, *who we really are* is Gadlus. One way to demonstrate this is with the following Mishnah. אבל פקח ונתחרש וחזר ונתפקח; פתוח ונסתמא וחזר ונתפתח; שפוי ונשתטה וחזר ונשתפה. כשר – כל שתחילתו וסופו בדעת – כשר / כשר. זה הכלל: כל שתחילתו וסופו בדעת – כשר / "If (a messenger) received (a *Gett* / bill of divorce to deliver it on behalf of another man) when he was able to hear, and then he became a deaf-mute, and then again he became able to hear; or if one received it when he was able to see, and then he became blind, and then again he became able to see; or one received it when he was competent, and then became an imbecile, and then again became competent, in all of these cases he is fit to bring the bill of divorce (in other words, he is a good *Shaliach*). This is the principle: Anyone who is competent in the beginning and in the end is fit, even if there was time in the interim when he was unfit" (*Gittin*, 23a).

BEREISHIS

Energy of the Week:
Reclaiming Our Greatness

Our existence originates from a place of light and purity, perfection and wholeness. True, we may have found ourselves estranged from our most authentic selves, alienated from our true spiritual greatness. Yet, Bereishis reveals to us that spiritual greatness is our birthright, our origin, and our ultimate destination.

At any moment of life we have the ability to lay claim to who we truly are, and live from that deeper place.

The way we conduct ourselves on the Shabbos of Bereishis becomes the template for the year to come.

While we need to work toward reclaiming our perfection every moment of every day, this Shabbos has a special power to do so, as it is the foundation and template of our entire coming year.

This week's Torah reading imbues us with the power to reclaim our original brilliance, to lay claim to our great goodness and, G-d willing, live from this expansive consciousness throughout the entire year.

PRACTICE OF THE WEEK:

**Recognize & Choose Greatness,
Moment by Moment**

Noach
A Vessel of Giving and Receiving

T HIS WEEK'S TORAH READING BEGINS WITH THE
words "These are the generations of Noach / Noah…
The earth was full of corruption…Hashem said to
Noach, 'The end of all flesh has come before Me, for all flesh
has corrupted its way on the earth… Make for yourself an
Ark'" (6:9–14).

Noach is instructed to build a *Teivah* / Ark to protect himself and his family, and the other creatures, when the Great
Flood would come.

Reasons given for the flooding and cleansing of the earth
are: a) "…The earth was full of corruption." Chazal, our sages,
say that this means that the inhabitants of the earth were consumed with robbery and theft (*Sanhedrin*, 108a). And b) "…For
all flesh had corrupted its way on the earth." This is understood
to mean that even the animal kingdom had become corrupt,
and there were interspecies physical relations occurring even
among the animals (*Ibid*).

A human being, as part of the natural, created world, is a receiver, whereas the Creator is the ultimate Giver. Yet, having been created in the *Tzelem Elokim* / Divine Image, a human being also has the potential to give and create. Receiving from life is our 'natural' tendency, and giving and creating is our Divine nature. To give is an expression of being 'a part of the Creator', as it were.

Living life fully requires creating a healthy balance between receiving and giving. Ultimately, we receive from life so that we can give and contribute to life. For example, we ingest food so that we can have the strength to bring our gifts to the world and do acts of kindness for others.

The devastation caused by the generation of the flood was in its total imbalance of receiving and giving. The entire generation was engaged in theft, promiscuity, and intimate physical violation. Theft is an act of 'receiving' from another without consent, taking something by force or deceit. Intimate physical violation, on the other hand, is an act of 'giving' without the other's consent, imposing oneself by force. In both actions, there is a massively destructive disconnect between the 'giver' and the 'receiver'.

Perhaps the Generation of the Flood allowed their selfishness to rule their lives. They took from others without giving in return, and even their so-called 'giving' was abusive.

The earth functions as a unified system, with the human being at its center — as its heart, as it were. A human being's role is to receive what they need from the animal, plant, and mineral kingdoms in order that they may distribute even more life and abundance to the world. The actions of each human being are so powerful that they affect all life forms. This is why the animal kingdom mimicked the unbalanced behaviors of the generation of the Flood. Nature itself became infected with their tyranny, and the animals began mating with other species. The masculine and feminine elements of Creation — the givers and receivers — are designed to work in sync. When they are out of sync and imbalanced, 'giving' becomes a method of controlling the receiver, and 'receiving' becomes a selfish act of taking. This set the stage for a pervasive culture of abuse, spiraling ever deeper into chaos and causing 'unbearable pain' to the Divine Presence, as it were.

Noach was commanded to build an ark, a vessel which contained the universe in a microcosm. Within this miniature world, Noach was obliged to give himself totally to the care of each of the animals, as well as the humans, that were enfolded within the ark. He labored constantly, feeding them according to the specific needs and schedule of each creature. At the same time, residing in the confines of the Ark protected him and his family from the catastrophic chaos outside.

Once, when Noach came late to feed the lion, the lion hit him with his paw, injuring him, the Medrash records. This physical injury can be understood as a manifestation of a spiritual defect: even though Noach was surely exerting himself in his service, whatever it was that delayed him also happened to cause discomfort to the animal in his charge. There was still some minor form of insensitivity in him, which he needed to correct through his path of selfless giving.

Interestingly, the Torah gives us the precise measurements of the Ark: 30 *Amos* / cubits high, 50 Amos wide and 300 Amos long. Since such specificity doesn't seem necessary to the narrative, it is a signal that we need to look deeper. Indeed, these dimensions correlate to the perfect cosmic balance between giving and receiving, also referred to as the masculine quality and the feminine quality.

To explain: Hashem is the Ultimate Being and the Source and Substance of all that is. The Name Hashem has four letters: Yud, Hei, Vav and Hei. In numerical values, Yud (the tenth letter of the Aleph-Beis) is 10, Hei (the fifth letter of the Aleph-Beis) is 5, and Vav (the sixth letter of the Aleph-Beis) is 6. As the Source of all interrelationships in Creation, Hashem's Name also includes and is the meta-root of the principal dynamics of giving and receiving. If the four letters of the name are visualized in descending order, the first letter, Yud, is on the top. This tiny dot or line (י) symbolizes an act of giving, and is thus a 'masculine' letter. The next letter below the Yud receives the 'Light' or nourishment bestowed by the Yud — the expansive 'feminine' letter Hei (ה). The third letter, the longer line is the Vav (ו), represents another level of 'masculine giving', which is in this case being channeled down to the lower Hei, the feminine dynamic of 'receiving'.

Using the numerical values for each of these four letters, with interpretive mathematical techniques called *Gematria*, we can understand deeper messages in the dimensions of the Ark.

- Yud=10, Hei=5; 10 x 5 = 50. The width of the Teivah was 50 cubits.

- Vav=6, Hei=5. Vav is like a channel between the upper Hei and the lower Hei. Based on the equation described above, the upper Hei now 'carries' the value of 50. The connection between the upper Hei (50) and the Vav (6) therefore manifests as 50 x 6 = 300. The length of the Teivah was 300 cubits.

- The connection between the Vav (6) and the lower Hei (5) is: 6 x 5 = 30. The Teivah was 30 cubits tall.

Teivah also means 'word'. As an out-picturing of the four-letter 'word', the Divine Name, the structure of the Ark contained a harmonious balance of the root elements of the 'masculine' and the 'feminine', giving and receiving.

By living inside the 'Divine Name' of the Ark, and by serving and maintaining the peace among all the creatures within it (שלום / *Shalom* / 'peace' in numerical value is 376; plus 4 for the four letters ש-ל-ו-ם, equals 380 — the total of the width, length, and height of the Ark), Noach undid the root cause of the Flood and laid the foundation for a brighter, more balanced world.

On the one hand, Noach was motivated to protect himself and his family from the flood. On the other hand, his function in the Ark was to give to all those who needed his care. The injury caused by the lion had motivated him to perform a *Tikun* / rectification on his own personal trait of giving. Ultimately, his unrelenting efforts in selflessly giving to all the creatures on the Ark became a Tikun for all the insensitivity, selfish 'taking' and selfish 'giving', that had pervaded his entire generation. Through Noach's concentrated activity in dedication to others, he was finally able to reverse the destructive course of history. The human being could then return to the status of caretaker and giver in relation to all of Creation.

In fact, as a result of this cosmic Tikun, none of the creatures, including Noach himself, initially wanted to leave the Ark, even once inhabitable dry land had appeared (Noach had to be *commanded*, "Come out of the Ark, you and your wife, your sons, and your sons' wives. Bring out with you every living thing of all flesh that is with you...": 8:16–17. "You and your wife" alludes to the balance of masculine and feminine: see Rashi, *ibid*). This was because they were all experiencing a level of redemption, a utopia of peace and balance within the Ark.

Based on achieving this redeemed state of existence, Noach was able to rebuild human culture, along with that of the animal kingdom, based on a Divine equilibrium of giving and receiving.

NOACH

Energy of the Week:
Giving and Receiving

Our life is a constant flow of giving and receiving. To create a harmonious balance, we must be sure that even as we protect ourselves and our loved ones, our primary purpose is giving to others. In order to give, we must know how to receive, and in order to properly receive, we must learn the art of giving; in this way, we complete the circuitry of life's flow.

This week's Torah reading imbues us with the power of attaining this balance, to be able to give openly and simultaneously be capable of receiving that which we need to continue this cycle of receiving and giving. We ourselves become an ark, a vessel, of reciprocity, and the quality of giving and receiving flow seamlessly through us, creating a harmonious, balanced universe. Through this, G-d willing, we are contributing to the great Tikun which will bring ultimate redemption to all creatures.

PRACTICE OF THE WEEK:

Be a Vessel for Flow

Lech L'cha
Movement & Growth

THIS WEEK'S TORAH READING OPENS WITH THE Divine instruction to Avraham "...*Lech L'cha* / Go forth from your land and from your birthplace and from your father's house, to the land that I will show you" (*Bereishis*, 12:1). Thus begins the journey of Avraham, leaving his homeland for the place of an undisclosed destiny.

Interestingly, there is no backstory. Why does Hashem speak to Avraham in this way; why is he chosen? Regarding Moshe, the Torah goes to great lengths to describe his unusual character before he was chosen, narrating his compassion for his fellow brothers and even compassion to utter strangers. Here, all we know about Avraham is from the end of last week's Parshah. He was born to Terach, and he is married to Sarah, but they are childless. Together with his father, his nephew Lot, and Sarah, Avraham travels toward the land of *Kena'an* / Canaan (which would eventually become *Eretz Yisrael* / the Land of Israel). "However, when they had come as far as Haran, they settled there" (11:31), and Terach dies.

On one level, Avraham is abruptly chosen in order to demonstrate that ever since, the chosenness of Klal Yisrael, his children, is not for any 'rational reason' or special qualities. Klal Yisrael is chosen only because it is the will of *HaKadosh Baruch Hu* / the Holy One. Hashem simply desired Avraham, and so Hashem simply desires us.

Avraham was "chosen" because he had already chosen himself; he chose to be open to a journey, to be sensitive to hear the Divine mandate to go beyond everything he already knew. The greatness of Avraham was that he was ready for a journey, not satisfied with the status quo and passionately open to his deeper calling. He had a burning desire to move, to grow, to become, to delve, to probe, to explore.

The Divine call of *Lech L'cha*, a call to go forth, to become, to journey, to make something of yourself, has and is being called to each and every individual person from the beginning of time. The greatness of Avraham is that he heard and acted on this call.

Indeed, this Divine call has resonated throughout Creation from the beginning of time — Avraham was simply the first human being to truly hear this perennial Heavenly voice. He became the forerunner who opened the way for us and all human beings to truly listen and integrate this call as well, and to take our own hero's journey.

Lech L'cha literally means "Go thou forth," but literally the words translate as 'go *to yourself.*' Avraham is invited to embark on this transformative inward journey that will allow him to become a great and influential person "for your pleasure and benefit" (*Rashi*, ibid). He is invited, as we all are, to go on a journey "to yourself," so that he can evolve into the great man he has the ability to become.

Listening closely to the text, we realize that 'Go to yourself' is even more than this. It is an invitation to Avraham to self-actualize and discover the essence of his being: 'Go and find your true self.'

Lech L'cha also literally means, 'Go *by* yourself.' It is a journey to find himself, which will allow him to become great, and as all such journeys are solitary, he needs to walk 'alone' (ואיש אל יעלה עמך כשירצה לעבוד את ה' / "And no one should ascend with you when you desire to serve Hashem: *Degel Machaneh Ephrayim*, Shelach).

"Go forth from your land…to the land that I will show you." It is important for Avraham, and by extension for all of us, not simply to 'go to the land Hashem will show you,' but first to 'go forth "from" your old land', and all that this means.

Lech L'cha is a call to each of us, and one that has been uttered since the beginning of time. It is just that the Torah establishes

Avraham as the model and template for how to heed this call. Ever since Avraham blazed the path, we can more clearly receive and respond to this Divine mandate, if we choose to open ourselves up to it. Hashem is always calling to us, saying, *Lech L'cha* / 'Go forward on your journey. It will bring great benefit to you. Step into the unknown, be "by yourself," and let Me guide you to a new place, to a new stage in becoming who you really are.'

To get to the "Land that I will show you," his highest destiny, Avraham is told that he must first leave three 'foundations' behind. He must depart *MeArtzecha* / from his 'land,' *MiMoladesecha* / from his 'birthplace', and *MiBeis Avicha* / from his 'father's house'.

At a later stage, he will also need to include and integrate his land, birthplace, and father's home. Yet these three contexts of ego are what he, and each of us, need to 'leave' and transcend — so that we do not settle within them forever, nor define ourselves by them, nor use them as excuses to avoid growing.

'Your land' refers to your context of *Olam* / 'space'; your physical location and circumstances.

'Your birthplace' infers your particular context of *Shanah* / 'time', the moment in history when you were born, and in which you live.

'Your father's house' references your unique context of *Nefesh*

/ personal 'perception', meaning thinking of yourself as your body and genetics which seem to shape your personality and direct your thought, speech, and action.

Sadly, many people 'know' what they need to do with their lives, but are simply too lazy to act on it. Then, to make themselves feel better, they find justifications for their immobility in life. It is common to make excuses for ourselves as to why we are staying in one place and not living our life to its fullest. We might sense what we might accomplish in our lifetime, but we don't act upon it. We often make excuses based on place, time, and our bodily self-perception as defenses against acting and becoming our greater self:

Space: 'Your land' refers to self-limitation using concepts of 'space'. The excuses are familiar; we know we must do, but we put it off: "Here, I'm being held back. If I move into a new apartment, things will be different, I'll be able to be myself. My career will take off, I will find my soul-mate, I will get a better job; i just need to wait until I can move." "I'm comfortable in this town; I know it's not good for me in some ways, but it's familiar. I can't see myself leaving...."

Time: "Your birthplace" refers to self-limitation using concepts of 'time'. Perhaps we tell ourselves, "I'm just not ready to start a path of growth right now..." "When I get married and settled (or when the children are older and out of the house), then I'll begin to live my dream..." "It takes too long to achieve the prerequisites for my ideal spiritual *Avodah* / work and learning; I wasn't raised in this, so it's too late for me…" "In this era, nobody reaches that level of righteousness. We are a weak generation; it's better not to attempt it." These are ways that people hold themselves back with excuses that the time is not right.

Self: 'Your father's house' refers to inaccurate self-perceptions, often connected to genetic tendencies. This is arguably the most insidious of justifications: "I would like to change, but it is impossible; I was born this way. This is me, it is my nature…." "I'm in many ways like my parents; they had the same basic weaknesses and character flaws…." "I don't have the inner resources and energy to change; I'm just not strong in this area of life, and there is nothing I can do about it." These resistances to change come from clinging to limited views of one's *Nefesh* / soul — that 'I am not the right person.'

However, the Torah tells Avraham to let go of his excuses. In order to take his journey to greatness, he must go forth and journey away from limiting his potential using his location, history, and inborn tendencies. He must release these albatrosses and simply start moving. He must go alone and become *Avraham.*

In our own lives, although our ultimate destination may be currently unknowable ("the land which I will show you"), our journey is not aimless, nor are we without guidance. When we take a firm step toward our greatness, we will have the sense that we are being guided at every juncture by the One Above.

"The land that I will show you" was not clearly revealed to Avraham in the beginning of his journey because if it were, his destiny would be limited to who he already was. But Hashem was telling him, "You are journeying to yourself, by yourself, to become more of yourself in a way that you cannot presently visualize. But your dream and your vision will continually develop and expand along the way, and you will be guided."

Hashem's call to Avraham is also a call to each one of us to leave behind our inner constricting perceptions and mindset. First, we must stop making excuses and let go of our 'land' and surroundings. 'Land', in Hebrew, *Eretz,* is connected to the word *Ratzon* / will and desire. *Ratzon* is a dimension of self that 'surrounds' everything we do; it is like a *Keser* / crown of 'surrounding light'. We must not let our limiting desires or lack of will 'box us in' and prevent our self-actualization.

'Our birthplace' refers to the *Midos* or emotional attributes which are 'birthed' in our mind and heart. We are called to put aside our old, limiting assumptions of what 'love' is, and what 'discipline', 'compassion', 'endurance', 'humility', and 'receptivity' are. We need to evaluate our emotional reactions to the hurts and obstacles in our past so that we can free ourselves up to journey into the future.

'Our father's house' refers to our limiting and inaccurate *Chochmah* / intuition and *Binah* / understanding about ourselves, which give birth to limited emotions and negative character traits. We need to leave our false 'intuitions', ideas, and outdated 'self-understandings', which hold us back.

In this way, Hashem is telling us, 'Let go of the understandings, emotions, self-perceptions, and beliefs which keep you stuck, and allow yourself to journey upward and outward, and become open to life. Do not box yourself into a certain vision of who you are and what you can do. I will guide you on a journey to realize your destiny, which is beyond your imagination, so "I will show you."

Why doesn't Hashem show Avraham his destination right away? Hashem is telling him that if he lets go of his personal or ego-based *Retzonos* / desires and the external influences in his life, then he will see *Eretz Yisrael* / the Land of Israel, which is his destiny. "This itself is the *Bechina* / reality of Eretz Yisrael: to nullify all one's *Chushim* / senses and desires to the will and desire of the Creator, and in this way truly experience Eretz Yisrael."

In the beginning, though, the most important directive is to go out of your limitations, your comfort zone, and stubbornness and set out on your journey; detach from your inertia and move forward in life. And we must do this "alone," meaning without clinging to egoic desires and perspectives.

On a deeper level, the Torah is not telling us to 'abandon' our surroundings. *Lech L'cha* means '*Go to yourself — for your benefit* — from your surroundings.' Your journey *begins* "from" your limiting and inaccurate perceptions of your space, time, and personal perception; these are your launching pad. But the journey itself is *"to"* yourself, 'toward' your highest truth. And thus it is also 'toward' true, de-limiting perceptions of space, time, and personality. Once we achieve a certain level of transcendence and growth, we should re-include the positive aspects of our previous period in life — including our 'land', our 'birthplace', and our 'father's home'.*

---

* The path of reintegration is related to a deeper reading of the word *Lech* / go. As the Baal Shem Tov teaches, *Lech* is numerically 50, which is the level of *Kerias Shema* (*Degel Macheneh Ephrayim*, Lech L'cha). There are 25 letters in the sentence of the Shema (שמע ישראל י-ה-ו-ה אלהינו י-ה-ו-ה אחד) and 24 letters in the *Baruch Sheim* (ברוך שם כבוד מלכותו לעולם ועד). Says the Zohar (*Tikunei Zohar*, Tikkun 21), in the future, the *Baruch Sheim* will also have 25 letters, as a Vav will be added as the first letter. Then, instead of the word *Baruch* / bless, it will say *U-Baruch* / 'and' bless, and the Shema plus the Baruch Sheim will equal 50. Parenthetically, this idea is connected to that of *Nun Shaarei Binah* / the 50 Gates of Understanding, and *Matan Torah* / the Giving of the Torah on the holy day of Shavuos, which is the 50th day after Pesach. The verse of Shema is called the "Higher Unity," as it refers to *Echad* / the Oneness that transcends all space, time, and personal consciousness. *Baruch Sheim* is called the "Lower Unity," and it contains the word *Va'ed* / forever, indicating that there was a beginning of time — a world. Normally, in our current world, the Shema and the Baruch Sheim are two distinct statements, not joined by a Vav. We declare the Higher Unity with our eyes closed and our voice raised so we don't see or hear the 'world'. This practice gives us a glimpse of the inner reality in which all is One, and the world of space, time, and personality does not truly exist. When we declare Lower Unity, we open our eyes and whisper it to ourselves, in an admission that there *is* a world of time-space and personal perception. Without the Vav, these are opposite statements. The Shema is the world of *Ayin* / 'no-thing-ness' or self-transcendence (*Hashem Echad*), and the Baruch Shem is the world of *Yesh* / 'existence' or the world of self. As there is a "higher" level and a "lower" level, then obviously we are meant to aspire to reach the higher level.

This will truly be for our "benefit," and like Avraham, we too will be blessed and become a source of blessing for others.

In the 'future', when we will have reached the destination that Hashem has shown us (*Lech* [50]...*El HaAretz Asher Arekah* / "Go...to the land *which I shall show you*), it will be a paradigm of *U-Baruch* / 'and' bless (the paradigm of 50). The Shema and the Baruch Sheim will be joined as one. This means it will be revealed that they are both an expression of a greater third principle which contains and integrates both (like a "land" which contains and integrates whatever appears there). In this way, the Essence of Hashem is expressed equally in the seemingly opposite modes of Higher Unity and Lower unity, in Ayin and in Yesh, in non-existence and self-existence. Likewise, even the aspects of our 'lower' self, our old space, time, and personality, will be revealed as part of *L'cha* — who we really are, our essential greatness.

LECH L'CHA

Energy of the Week:

Movement and Growth

This week's Torah reading infuses us with the *Ko'ach* / power of movement and the ability to grow despite any resistances. We can challenge ourselves by emerging from our comfort zone and entering the unknown, moving forward and journeying toward discovering our true self.

Feel empowered to overcome any stubbornness or inflexibility, or abdication of your potential to ideas of space, time, and personality. Simply drop all excuses and step out of our perceived limitations. Make a move this week, be it physically, financially, spiritually, intellectually or emotionally.

Perhaps there is an opportunity that has been presenting itself that you have felt you are not ready to take on. Take advantage of this week's additional *Shefa* / Divine flow of forward movement and growth, and make the leap. There will always be excuses available if we desire to stay in one place. But if we are to step toward growth, then we must let go of our limiting beliefs, and march forward with faith and trust.

Never stop listening to the eternal Heavenly Voice that invites or inspires us to *Lech L'cha* / to go to yourself, by yourself, toward the revelation of your greatest self, and to become a blessing for all Creation.

PRACTICE OF THE WEEK:

Make the Leap

Vayera

Correct Vision

THIS WEEK'S TORAH READING OPENS WITH THE words, "And now Hashem appeared to him …and he was sitting at the entrance of the tent" (*Bereishis*, 18:1).

In this *Pasuk* / verse, we are not told to whom Hashem appeared. We eventually learn from the narrative that it was Avraham, but his name is not mentioned in the Pasuk.

"And he lifted his eyes and saw, and behold, three men were standing near him, and perceiving this, he ran toward them from the entrance of the tent." Avraham was sitting by the entrance of his tent, experiencing a mystical vision of the Divine Presence, when he lifted his eyes and saw three men standing there. He interrupted his vision and rushed to greet them and offer them hospitality. From this, we learn גדולה הכנסת אורחים

מהקבלת פני שכינה / "Greater is the welcoming of guests than receiving the *Shechinah* / Divine Presence" (*Shabbos*, 127a). But how did Avraham know this principle?* We learn this teaching from him, but how did he know?

The Pasuk begins as a sequel to the previous portion in which Avraham circumcised himself. This is inferred by the first words of the Pasuk, 'And now…,' making it a continuation of the circumcision story. As the Zohar teaches, Avraham's circumcision was the cause of the revelation. Physically speaking, circumcision is an act of peeling away external parts of oneself to reveal something deeper. Yet, by doing this physical act of revelation, he merited to experience a spiritual revelation as well.

Avraham experienced this spiritual revelation from the perspective of his own essence, beyond his name. This is why the verse does not mention the name of Avraham, rather: "And now Hashem appeared to *him*…." "Him" indicates his essence.

---

* How did Avraham know this, and why exactly is it true that "Greater is the welcoming of guests than receiving the Divine Presence"? The Brisker Rav answers that it is because *Hachnasas Orchim* / welcoming guests is a Mitzvah, and a Mitzvah takes priority over *Deveikus* / mystical union. On the other hand, the Netziv writes that *Kabalas Pnei HaShechinah* / receiving the Divine Presence is also a Mitzvah, the Mitzvah of Deveikus. However, *Hachnasas Orchim* / welcoming guests is a *Mitzvah Overes* / a Mitzvah whose opportunity is passing. The three men would have left if Avraham did not run to welcome them, so he knew that in this case, the Mitzvah of Hachnasas Orchim pushes aside the Mitzvah of receiving the Presence of the Shechinah. Here are the words of HaAmek Davar (the Netziv): שהיא גדולה לדחות שכך הוא רצונו ית' שיהא מצוה מעשית דוחה מצוה זו שאין לה שיעור זמן…אכן זה אינו אלא במצוה שא"א להעשות ביד אחרים.

A name is a description, a means of human interaction. One person may call you 'father' or 'mother', another person may call you 'daughter' or 'son', and yet another, 'boss' or 'employee'. Your friends may call you one thing, while your family calls you something else. To each person, you are known by a different name, as you have a different relationship to everyone you encounter.

When Hashem 'appears' to someone and their name is used, it is a revelation of the Infinite One to an aspect of who that person is. In this case, however, there was a revelation to 'all' of Avraham, to the all-inclusive essence of who he was, which is too open-ended to have any title or name.

Avraham received a revelation into his essence because he had revealed his essence in the heroic act of circumcising himself. Avraham became fully open with nothing concealed, and so the Creator also became fully revealed to him, to all of him. Nothing remained hidden between Hashem and Avraham. It was an Essence-to-essence encounter.

This revelation occurs at the beginning of this week's Torah reading. At its conclusion (22:12), we read that Avraham is called a *Yirei Elokim*, which is generally translated as 'a G-d-fearing person', but can also mean 'a G-d-*seeing* person'. Avraham becomes a 'seer'. He is not 'merely' one who sees the Hand of G-d in his day-to-day life; rather, he sees himself and the world around him from within a Divine prism — as one with the Essence of the Creator, as it were. And as the Creator always sees "that it was good," so too, he sees goodness, possibility, and hope within everyone and everything in Creation.

When the Essence of the Creator is revealed in his own essence, Avraham acquires a more spiritually sensitive power of vision. He "raises his eyes," and he can now access the inner reality within everything, the Divine animating force within all of Creation, without any concealment. Thus, his seeing the arrival of guests is, in fact, a part of his mystical vision, his new way of seeing.*

---

* It is instructive to look closely at the words the Torah uses in these verses. Avraham is "sitting," the angels are "standing," and then he "runs" towards them. The Medrash adds, "The coming and going of people had ceased due to 'the heat of the day.'" However, despite this heat, there are men, who are really angels, "coming and going."

There is a *Ratzu V'Shuv* / running and returning of Asiyah, and there is a Ratzu V'Shuv of *Yetzirah* / the world of angels. The running and returning of Asiyah represent the "ways of the world," the ups and downs of life. Avraham has transcended worldly ups and downs. In the previous Parshah, Avraham is pre-Bris, but now he is post-Bris. The difference is that now he is one with Hashem, even in his body. So now, in the "heat of the sun," meaning in the 'higher' form of revelation in Asiyah, he is "sitting" in stillness, and there are no "passersby" — no Ratzu and Shuv of Asiyah. Yet, from this place of stillness and freedom from ego attachments, he beholds a higher level, a world of "angels."

The angels are "standing" (as the Book of Zecharyah tells us: angels are called *Omdin* / standing still, as there is no genuine movement or growth in their realm). Yet, Avraham sees them and "runs" towards them. This is because to him, they appear as if they *are* in the world of Ratzu and Shuv.

In other words, movement on the level of Yetzirah comes from a place of stillness, the stillness at the peak of the World of Asiyah. Movement in Asiyah is fundamentally restless, as it is driven by a constant desire and yearning for more. One may ascend within Asiyah to a state of stillness in which

When we read this passage, גדולה הכנסת אורחים מהקבלת פני שכינה / "Greater is the welcoming of guests than receiving the Divine Presence," we assume it means that greeting guests is greater than any mystical vision, and so it makes sense to us that Avraham appears to put his vision on hold to run to greet his guests. This is a valid explanation, but there is also a deeper meaning: גדולה הכנסת אורחים מהקבלת פני שכינה / "The greatness of greeting guests *is* the 'greatness' that is received from receiving the Divine presence." In other words, the effect of receiving the Presence of the Divine Essence is not separate from recognizing the essence of other people and bringing them into your home.[*]

Avraham did not have two experiences: one, a revelation of the Divine Presence, and two, seeing the arrival of guests. Rather, the experience of receiving the Divine Presence was materialized as seeing the guests.

---

there is no desire. This was Avraham's state of "sitting." But if one then is beckoned to an even higher level, one may "run"; one may enter the movement 'above' stillness, the movement of Yetzirah. In this higher movement, there is again desire, but it is not attached; it's lighter and more 'angelic'.

[*] Avraham was sitting in a state of *Deveikus* / unification with the Divine Presence, and in this state, וישא עיניו וירא והנה שלשה אנשים / "He lifted his eyes, and behold there were three men...." Hashem allowed him to see three guests while within his meditative state, and thus, he realized that serving them was *part* of *Kabalas Pnei HaShechinah* / receiving the Divine Presence. Not only that, but since it was Hashem's will that he perceive the guests *during* the meditative state, it was clear that running to serve them was a deeper level of Kabalas HaShechinah than merely sitting in silent mystical absorption.

Truly seeing a human being *is* the depths of seeing Hashem.

The first time 'seeing' is mentioned in the Torah is at the beginning of the Creation story, when Hashem creates Light. The Torah says, "And G-d saw that the Light was good." Divine seeing is seeing the goodness within Creation, beholding the *Nekudah Tovah* / the point of goodness, hope, and redemption in everything, everyone, and every situation.

VAYERA

Energy of the Week:
Essence Vision

Upon encountering another person, we tend to in-stantly label them and feel like we know who they are based on their appearance, dress, life station, man-nerisms, and so forth. The same can be true for all objects, places, or events we come in contact with ev-ery day. We tend to be easily influenced or impressed by external appearances and overlook the essence of who or what we are seeing. Without considering what lies deeper, we define them by what we see at first glance. However, this is often no more than a projection of our own conditioning and associations. This tendency extends even to the way we look at ourselves.

This week's Torah reading enables us to see beyond outer 'garments'. It 'raises our eyes' beyond names and labels and allows us to glimpse deeper truths. We learn to see beyond the concealments and trappings and behold the essence of the matter in its entirety, recognizing the spark of goodness within all.

This power of higher vision allows us to see each person for their essence, their essential Divinity and goodness, and extends to every event that occurs in our life. The Torah reading this week inspires us to everywhere perceive the Divine Hand of the One whose nature is to create, to give life and goodness: טבע הטוב להיטיב / "The Nature of the Good One is to bestow goodness" (*Sha'ar HaYichud veHaEmunah*, 4. See also *Shomer HaEmunim* (HaKadmon), 2:14. *Derech Hashem*, 2:1. Beginning of *Da'as Tevunos*. Shu't *Chacham Tzvi*, 18). Hashem is present in every life event and circumstance.

Essence-vision is the ability to see the Divine animating force, the goodness, and the life-affirming truth within everyone and everything. We view all of life as an opportunity and invitation to connect more deeply with the Creator, the Creation, and ourselves.

PRACTICE OF THE WEEK:

Train Yourself to See the Goodness Within Others & Life

Chayei Sarah
Death within Living

THIS WEEK'S TORAH READING IS CALLED *Chayei Sarah* / 'The Life of Sarah'. Its narrative opens with the words, "And the life of Sarah was 100 years and 20 years and seven years… And Sarah passed on" (23:1–2). Avraham then begins mourning her and purchases a plot of land in which to bury her. The Parshah speaks only of her death and the events that follow, yet its title is "The *Life* of Sarah."

A simple reason for this title is that this portion speaks of the living legacy of Sarah, the continuation of her progeny, the story of Yitzchak, her only son, and his marriage. So in this sense, the "life" of Sarah means the 'legacy' of Sarah.

A deeper reason for the title is the message that for "life" to be lived to its fullest, it must also include the element of death. A life cycle is a flow of life and death, inhale and exhale.

This is true both personally and cosmically. The flow of Divine life-force into this cosmos is similar to the cycle of our breath, as the creation and re-creation of the universe is a continuous process. The Divine 'exhale', as it were, fills all of Creation and gives it existence and life. Then, almost simultaneously, Creation exhales and gives its life back to its Creator as a cosmic 'exhalation' into the Creator's 'inhalation'. And again, instantaneously, the Creator breathes the breath of life back into us; back and forth, exhalation and inhalation, expiration and inspiration, 'running and returning' (*Ohr HaEmes*, Imrei Tzadikim, p 4).

Every moment thus has the Divine attribute of *Chesed* / 'giving' new existence and reviving the 'dead' — and the Divine attribute of *Gevurah* / 'retracting' existence and reabsorbing life (*Pri HaAretz*, Vayeshev. *Avir* / air or oxygen is numerically 216 (217), as is three times the word *Chesed*: 72+72+72=216. The word *Gevurah* is also 216: *Eitz Chayim*, Sha'ar 25, Derush 1. This means *Avir* includes both Chesed, the Creator's exhale into us, and Gevurah, our exhale into the Creator).

Bridging this ever-present oscillation of expansion and contraction, including both giving and restricting, Chesed and Gevurah, coming alive and passing away, is the third element, *Tiferes* / splendor. Tiferes is also the retention in between breaths.

This process is continuous. Every moment, there is the cosmic exhale of Hashem into the world — creating, forming, animating, and sustaining creation anew at all times, and an immediate return, a Divine inhale, as it were.

On the microcosmic level, our every inhalation is our per-sonal reception of the cosmic flow of new vitality and strength that rushes into Creation. This represents our instinctual am-bition to succeed and thrive and fill ourselves with more and more abundance. Our every exhale is the emptying of our-selves into the Creator, 'expiring' back into our Source. This represents our moments of surrender, serenity, and letting go, gratefully offering our abundance back to the Giver.

To live life fully, we need to also know how to 'die' הרוצה לחיות ימית את עצמו / "One who wants to truly live, let him 'kill' himself'"" (Tamid, 32a). In the simplest interpretation, this means 'let him live moderately'; to 'surrender' his addictive urges for wealth and pleasure. On a deeper level, this means we need to be able to let go, to be comfortable taking a break from the world of striving, and to be grateful for what Hashem has giv-en us. This can be emotionally painful at times. For example, there can be a little 'death' of our ego when we refrain from indulging in a food that is objectively not healthy for us.

We do need to work hard, create ambitious goals, contin-ually strive for more Divine goodness, and be fully engaged in the world. Yet, simultaneously, we must also have a strong awareness that our lives are in the hands of our Creator, and that every breath we are given is a gift. And with every exha-lation, we are returning our life back to the Source of Life. In this way, even in our striving to achieve, we won't be attached to results. We will know that at the end of the day, Hashem runs the world, not us.

Our life-force is symbolized by (and embodied in) our blood flow. If it is held back and not allowed to flow properly, it will begin to coagulate and clot. The viscosity of our blood must constantly be in balance so as to maintain a healthy flow of Chesed and Gevurah, the flow of 'receiving life' and 'releasing life'.

CHAYEI SARAH

Energy of the Week:
Letting Go

This week's Torah reading gives us the strength to let go. We harness the power to surrender and be at peace with what we have and what we have achieved so far in our lives.

We are, of course, human, and we have an inborn drive to constantly strive, live, and grow. While this drive is essential to the human condition, the need to surrender and understand that our life rests in the Hands of our Creator is equally essential to our growth and success in life.

This week's Torah reading enables us to exhale deeply and allows us to surrender and 'rest in peace' and
acceptance. Allow yourself to experience surrender-
ing your life to Hashem and sense how this, too, is an
essential part of being fully alive. Wait for a moment
at the end of your exhale until the Creator gently
places within you your next inhale — a gift of 'inspiration' from Above.

PRACTICE OF THE WEEK:

Surrender

Toldos
Utilizing Tension to Create the New

"And these are the generations of Yitzchak... he was 40 years old when he took Rivkah...for a wife...And he prayed...opposite his wife, because she was barren... and his wife conceived" (25:19–21).

Yitzchak and Rivkah have already been married for a while and She has not been able to conceive a child. Now something shifts. Although we already know that Yitzchak is married to Rikvah, the Pasuk goes out of the way to inform us, "He was 40 years old when he took Rivkah...as a wife." This surprising interjection invites us to look more closely at the unique wording of the verse: "...he *took* Rivkah...as a wife." And directly following this, it says, "And he prayed *opposite* his wife...." Reading between the lines, it becomes clear that although he had married her already, he was now truly 'taking her as a wife', and specifically by 'praying opposite her'. And with this new approach, they are finally blessed with children.

There are two dynamics permeating Creation from the macrocosmic to the microcosmic realms: the 'masculine' dynamic, meaning 'giving' — and the 'feminine' dynamic, meaning 'receiving'. All of life is composed through articulations of these two fundamental dynamics, which are *Zeh LeUmas Zeh* / "one opposite the other" (אמר רב יהודה אמר רב כל מה שברא הקב"ה בעולמו זכר ונקבה בראם / "Rav Yehuda says that Rav says, 'Everything that the Holy One, Blessed be He, created in His world, He created male and female'": *Baba Basra*, 74b. 'Male and female' also means משפיע ומושפע / 'giver and given-to': Shaloh, *Torah Ohr*, Shemini, 6).

In the most basic form of this theme, the Creator is the Giver, and the Creation is the receiver. Although, 'within' the Creator, there are attributes of both Giver and Receiver. Within Divinity, there is the 'Giver', called the *Ohr* / Light, and within Divinity, there is also a revelation of the *Kli* / vessel for the Light, the receiver. In another way of saying this, Hashem has a *Ko'ach Bli Gevul* / an Infinite Power, and a *Ko'ach HaGevul* / a Finite Power (אין סוף הוא שלימות בלי חסרון וא"ת שיש לו כח בלי גבול ואין לו כח בגבול אתה מחסר שלימותו — Rebbe Azriel of Gerona, a student of Rebbe Yitzchak Sagi-Nahor and a Rebbe of Kabbalah to the Ramban: *Bi'ur Eser* Sefiros, 3. *Avodas HaKodesh*, 1:8).

Although found within both men and women, the dynamic of 'giver' is generally termed 'masculine'. It is expressed in forward or outward proactive movement, and is often characterized by assertiveness, extraversion, and ambition. The dynamic of 'receiver', also found within both men and women, is expressed in inward movement and characterized by 'feminine' receptivity, introspection, hiddenness, and presence.

In our narrative, the protagonist Yitzchak was raised, fed, and housed by his loving parents, Avraham and Sarah. While the Torah tells us a tremendous amount about his parents, and details many conversations between Avraham and others and between Avraham and Hashem, the young man Yitzchak is basically portrayed as voiceless. Life seems to occur *to* Yitzchak; he doesn't seem to choose anything proactively. When he is already in his late thirties, he has yet to be married and still doesn't seem to be looking for marriage. His father needs to send his servant Eliezer to find him a wife. Outward or assertive movement does not seem part of Yitzchak's constitution. Indeed, the saintly Arizal, Rebbe Yitzchak Luria, reveals that Yitzchak was born with a feminine soul and only received a masculine soul at a later point in life.

In mentioning that Rivkah was barren and could not have children, the Torah says, "And he prayed...opposite his wife, כי עקרה הוא / "because she was barren" (*Bereishis*, 25:21). Interestingly, the word "barren" here is a feminine adjective, but the pronoun "she" here is written with a Vav instead of a Yud, spelling הוא / *Hu* / he meaning "*he* was barren." Now, the tradition is to pronounce this pronoun verbally as if it is written היא / *Hee*

/ she, as in "*she* was barren." And still, we need to understand that both the written spelling and the spoken pronunciation are true readings. Clearly, in the external world, it was obvious that Rivkah was 'barren' as she was not becoming pregnant. Yet the written spelling alerts us to something hidden from view: he himself was in fact barren. And since both are true readings, we learn that שניהם עקורים היו / "they were both barren" (*Yevamos,* 64a).

In order to create a new entity, opposing forces need to come together. When a thesis and an antithesis unite, there is a possibility of synthesis, which is something new. From the tension and eventual fusion of opposites, masculine and feminine, a third reality, a new life can emerge. Although they were already married for a while, both Yitzchak and Rivkah had both been embodying the feminine dynamic, and thus, they were not able to create new life together (To create a 'third' there needs to be a masculine Chesed (the Name *MaH*) and feminine Gevurah (the Name *BaN*), but both Yitzchak and Rivkah were both connected originally to feminine Din / Gevurah).

They were not able to have children because they were on the same 'side'.

When Yitzchak finally stood נכח / 'opposite', meaning 'in front of', his wife,* he moved to the other 'side'. He then em-

---

* Regarding the word נכח, the Arizal teaches that when the Pasuk says, עיניך לנכח יביטו / "Let your eyes look forward" (*Mishlei,* 4:25), the word נכח in numerical value is 78, the same as the Name of Hashem three times (3x26=78). Thus, to be נכח means to place the Name of Hashem literally

bodied the quality of the proactive masculine 'giver', and she stood opposite him as the embodiment of the feminine 'receiver'. In this way, as they prayed 'opposite' each other, they could finally come together as opposites and create new life.

In general, the posture of *Tefilah* / prayer is to take a stand 'opposite' to what life presents to us, requesting or pleading from the Creator of All Life and Infinite Possibilities, to alter reality. For instance, we pray that a sick person be healed. Life presents that individual as sick, and yet, we counter this status quo and request that the individual should be healed. Indeed, this is precisely what Hashem wants from us; to have 'limited vision' and look at life on face value, and then to plead for change (Although we must simultaneously have complete faith that from a higher perspective, life is exactly how it should be). The act of prayer is a brazen, almost, 'heretical' act: Hashem tells us, 'This is the way it is,' and yet we 'demand' that it change. In fact, it could be said that if praying was not a Mitzvah, it would be the greatest of sins.

---

in front of you 'three times': once to your right, once directly in front, and once to the left. These are the directions that your eyes naturally see: *Likutei Torah*, Parshas Toldos, on the Pasuk *l'Nochach Ishto*. See *Sha'ar Ruach Ha-Kodesh*, 8a. In the context of Yitzchak praying, this means they were both 'front and center' in relation to the other, such that in 'every direction', in every natural visual angle, she was his 'opposite'. It is interesting to note that we bow to Hashem in these three directions at the end of the Amidah prayer. Perhaps this practice helps to trigger a Giver-receiver relationship between Hashem and ourselves, as it were, allowing something new to be created.

Standing up, being proactive and assertive, and being so forward as to try and 'influence' the Creator to change, so to speak, is a gift that the Creator gives us and wants us to use. This is only one of the postures of prayer: it is the masculine dimension of Yitzchak. Yet, both Yitzchak and Rivkah prayed. While Yitzchak assumed an active, demanding stance, Rivkah remained with the 'radical acceptance' aspect of prayer. Prayer includes both assertively making requests, and being gratefully receptive to what Hashem has already given us. We need both. As an allusion to this dual function of prayer; the numeric value of *Tefilah* / prayer is 515, the same value as the sum of the names Yitzchak (208) and Rivkah (307).

Yitzchak and Rivkah created new life by embodying opposite dynamics in prayer. The uniting of these opposites allowed for the creation of a 'synthesis': their children.

TOLDOS

Energy of the Week:
Utilizing Tension to Create

This week's Torah reading gives us the strength to create new realities and paradigms through the power of opposites. Whether these opposites exist within yourself, or between yourself and others, the idea is to use the tension to create a new force. At some point, there may be a merging of these opposites in such a way that a third force emerges to synthesize the two.

Understand that it takes polar opposites to create a new entity. Embrace the opposing energies within yourself and within your relationships and observe how they bring about new consciousness and new creativity.

In the workplace, this may translate into finding that the person with whom you experience tension is actually capable of increasing your productivity — through that very tension.

As another example, the ways that you differ from your partner, spouse, friend, or child may create a tension that can be utilized to engineer change and new direction. Too much 'yes' and like-mindedness doesn't usually stimulate growth. An occasional pull in the opposite direction can create just the right amount of tension which will increase the energy and produce change. In the arts, as in prayer, the tensions of pain, cognitive dissonance, or great need are often the factors that trigger the greatest creativity and productivity. What's important is that, like Yitzchak, we take the initiative to harness these experiences.

This week, proactively take the view that the things which 'oppose' you are really creative opportunities. Actively utilize the spark which is created from the friction of opposing forces to bring forth new light. Stand 'opposite' the Creator and leverage the discomfort of your unmet needs to pray with intensity and sincerity for fulfillment.

PRACTICE OF THE WEEK:

Be Proactive

Vayetzei
Steadiness Within Turbulence

ayeitzei / And Ya'akov 'went out' from Be'er Sheva, and
he went toward Charan. And he arrived at 'the Place'
and lodged there because the sun had set...and he lay
down in that place... and he dreamed, and behold, there was
a ladder set up on the ground and its top reached to Heaven,
and the angels...were ascending and descending... and behold, Hashem was standing above it...(Upon awakening) he
said, "Indeed, the Divine is in this place, and I did not know"
(*Bereishis*, 28:10–16).

Our journey this week begins with Ya'akov, who is already
in his sixties, leaving his homeland. He is not merely "going

to" Charan; rather, he is also "leaving from" Be'er Sheva, and stepping away from his previous life. Up until this moment in Ya'akov's life, he has been living a sheltered life with his parents. This is why he is called 'a man of tents', in contrast to his wild, aggressive brother, who is called a 'man of the field'. He is secluded and protected, hidden away from the harsh realities of physical, mundane life.

At his mother's urgent instructions, he leaves the Holy Land, from the town of Be'er Sheva, which can be translated as 'the Well of Satisfaction'. In doing so, he leaves the protection and spiritual satisfaction of the Holy Land. He leaves his parents' home, his comfort zone, and journeys to the city called *Charan*, which can be translated as 'Divine Wrath' (חרון אף של מקום בעולם: Rashi, *Bereishis*, 11:32). This name implies it is a place of corruption and deceit, and thus a place that is in total opposite to the holiness of *Eretz Yisrael* / the Land of Israel.

Ya'akov is essentially departing from a place of spiritual elevation and safety, a place of clarity and a life of introspection and contemplation (the 'tent'), and moving into the unknown. Indeed, the debased Charan, a place of conceit and materialism, is bewilderingly unknown. Now, he is in limbo, neither dwelling in his settled past nor yet reaching the future that he hopes for.

The first place he encounters on his journey from Be'er Sheva to Charan, is called במקום / *BaMakom* / '(In) the Place'. This is an ambiguous, uncertain, and undefined location, and it is here that he experiences nightfall all of a sudden, upon arrival: ויפגע במקום וילן שם כי־בא השמש / "He encountered 'the Place' and lodged there as the sun had set" (28:11). Not only is this 'place' itself uncertain, but he encounters it in the dim light of uncertainty. "He encountered the Place" also means 'he bumped into the Place' — he finds himself there without intention or prior knowledge. Something about this place is 'beyond' him.

It seems his 'sunny days' are behind him; the life of 'day' and clarity is left behind, and he is entering a world where 'the sun has set', and darkness is descending. He is frightened and vulnerable, and lacking the clear vision to continue on his journey, he simply lies down to rest and sleep.

'In' this unnamed and unmarked location, amid the darkness, he has a strikingly vivid dream: "A ladder was set up on the ground and its top reached Heaven, and angels…were ascending and descending… and behold, Hashem was נצב / *Nitzav* / standing above it." Amid great movement, he beholds above the ladder and above all movement the "standing" or unmoving Presence of Hashem. The word the Torah uses is נצב / *Nitzav*, which can be translated as 'standing' or as 'steady'.

When he awakens, the sun rises and he experiences unprecedented clarity of vision. Now he is able to declare, "Indeed, Hashem is in this place, and I did not know!"

Angels are conduits of energy and transmitters of information; they are communicators. Through their ascents and descents, the angels are communicating something about the world of ups and downs. At first, Ya'akov senses that he is witnessing the ups and downs, the onrushing experiences of his own life. He is dazzled by this constant movement, and he is attached to this 'content', this narrative. But then he beholds Hashem, standing Above, steady and still through it all, beyond all the intense ups and downs.

When he awakens, he realizes that Hashem is in "this Place", right here, right now.*

---

* The Pasuk says the word *Makom* / 'place' three times: ויפגע במקום וילן שם כי בא השמש ויקח מאבני המקום וישם מראשתיו וישכב במקום ההוא / "He came upon a certain Makom and stopped there for the night, for the sun had set. Taking one of the stones of that Makom, he put it under his head and lay down in that Makom" (*Bereishis*, 28:11). These three references to Makom represent the three essential contexts of existence: the context of location, the context of time, and the context of consciousness:

Location: *HaMakom* is Mount Moriah, which is the place of the Foundation Stone, the essence and source of all space: *Yuma*, 54b.

Time: Hashem, the Yud-Hei-Vav-Hei represents Infinity. The letters of Yud-Hei-Vav-Hei spell out, *Hayah* / 'it was' (past), *Hoveh* / 'it is' (present), *Yihyeh* / 'it will be' (future) — the infinity of time. In full numerical value, that involves multiplying each letter, the Yud/10, Hei/5, Vav/6, Hei/5, thus 10x10 + 5x5 + 6x6 + 5x5 = 186. *Makom* is also 186 (Mem/40, Kuf/100, Vav/6, Mem/40 = 186).

Consciousness: *Ya'akov* is numerically 182. Yud/10, Ayin/70, Kuf/100, Beis/2, plus 4 for the four letters = 186.

Ultimately, "the Place" is singular. As space and time are really one, HaMakom is the singular essence of all space-time. And since consciousness observes and gives reality to space-time, it is, in turn, the context and essence, the Makom, of space-time. Ya'akov is the observer, the very 'locus' of consciousness, in the dream. In this way, when Ya'akov encounters 'HaMakom'

Hashem's Presence is the unmoving 'Place', the transcendent context or 'container' of all movement. The Divine Presence is the backdrop behind all ups and downs, beyond or prior to all the ladders of life. Indeed, one of the names of Hashem is *HaMakom* / 'the Place', the unmoving Divine Space within which the world appears.

Just as Hashem can be found within our moments of clarity, spiritual satisfaction and redemption, Hashem is present within all our moments of ambiguity, spiritual turbulence and exile. In day and night, light and darkness, Hashem is equally present, without exception. The question is, why don't we always recognize Hashem's Presence in darkness and dissatisfaction?

"Indeed," he says, "Hashem *is* in this place, but I — *I* did not know." In Hebrew, if he had said *V'Lo Yadati* without the word *Anochi* / 'I', it would still mean "I did not know." Why the 'double I'? In the 'daylight' of clear perception, Ya'akov suddenly realized that it was his 'I', his ego, which had not allowed him to know the truth of the Makom: "(My) 'I' did not know." His 'small self' had been concealing the expansive perception of his essence, and of Hashem's Presence dwelling there, but this concealment had dissolved in his dream state, and he awoke in an egoless mode of perception.

Even when we are on a high, our small 'I' is actually pronounced; we can still be obsessed with how we feel. And when

---

he is encountering the essence of time, space, and consciousness in and as himself. In simple terms, he is encountering his own essence.

we are at a low point, we can still have an arrogant preoccupa-
tion with our fragile ego. In both cases, the real self is obscured.
Thus, "And I did not know" also means, 'I did not really know
myself.' And that's the reason one doesn't know that Hashem
is there in a place that feels 'static'. The part of self that doesn't
really 'know' anything because it just lives in its own thoughts,
is always on a rollercoaster of highs and lows. Identifying with
this false self eclipses one's perception of the space-like steadiness of their true self, and as a result, they cannot know the
ultimate steadiness of the Creator and Essence of Life.

Ya'akov was coming from Be'er Sheva, a higher location, to
the lower place of *Charan* / anger — and he was scared. But he
was even more scared of a place that is 'neither high nor low',
where life is just *Nitzav* / static. Therefore, when he 'bumps
into' the Place, the unmoving Space, and it startles him. However, this liminal space is precisely where Ya'akov can take a
completely accurate inventory of his life and prepare for the
next step in his journey through life.* This gives Ya'akov the

---

* *Shacharis* / the morning prayer, *Mincha* / the afternoon prayer and *Ma'ariv*
/ evening prayer were initiated by the three corresponding *Avos* / Patriarchs, Avraham, Yitzchak, and Ya'akov. We observe how Ya'akov initiates
Ma'ariv, as he prays when the sun sets and it is dark. Yet, technically speaking, Ma'ariv is not a חובה / obligatory prayer; rather, it is a רשות / *Reshus* /
optional prayer (*Berachos*, 27b. Although today, we have accepted Ma'ariv
as an obligation upon men, and it remains optional for women). Why was
the Tefilah that Ya'akov prayed considered only a Reshus? In life, there
are things that we are obligated to do, for example, positive Mitzvos, and
there are things we are forbidden to do, as in negative prohibitions of the
Torah. Yet, there are also the 'in-between' things that are neither Mitzvos
nor *Aveiros* / prohibitions. This is the place of Reshus; hence, while in this
in-between space, Ya'akov initiated the evening Tefilah which was a Reshus.

strength and stamina to journey 'downward' into the darker world of Charan, while remaining connected to *HaMakom* / Hashem's Everpresence.

In that liminal Space, Ya'akov has a dream of angels moving up and down, with Hashem standing still above them. He realizes that his 'ups and downs' in life are just like 'angels' — different manifestations of duality and ever-shifting feelings. And yet, Hashem is 'standing' in stability and stillness, encompassing all of them from above.

The small 'I' thinks that G-d is only in the high spiritual experiences. But this 'I' is what does not allow one to see that "indeed Hashem is in this Space" right here, right now, deep within my essence, no matter how high or low I feel. Discovering this, we cry out, 'I did not know that a higher Stability encompasses all my life!"

Anochi / I, refers to the unchanging essence of who we are. Ya'akov says, *Anochi Lo Yadati* / 'It is my *Anochi* that I did not know!' This awakening as essence occurs precisely after he has left the heights of Eretz Yisrael, and is descending towards the depths of Charan. 'Between' the angels that are ascending and descending, 'between' all ups and downs in his life, he senses who he is in essence: a revelation of the Ultimate Self, Hashem's ever-steady Presence.

When we are spiritually excited, moving, or making progress, and great things are happening to us, that excitement can distract us from consciously knowing our stable, essential self. Similarly, if we get caught up in a drama or tragedy, we can lose perception of essence.

Like Ya'akov, sometimes we're moving and traveling, and suddenly we bump up against darkness, limbo and vulnerability. A seemingly 'negative' experience may trigger a fight or flight reaction in our body and mind. We may instinctually fight the darkness, perhaps by trying to change it or to push through the experience. Or we might attempt to 'flee' the experience and deny or avoid the unpleasant sensations and narratives that are arising.

Ya'akov's brilliant response is simply to stop and rest. He allows himself to be in this in-between state, beyond his comfort zone, without acting upon any reactive thoughts or feelings. In fact, when night falls, he allows himself to become even more vulnerable by going to sleep there, in the open air. He is not grasping at the past nor at the future; he is just being still and open. This is a deep *Avodah* / a mode of spiritual work in which your Anochi can emerge and you can receive the gift of unconditionally clear vision.

VAYETZEI

Energy of the Week:
Steadiness Within Turbulence

This week's Torah reading gives us the strength to uncover our true self, when we are precisely in the 'in-between' moments of life, neither going up nor going down, not feeling 'high on life', but also not feeling particularly low, just in-between. When we can sense Hashem's steady and constant presence in these undefined or uncertain moments, we will strengthen our ability to sense the Divine through-out all ups and downs.

As a response to uncertainty, we may sometimes build up the courage to move forward, but other times we are 'forcibly' removed from all familiarity and place into a new 'story'. Being outside of our comfort zone is difficult, especially when we have set out with confidence or determination but then quickly bump into darkness and the unknowable.

The initial excitement and adrenaline rush of a new journey can quickly drain away when we encounter ambiguity. The most challenging feelings can be those of emptiness, loneliness, and alienation, and being unmoored, without a foothold.

The revelation of Ya'akov's dream is the deep realization of Hashem's constancy throughout all our journeys. Hashem is a steady and constant presence, throughout the roughest parts of our path, and in the times of illumination, as well. This week, we receive the strength and stamina to continue onward in our journey through life. We move forward in the knowledge that Hashem is present, standing above every experience and movement. In the greatest turbulence, there is always a 'Place' of stillness and steadiness. Even in the darkest of moments, we are never alone.

PRACTICE OF THE WEEK:

**Stillness of Presence
within the Drama of Life**

Vayishlach
Re-establishing Bonds, Healing Rifts

Y A'AKOV NOW RETURNS HOME AFTER MANY YEARS of exile. He had left his home many years earlier to escape his elder brother Eisav, who wished to kill him. Ya'akov is now returning home and wishes to make peace with his brother.

"Ya'akov sent angels ahead of him to his brother Eisav" (*Bereishis*, 32:4).

He begins his return by sending 'angels' to precede him. In the broadest definition, a *Malach* / angel is a 'messenger'. This suggests that an angel is a carrier, conduit, or transmitter of some form of information or energy. In fact, since everything in life carries a distinct flow and quality and transmits information or energy, all natural phenomena can be seen as 'angels' (Rambam, *Moreh Nevuchim*, 2:6: וכבר ידעת, שעניין 'מלאך' שליח, וכל עושה מעשה

מצוה הוא 'מלאך' עד שתנועות בעלי החיים ואפילו שאינם מדברים סיפר הכתוב עליהם שהם 'על

ידי מלאך' כשתאות התנועה ההיא לכונת האלוה אשר שם בו כח יניעהו התנועה ההיא / "'Angel' means 'messenger', and hence everyone that is entrusted with a certain mission is an 'angel'. Even the movements of the brute creation are sometimes due to the action of an angel, when such movements serve the purpose of the Creator, who endowed it with the power of performing that movement." See also *Likutei Sichos*, 5. p. 82–83).

Another kind of 'angel' is the energy and information that we continuously create through our thoughts, words, and actions. Everything we think, say, and do releases and transmits a spark of subjective energy into the interpersonal atmosphere. When Ya'akov consciously sent "angels" toward Eisav, he may have sent physical messengers or actual angels, and he did send gifts — but he also generated subtle 'angels' of thoughts of love and reconciliation and sent these out to precede his arrival.

The message had been relayed to Ya'akov that Eisav was approaching him with four hundred men, apparently ready to wage war. Ya'akov senses that Eisav has not forgiven him for buying the rights of the firstborn when Eisav was exhausted, hungry, and vulnerable. Realizing that Eisav is not in favor of a peace agreement, Ya'akov strategizes for the worst scenario and prays for guidance. He prepares for the encounter on three levels: 1) he sends love and gifts; 2) in case those do not help, he is ready to battle; and 3) through it all, he continuously prays for protection and guidance to make the correct choices (This three-pronged approach (gifts or appeasements, battle, and prayer) was learned from his grandfather, Avraham: Rashi, *Bereishis*, 18:23, and replicated by his son, Yehudah: *Medrash Rabbah*, Bereishis, 93:6).

When he was finally about to encounter Eisav, upon seeing him, "Ya'akov prostrated himself to the ground seven times, until he came close to him, to his brother. And Eisav ran toward him and embraced him, and he fell on his neck and kissed him, and they wept" (32:3–4).

Something crucial and profound occurred to Eisav; he originally approached Ya'akov to wage battle but embraced him instead. Between the intention to fight and the embrace were Ya'akov's seven prostrations, and this is what seemed to change their entire relationship.

When a person prostrates him or herself, they are physically 'breaking' and softening the straight line of their body, bending their head and spine. Spiritually, this represents a 'breaking' of negativity or concealment (*Kidushin* 29b: אידמי ליה כתנינא דשבעה רישוותיה כל כריעה דכרע נתר חד רישיה / "The demon appeared to him like a serpent with seven heads (Rav Acha bar Ya'akov began to pray, and with) every bow that he bowed one of the demon's heads fell off, until it eventually died").

Bowing is a movement that allows for a seemingly immutable outer reality to crumble, and a new reality, one that reflects an inner truth, to emerge. Seven is symbolic of the natural order of the world, a world created by seven (Divine 'attributes') in seven (days) and exists for seven (millennia). The world of nature is an outer concealment that hides the miraculous, the enlivening Divine animating force and potential of everything, within it.

By prostrating seven times, Ya'akov broke the old reality that once seemed so unshakeable and revealed the truth of their story, the natural love between brothers that was always there beneath the concealments and friction.[*]

[*] In contrast to Ya'akov bowing, breaking open the apparent 'concealment' of brotherly love and revealing it, Eisav sets out to greet him with 400 men. The final letter of the Aleph-Beis is Tav, which is numerically 400, and represents concealment. Letters and words conceal one's thoughts, albeit they also reveal them. Cosmically, the world is created through the Aleph-Beis. The letter Aleph ('1'), is still connected to the Light, revealing more of the original Oneness, and thus the final letter represents the ultimate 'concealment' of the Light. Another way of saying this is Tav equals 400 Alephs (*Toldos Ya'akov Yoseph*, Bereishis. *Toldos Aharon*, Likutim, p. 493). Thus, the original and primordial exile of Klal Yisrael, the 'concealment' of their purpose and destiny, was living in Egypt for 400 years. *Ayin HaRa* / evil eye, concealing the goodness of what is being seen, is also numerically 400, and thus the concept of Ayin HaRa is always present when 400 is mentioned: see, for example, *Berachos*, 4b. *Eiruvin*, 54b, *Ben Yehoyada*, ad loc. The root of the descent into Egypt was the sale of Yoseph, toward whom the brothers projected an Ayin haRa, and were, as a result, condemned to 400 years of exile. *Rabbeinu Bachya*, 15:13. The hidden, 'concealed' Cave of Machpelah was purchased by Avraham for 400 *Kesef* / silver (connected to the 400 men of Eisav. *Likutei Torah*, Vayishlach, first two Ma'amarim). Indeed, the name of the person from whom Avraham purchased the cave, *Efron*, without a Vav is 400: *Gur Aryeh. Rokeach. Hadar Zekeinim.* Baal HaTurim, *ad loc*. The mission and purpose of Amalek, the archenemy of Klal Yisrael, is connected to 400, as represented by the 400 men with Eisav. Thus, Mordechai, who wages battle against Haman-Amalek, wears שק / sackcloth, which is numerically 400. And eventually, the House of Eisav, which became intermingled with Amalek, will be nullified by Yoseph, who is beyond the reach of Ayin HaRa (*Berachos*, 55b) והיה בית־יעקב אש ובית יוסף להבה ובית עשו לקש / "The House of Ya'akov shall be fire and the House of Yoseph a flame, and the House of Eisav shall be קש straw" (*Ovadiah*, 1:18), קש / straw is also 400. The root of this world of Asiyah is the letter Hei (*Menachos*, 29b), the letter of breath, as breath comes before speech. Hei is shaped like a Dalet with a Yud next to it. The Dalet / 4 represents the four corners of this world of dimensionality, and the Yud, the 'point', represents the focus on the central *point* of life, the dimension of Divine life. Without this Yud, there is just

Even years after a conflict, one can still be stuck, rigidly holding a frozen image of the experience in their mind, subliminally rehearsing the story over and over how that person did such and such to them. The instinctual self responds to this stressful mental narrative by etching into the nervous system certain self-preservation strategies. The system remains in an unresolved, low-level or subconscious fight or flight response. This rigidity can block freedom of movement and growth, and sometimes even prevent the inner revelation that the past

the fullness of Dalet, 400, thus the world of exile and concealment, and the power of the 4 exiles. Exile and estrangement manifest when there is no realization that there is a central *Nekudah* / point to life.

The *Megaleh Amukos* speaks of the 'hidden five (Hei)' alluded to at the beginning of the Parshah. For example, ארצה / *Artzah*, with a Hei instead of a Lamed (as in *LaAretz*). Also, when Ya'akov says, "I have שור וחמור צאן ועבד ושפחה / cattle, donkeys, sheep, and male and female servant(s)" (32:6), five objects are listed.

Ya'akov is drawing down and sending "five" to Eisav. When Eisav is born, Ya'akov takes away his 'Yud'. When Eisav is born, they name him 'Eisav', which comes from the word complete (עשוי) since he was born complete with hair, as Rashi says. Some sources say he was born with teeth. But if so, why is he called Eisav, without a Yud, and not Asuy, with a Yud? After Eisav's birth, Ya'akov is born, with "his hand grasping Eisav's heel, and (Yitzchak) named him Ya'akov." But 'heel' is *Ekev*, not *Ya'akov*, so why is he called Ya'akov with a Yud? Says the Zohar, this is because Ya'akov 'stole' the Yud from Eisav. And thus, *Ya'akov* has a Yud in the beginning and *Eisav* lacks a Yud at the end.

Perhaps an allusion to sending back the Yud, in the form of the Hei / 5, are the five *Nekudos* / dots above the word "and he kissed him" (see *Sifsei Chumim*, ad loc, although most sources speak of six Nekudos), when Eisav finally meets again with Ya'akov (a Yud is like a 'dot').

is past and one can let go and move forward. By bowing in front of Eisav, Ya'akov softens the rigidity in his own spine, and reveals his willingness to move on, to forgive. A person of deep *Emes* / truth and faith, Ya'akov has the courage to become malleable, break his traumatic narrative, draw out his brotherly love from within, and send it out to Eisav.

The Zohar teaches that by bowing down to the Divine spark / the Shechinah, within Eisav, essentially, to the purity, holiness, and perfection within him, he was softening Eisav's external heart as well. As a result, the hidden, deep natural love of Eisav towards Ya'akov was also released. As the layers of accumulated hurtful narratives fell away, Eisav's love spontaneously became revealed, and instead of threatening war, he opened to a tearful embrace.

"Until he came close to him, to his brother." Ya'akov prostrated himself until he could reach "his brother" — not the external form of Eisav who still hated him, tied to his old narrative, but the real Eisav, his twin brother, and the son of the righteous Yitzchak and Rivkah. Once Ya'akov reached who Eisav really was, they could both reach out to embrace each other.

VAYISHLACH

Energy of the Week:

Re-establishing Bonds / Healing Rifts

This Torah reading gives us the strength to repair our relationships with others — in particular, with family members from whom we may have felt alienated. This is a week for reconciliation.

Ya'akov established a map for reconnecting with others. We should begin by 'sending messengers', or messages if you will. This means finding willingness in yourself to reconcile and to wish true well-being for the other person. Dwell on these thoughts of goodwill and they will invisibly transmit the opportunity to reconcile. Look for the inner truth of that person; know that their innermost essence is pure and luminous. Reach out carefully, being aware of the other person's current feelings. Prepare for the possibility that you may not at first be successful.

To prepare for 'war' means understanding that you are only half of the equation — you cannot force your choices onto another, and they, too, have free choice and may choose not to engage civilly. If goodwill is not reciprocated, you may have to acknowledge temporary defeat and wait for another opportunity.

'Prayer' is reaching out beyond yourself — understanding that the Creator is infinitely greater than yourself and the estranged person. Ask Hashem for help, knowing that healing the rift will affect a *Tikun* / a change for the better throughout the entire universe.

Finally, assume a posture of softness, an inner 'position' of bowing. This means to humble our voice that wishes to perpetuate old narratives, and to break free of what you have felt to be true until now. This allows us to reveal and "reach" the deeper truth that has been there all along: the other person is your 'brother' or 'sister', in that you both come from the same Ultimate Source. They too are a son or daughter of the Creator.

PRACTICE OF THE WEEK:

Reach Out to Someone Who Is Estranged

Vayeshev
Trustful Waiting

V*ayeshev* / 'And Ya'akov settled' in the land of his father's sojourns…These are the chronicles of Ya'akov, when Yoseph was seventeen years old" (*Bereishis*, 37:1–2).

Ya'akov has been journeying for many years. Having toiled and struggled throughout those years, he now expects to arrive at a place of peace and tranquility — the home of his father. He expects his experience of life to change from darkness to light, like from the cosmic *Tzimtzum* / withdrawal of Divine Light, to the subsequent revelation of Light — "There was evening (darkness) and there was morning (light), Day One." Indeed, ever since the Tzimtzum, all holy and positive narratives move from darkness to light and from tension to release and resolution. The universe is in transit from a world of effortful toil to the World to Come, 'settledness' and ease.

As Ya'akov is now ripe of age and has lived a full life, he imagines that he can reap the 'rewards' of his toil. After thirty-plus years of journeying, he yearns to go 'home', literally and metaphorically, as Rashi says: ביקש יעקב לישב בשלוה / "Ya'akov wished to settle in peace...." Yet, at that very point, קפץ עליו רוגזו של יוסף / "...the difficulty (regarding) Yoseph sprang upon him" (Rashi, *Medrash Rabbah* on Bereishis, 84:3).

First, we need to ask why a *Tzadik* / illumined, righteous person such as Ya'akov would wish to לישב בשלוה / "settle in peace." Surely he is conscious of the fact that "a human being is created to toil" (*Iyov*, 5:7), and there is no question that he is dedicated to striving and to growing until his last breath. But it sounds as if he wishes to 'retire' and settle into a state of 'reward'. Rashi continues, "When the righteous wish to live at ease, the Holy One, blessed is He, says to them: 'Are not the Tzadikim (by nature) satisfied with what is stored up for them in the World to Come? (How is it) that one would wish to live at ease in this world, too!'"

Again, on the macrocosmic level, all movement is from darkness to light. From a broad perspective on our individual lives, too, it can be seen that our overall trajectory is upward toward the light, for it is clear that even descents are for the sake of the ultimate ascent. Yet, when viewed from within a normative sense of time, our lives may sometimes seem to be devolving or slipping gradually into chronic habitual mistakes, weakness, or darkness.

In any case, on a personal, day-to-day level, moving from darkness to light is never inevitable; it is caused by our actions. If we consistently put in the effort to bring light and redemption, eventually it will come. Every action causes a reaction, for better or the opposite. Every thought and feeling we repeatedly entertain also creates ripples in our life and eventually in the world at large.

Unfortunately, perhaps, the payoffs or consequences of our actions are felt only much later on. Some effects of our thoughts, words, and actions may only be felt in an afterlife or a subsequent incarnation.

The Zohar (1, 180b) explains at the beginning of this week's Torah reading that in a world of pure *Din* / judgment, every action has an *immediate* reaction. If a person steals with his hand, for example, his hand would instantaneously cease to function or exist. Our world, however, is a world of compassion. Here, we are granted a waiting period between action and reaction, and in this space, we have a chance to rectify our actions and reverse their effects.

Ya'akov desired to sit in *Shalvah* / rest, and observe the fruits of his efforts, to finally see the light, resolution, redemption, and peace that he had worked so hard to create. But instead, he experienced the tremendous hardship of believing that his beloved son Yoseph had been killed.

Only many years later did Ya'akov see the effects of his life of positive action. Yoseph was still alive, and not only that, but he had risen to become the demi-ruler of Egypt, in the position to save his family from famine and starvation.

Thus, the last 17 years of Ya'akov's life were *Tov* / good (numerically 17). For 17 years, he was able to see the light, resolution, redemption, and reward of his actions; he lived in peace and tranquility, surrounded by his entire family, who had reunited and overcome their conflicts. On a deeper level, he had the rare experience of deep, ongoing *Shalva* / rest, peacefulness, and tranquility within this world of tribulation and restless movement.

On the other hand, the state of לישב בשלוה / settling in peace that Ya'akov desired was not to 'retire' and stop striving, aspiring, and living. Rather, he desired to live from a settled, peaceful state of stillness and wholeness, and nevertheless still strive for higher good on the behalf of his family and all of us throughout history.

From within the paradigm of 'reward', one may experience the uncertainties of life and even the pressures of toil, yet he will experience these without the normal accompanying sensations of anxiety and inner suffering. In fact, Ya'akov opened the door to this higher way of living and possibility for all of us, his spiritual offspring. He made it possible for each of us, on our own level, to eventually live in a certain level of *Geulah Pratis* / individual, personal, inner redemption and wholeness — even as we experience difficulty, and even as we continue to strive to bring the *Geulah Klalis* / redemption for all humanity.

VAYESHEV

Energy of the Week:
Trustful Waiting

We live in an era of instant gratification. With the increasingly rapid proliferation of so-called 'intelligent' technology providing us with all kinds of instant results, information, and tasks, we have forgotten that sometimes we need to work for and wait for what is truly *Tov* / good.

As instantaneous as our communications and tasks may become, there are many endeavors that will always require patience and trust. We will still be faced with waiting periods in which we don't see immediate results or the fruits of our efforts. We may even reach a point where it seems that all our striving has been in vain. This is where we must stop and recognize the tremendous value in 'trustful waiting'.

When we believe that compassion has been woven into the fabric of life, and that every positive effort has a far-reaching effect, then we can trust that our efforts will eventually manifest tangible, positive results. In the meantime, we need the wisdom and strength to be patient, and to trust, and to continue working for what truly matters.

This week, we can strengthen our practice of trustful waiting and believing. Things will eventually turn around for us outwardly. Yet, we do not have to wait for that turnaround in order to be at peace inwardly. True peace is already available here and now.

"

PRACTICE OF THE WEEK:

**Settle Yourself & Wait for Things
to Turn Around**

Miketz
Proactive Dream Fulfillment

I T CAME TO PASS...PHARAOH WAS DREAMING, AND behold, he was standing by the Nile, and coming up from the Nile were seven cows, handsome and sturdy...seven other cows came up from the Nile close behind them, ugly and gaunt, and stood beside the cows on the bank of the Nile... And he woke up...And he fell asleep and dreamed again, and behold, seven ears of grain were growing on one stalk..." (41:1–7).

Pharaoh, the mighty ruler, has two dreams. In the first, the seven gaunt cows go on to eat the sturdy cows. In the second dream, the seven healthy ears of grain grow, and close behind them sprout seven thin and scorched ears, which proceed to swallow the seven healthy ones. Both times that Pharaoh awakens, he is utterly perplexed as to the meaning of the dream, but he is not satisfied with the allegorical, metaphorical interpretations being offered by his Egyptian advisors, such as seven of his children will be born and seven will die, or he will win seven wars and then lose seven. As Yoseph has already established a reputation as a prophetic dream interpreter, Pharaoh summons Yoseph from his prison cell.

Yoseph unlocks the dreams for Pharaoh brilliantly and quite literally: the cows and grain indicate food. Thus, there will be seven years of plenty, followed by seven years of famine, and if provisions are gathered during the years of plenty for the years of famine, then the cows can appear together standing at the bank. Pharoah is overwhelmed by the simple genius and the clear Divine message conveyed through Yoseph, that he immediately promotes him to royal vizier, the second most powerful person in the entire land of Egypt — and, by extension, the entire world. Miraculously, he has risen from being a convict long forgotten in a dark dungeon to the demi-ruler of the most powerful civilization of the time.

Yet, puzzlingly, he does not take this opportunity to send a message to his father that he is alive and well.

Many years earlier, Yoseph himself had two dreams, dreams that indicated to him that he was destined to become a powerful ruler. Now, through Pharaoh's two dreams and his interpretations, his own dreams are realized and actualized.

There are many differences between the two sets of dreams. One noticeable difference is that in Yoseph's first dream, he sees, "We were binding sheaves in the field, when suddenly my sheaf stood up and remained upright, and then your sheaves gathered around and bowed low to my sheaf" (37:7). In this dream everyone was hard at work, including himself, while in Pharaoh's dreams, the King was merely a spectator, observing cows pasturing and grains growing (41:1–7).

In Yoseph's dream, there is human activity and participation. Being a spectator or participator in life can be the difference between *Kedushah* / holiness and the opposite, the way of *Kelipah* / impurity and the 'other side'. The true, lasting, and eternal gifts of life, the ones that are appreciated and truly a blessing in our lives, are those we worked on achieving, not the ones granted to us by birthright, inheritance, or a lottery. To receive sustenance or benefit without earning is called "bread of shame," for in the end, it brings an unholy sense of unworthiness and even resentment toward the giver.

To ensure that what we receive is 'holy' and not the opposite, even when we do receive a free gift from life, we need to ensure that we then 'invest' and use that gift to fuel or motivate greater *Avodah* / spiritual-mental-emotional-physical work.

As a young lad, Yoseph is destined for greatness and leadership. He is gifted with the sparkle of beauty, and he automatically finds *Chein* / grace, favor, and charm in the eyes of all he meets. Despite the fact that all this seems to be his 'birthright', in his dream, he is an active participant in the work in the field, actively engaged in his own story, not a mere 'recipient' or spectator.

Yoseph's dreams of leadership are realized when he is asked to interpret Pharaoh's dream and rises to the occasion. And not only does he respond by 'participating', but he takes his role a step further and offers advice on how to save the Egyptian people from starvation. If, during the seven years of plenty, hinted at by the seven handsome and sturdy cows, Pharaoh would gather enough produce for the seven years of famine, hinted to be the seven ugly and gaunt cows, his kingdom will survive.

In Pharaoh's dream, the seven ugly, gaunt cows "stood beside the (handsome and sturdy) cows on the bank of the Nile." This represents a merger between these two sets of years: the 'active' years, during which they will work to save up for the famine, and the more 'passive' years, during which they will 'receive' and eat the grain in the storehouses.

A lowly prisoner giving advice to the mightiest man alive is a bold act. Perhaps in other circumstances, it would have cost him his life. Yet, Yoseph was certain that he would be successful. Hearing that the fat and lean cows were standing next to each other on the Nile — that they existed simultaneously — he knew that his 'inheritance' would coexist with his 'work'. It was clearly the right time to manifest his own dreams of leadership, and indeed, he was promoted to a role of great power and responsibility.

Yoseph always understood that his life was a dream unfolding; he knew at which junctures in life he was called to make a move toward fulfillment. When he was offered a chance to stand in front of Pharaoh, he did not shy away from making a move. Years later, when all his brothers, including Binyamin, finally came and bowed in front of him, he saw that his dreams were finally being fulfilled. Thus, he began to reveal himself to his brothers, telling them that it was all part of a Divine plan, and that they should bring Ya'akov to Egypt so that he would not starve in Eretz Yisrael.

This is the reason why he does not send messengers earlier to tell his father that he is still alive. He is waiting for his original dreams to be fulfilled: all his brothers prostrating before him. As the master interpreter of dreams, he knows when a dream is over and needs interpretation, as in the dreams of Pharaoh. And he knows when a dream is still in process and should not be disturbed, and rather should just be allowed to unfold.

We can learn many profound lessons from this Parshah about proactive dream fulfillment.

MIKETZ

Energy of the Week:
Proactive Dream Fulfillment

Last week's reading provided us with the power of trustful waiting and coming to life from a settled state of mind. This week's reading builds on that Ko'ach, and gives us the strength to act and take a step forward with complete faith in our ability to realize our dreams.

We begin celebrating the festival of Chanukah during this week. Chanukah is a story of a small group of courageous people, the Maccabees, who stood up to their Greek-Assyrian oppressors because they had a dream of a better and holier world.

Despite all odds, their courageous actions bore fruit and they were victorious. Because they trusted in the possibility of miracles, miracles occurred for them, and through them, for us.

When they finally entered the Beis HaMikdash, it was in shambles.

It had been defiled and vandalized, grass had over-
grown the holy courtyard and chamber floors, and
breaches had been made to the Beis HaMikdash in
thirteen places (לפנים ממנו, סורג, גבוה עשרה טפחים. ושלש עשרה
פרצות היו שם שפרצום מלכי יון: Mishnah, *Midos*, 2:3). There was
no rational hope of finding any undefiled sacred oil,
whatsoever. Yet, they had a vision of rededicating the
Beis HaMidash by kindling the Menorah lights with
pure, untouched oil.

Given the circumstances, it would have been understandable to simply kindle the Menorah with defiled
oil, as the laws allowed. Instead, they acted on their
dream. They searched for pure oil and found one tiny
jug tucked away and protected.

Only because they sought, did they find. Their unwavering trust and belief in the miraculous caused
this miracle to occur, and as an additional sign of
Hashem's Pleasure, the oil remained miraculously lit
for eight transcendent nights. Had they not acted,
their dream of self-rule and rededication of the Beis
HaMikdash would have remained just that, a dream.

This week, take a bold step forward toward actual-
izing your dream, with trust in Hashem. Believe in
miracles; know that the seemingly impossible is possible.

PRACTICE OF THE WEEK:

**Have Faith in Your Ability
to Manifest Your Dreams**

Vayigash
Personal Encounter

V AYIGASH BEGINS WITH THE DRAMATIC ENCOUN-
TER between Yehudah and Yoseph, representing two
archetypes of service:

Yehudah, the son of Leah, is a person of good deeds. He is
a struggler and is constantly overcoming obstacles within the
paradigm of separation. He is the root of Moshiach ben Dovid
(a descendent of the *Sheivet* / tribe of Yehudah), who brings
redemption from the constrictions of exile.

Yoseph, the son of Rochel, is more ethereal and heady, representing one who studies much Torah, the *Tzadik* / righteous
individual who can descend to a place of immorality and remain pure and unscathed. The paradigm of integration and
unity, Yoseph is the root of Moshiach ben Yoseph, who brings
redemption *within* the confines of exile.

As the story unfolds, there is a famine in Eretz Yisrael and Yoseph's brothers journey to the land of *Mitzrayim* / Egypt to purchase food. They are unaware of the fact that Yoseph has risen to power in Mitzrayim after they had sold him into slavery many years before. Upon encountering Yoseph, the brothers do not recognize him as their brother, but Yoseph knows who they are. Yoseph accuses his brothers of being spies and threatens to take the youngest brother, Binyamin, the other son of Rochel, who he accuses of theft, as his slave.

Yoseph is testing them and trying to evaluate whether the children of Rochel and the children of Leah are currently a family unit in which the members protect each other, or whether the integrity of the family has fallen apart once he was sold into slavery. His own father and uncle, Ya'akov and Eisav, parted ways and became two separate nations. Are *Bnei Yisrael* / the Children of Ya'akov, Israel, still one nation, or are the children of Leah and the children of Rochel now divided into two nations, Heaven forbid?

If there is unity among the brothers, he knows the time is right to reveal himself to them and reunite with the family.

Yoseph puts the brothers through trials to see if the children of Leah will stand up for their younger brother, Binyamin, who, like himself, is a son of Rochel. If they are willing to put themselves in harm's way to protect a child of Rochel, and even to become a slave in his stead, then it will be proof that the rectification of the brothers' crime against Yoseph is underway. Since the children of Leah sold Yoseph, the child of Rochel, as a slave, he hopes to see that now a child of Leah will be willing to become a slave in place of Binyamin, the child of Rochel. This will demonstrate that they are a unified nation, no matter how diverse.

ויגש / *Vayigash*... / "Then Yehudah 'approached' him (Yoseph) and said, בי אדני / *Bi Adoni* / 'Please, my master, let now your servant speak something into my lord's ears...for you are like Paroh'" (44:18).

Yehudah, the powerful leader of the brothers, goes on to explain how he took personal responsibility for their younger brother Binyamin, and how Binyamin's mother passed away, and her other son has 'died' (referring to Yoseph), and how his father would greatly mourn his disappearance. Yet, all this seems very familiar — indeed, the brothers have already told this to Yoseph, so what is different? What new argument is Yehudah presenting?

After Yehudah presents his case and the whole story, Yoseph can no longer contain himself: ויקרא הוציאו כל־איש מעלי ולא־ עמד איש אתו בהתודע יוסף אל־אחיו / "And he cried out, 'Have every *Ish* / person withdraw from me!' and there was no Ish with him when Yoseph made himself known to his brother" (45:1).

On a deep level, this means that when Yoseph and his brothers reunited, there was no *Ish* / איש / 'man' present. They were, of course, present, but not as an *Ish*; none of them were a separate 'person' or ego-based individual. They were a unity.*

ויגש / *Vayigash* means there was an 'encounter', a genuine meeting of minds and hearts. Years of misunderstanding and anguish between the brothers continued until this moment when Yehudah, the representative of all the brothers, approached Yoseph and said, *Bi Adoni* / "Please, my master...."

It seems that somehow, this utterance, *Bi Adoni*, enabled Yoseph and Yehudah to encounter each other in a true and meaningful way, moving Yoseph to reveal himself to his brothers and begin the reconciliation and reunion with the entire family.

בי אדני / *Bi Adoni* can also be translated more literally as, "You are within me, my master." Yehudah says, 'You are within me! I identify with you. I understand you.' He is finally seeing the "other" as part of himself, within himself, and himself within the other. To encounter another, we need to identify with them completely. When Yehudah says this phrase, Yoseph is moved because he resonates with the fact that Yehudah is finally identifying himself with him and his struggles.

---

* In contrast, right before the sale of Yoseph, the Torah says, that Yoseph was looking for his brothers, וימצאהו איש והנה תעה בשדה וישלאהו האיש / And an ish/man came upon him wandering in the fields. The ish asked him... ויאמר האיש נסעו מזה / and the ish said "they have departed from here." Rashi says regarding this, "They have departed from all feelings of brotherhood." *Bereishis*, 37:15-17

Yehudah overcomes his 'separate' egoic self and sees Yoseph as within himself. Yoseph is then also moved to see himself within Yehudah's narrative, and as a result, there is no 'Ish'. And then Yoseph can begin to reveal who he really is, in a way that unifies the family.

Once I can 'see you' and experience you without my prism of separation, this opens the path for a genuine, ego-less encounter. In the words of the Arizal, Yehudah experiences *Hiskallelus* / inter-inclusion with Yoseph, and this compels Yoseph to experience Hiskallelus with him and the other brothers. Once there is a collapse of each of their narratives of separateness, conflict, and what they are still holding onto, they let go of their איש / *Ish*. Then and only then can they truly unify — and this unity is greater than it ever had been before.

It is due to the absence of 'an Ish' that the brothers are reunited, not only among themselves but also with Yoseph. Eventually, Ya'akov arrives and, witnessing the aura of unity, proclaims the Shema, the affirmation of *Echad* / Oneness. Yoseph's children are then blessed as two tribes, Ephrayim and Menashe — the total number of tribes coming to 13, the numerical value of the word *Echad*.

VAYIGASH

Energy of the Week:
Letting Go of Personal Narratives

This week's Parshah infuses us with the power to have true and meaningful encounters and make breakthroughs in peace with others. We are gifted with the ability to resolve difficult matters through meeting others, fully present and in person.

In this age of 'virtual communication', we need to remember to make *real* 'face time'. We need to remove our senses from the mirage of digital renderings and the other veils of artifice that divide us, stop rushing and multitasking, and take the time to truly see and hear others face-to-face. Then, we can focus on what is similar between us and begin to sense the dawning resolution of any misunderstanding.

Look into the reality of the other person and see that you are a part of their inner presence, and they are a part of your inner presence. As deeply as we know ourselves, we can know another. Not only can we, from our own experiences, relate to the similar experiences of the other — but also from our simple sense of existence, we can be 'within', or one with, the other's existence. Ultimately, there is one existence; there is only One.

The Zohar reads the encounter between Yoseph and Yehudah as a metaphor for our intimate embrace with *HaKadosh Baruch Hu* / the Holy One, in the act of *Tefilah* / prayer (בזמנא דקודשא בריך הוא אתי לאזדווגא בכנסת ישראל...דהא בזמנא דא, איהו קודשא בריך הוא בלחודוי, בחבורא חדא עם ישראל: *Zohar* 1, 208b). Just as we need to put aside our external digital devices and take up our own G-d given 'devices' of seeing, hearing, and empathic feeling to relate to and reconcile with another person, so in prayer, we eventually need to let go of our limited narratives and external prisms, so that we can enter into a true encounter with our Creator.

We may, in fact, have a long list of requests, perceptions of what we think we need, want, and should
have, and this, too, is an important stage of prayer.
But then, at some point during our Tefilah, we need
to turn to the Master of the Universe and say, 'All
that is just *my* story, my feelings, my sense of separation. Now I am letting go of that, and, with empathy
for Your Presence in this world of separation, I am allowing Your story to manifest within me: "Open my
lips Hashem, and let my mouth tell *Your* praise…" It
is not merely 'me' who is praying; it is Your Presence
praying in and through me! *Bi Adoni* / "My Master
is within me!"'

PRACTICE OF THE WEEK:

Empathy

Vayechi
Panoramic Vision

T he Torah reading this week speaks of Ya'akov's final years of life, the seventeen years he spends reunited with his family, and the blessings and encouragement he bestows upon them for the future. The reading opens with the words, "And Ya'akov lived in the land of Egypt for seventeen years, and Ya'akov's days, the years of his life, were seven years, and forty, and a hundred year(s)" (47:28).

In simpler terms, he lived to the age of one hundred and forty-seven. Yet, the way the verse says, "seven years, and forty, and one hundred year(s)" should draw our attention. In most cultures in history, the digits in numeral notation progress from the largest unit to the smallest unit. This is also the way the Torah usually enumerates years. For example, when speaking of the years of Sarah at the time of her demise, the Torah says she was "one hundred year(s), twenty year(s) and seven years". Similarly, when speaking of Avraham, his age is "one hundred year(s), and seventy years, and five years." Why does Ya'akov's age stand out by moving from the smaller unit to the larger unit?

Another interesting detail to observe is that the next verse reads, "And the days of Yisrael neared death." Why, when it speaks of his life, does it say, "Ya'akov lived in Egypt," while when it speaks of his death the Torah uses the name Yisrael? Why is there a sudden switch of his names?

Also, the terms for 'one hundred years' in the lifespan of Sarah, Avraham, and Ya'akov are written in the singular: "... one hundred *year*." What is the meaning encoded in this fact?

To offer an answer to the last question, 'years', in the plural, refers to the countless intricate details and ups and downs in a person's life. 'Year', in the singular, refers to the singular overall picture of one's life, their overarching goal, trajectory, or 'reason for being'.

Avraham, for example, experienced a clear Divine *Nevuah* / prophecy, telling him, *Lech L'cha* / 'Go on a journey from your homeland to the land I will show you.' This initiated him in his overall direction in life, whereas he then needed to live out all the details of that direction. Here, too, the singular, more 'general' or 'larger' unit is revealed first. This is the meaning of 'one hundred year', in the singular. And wherever 'years' is written in the plural, it refers to the details.

It makes sense that one would first have a revelation of their general trajectory, and then begin working out the practical details of getting there. Yet, Ya'akov, for the most part, experiences Nevuah in the form of a dream, not like the crystal clear prophecy of Avraham. The defining quality of a dream, even a prophetic one, is unclarity. Even a prophetic dream could have some amount of untruth woven into it (as in the prophetic dreams of Yoseph: Rashi, *Bereishis*, 37:10. The life of a 'dreamer' is more ambiguous than the life of a prophet. Ya'akov Avinu was a prophet, yet for most of his life, his prophecy came in the form of dreams).

At the beginning of Ya'akov's journey, he goes to sleep and dreams of a depiction of 'ups and downs', of details. Only after many years of living 'in the details', being away from home, marrying, having children, and becoming a wealthy man, at last, the angel of Hashem comes to him and tells him a clear prophecy about his journey: 'It is time to go back home, to the land of your birth.'

Throughout his life, Ya'akov is repeatedly taken by surprise. This begins with taking the blessings from Eisav and suddenly needing to flee, being tricked into marrying the sister of the woman he loves, and finally, experiencing the disappearance of his beloved son, Yoseph. Ya'akov wished to live at ease, but this trouble in connection with Yoseph, קפץ עליו / "suddenly came upon him" (Rashi, Bereishis, 37:2) as if by surprise (Although the actual language of the Medrash is נזדווג לו: Medrash Rabbah, Bereishis, 84:3). Never knowing what move to take next, he lives in a space of disjointed 'details'.

When Ya'akov goes away from home, ויפגע במקום וילן שם כי־בא השמש / "He accidentally encountered (פגע / Pega) this space." פגע / Pega also means 'strike'. In other words, he is struck, or surprised, when the sun suddenly sets. The same word means 'Tefilah' (ואין "פגיעה" אלא תפלה: Berachos, 26b), and specifically a type of Tefilah when a person has suddenly encountered darkness.

Thus Ya'akov, who wanders among the Peratim / details of his life, is engaged in finding HaKadosh Baruch Hu within the darkness and seemingly disjointed details. Within the Pega / sudden surprises, he quickly develops the ability to create Tefilah, and to connect to HaKadosh Baruch Hu even in darkness and unclarity.

Yet, the seventeen final years of his life, the years at the end of his life, are his best years, illustrated by the fact that 17 is the numerical value of the word Tov / good. Ya'akov's entire family is by then united and living in peace, unlike the family of his father or grandfather, from whom conflicting nations emerged. All of his descendants are part of Klal Yisrael, the singular Nation of Israel. Indeed, in these final years, he is able to recognize the patterns of his journey. He sees the intent of each step along the way, realizing the bigger picture. It becomes clear to him that all the details of his life were bringing him to this culminating state of unity and clarity.

Thus, at the end of his life, and in retrospect, he sees the overall unity and coherency of his life. He has moved from 'years' to 'year', from the minute details of 'seven years' and 'forty years', to the singular 'one hundred *year*'.

Similarly, his name *Ya'akov* is related to the word 'heel' and also 'trickery', while his name *Yisrael* is connected to the word *Sar* / prince or master. *Yisrael* also has the letters of the word *Rosh* / head. When the Torah calls him *Ya'akov*, it refers to his life on the level of the 'heel', the lower perspective of the multiple details and 'tricky', unexpected twists and turns. When the Torah calls him *Yisrael*, it refers to his life on the level of mastery, the higher perspective of the unitive vision and clarity of the 'head'.

Yisrael is the idea of *K'lal* / generality, while *Ya'akov* is the idea of *P'ratim* / details. *Yisrael* is his life of vision, joy, soul, and purpose. *Ya'akov* is his life of constriction and anguish (*Ohr HaChayim*, 47:28: כל זמן שאין שם עצבון וענף הנגדי קצת לשמחה ולשלימות הקדושה והטהרה, ובהעדר כן וינפש יוצאה ממנו כיציאת נשמה יתירה של יום שבת ובאותו זמן לא יקרא לו ישראל, כי בעלת השם הלכה לה ואינה אז ויקרא שמו יעקב / "Whenever Ya'akov experienced the kind of spiritual serenity…he was qualified for the name Yisrael. Whenever Ya'akov experienced worries, etc., this serenity departed from him, similar to the departure of the additional soul from every Jew at the end of

Shabbos. At such times, the Torah reverts to referring to our patriarch as being merely Ya'akov").

During his life, he is called Ya'akov and he lives as Ya'akov, but when the Torah says he is about to pass on, it uses the name Yisrael, meaning, he passes on in the state of Yisrael (*Zohar* 1, p. 221b). He has realized the 'general', unified, Divine intent within the unfolding of his life. This is why, before he passes on, he tells his children to gather, to 'unify'.

Ya'akov tells Pharaoh, when he arrives in Egypt as a 130-year-old, "The days of my life are מעט ורעים / 'little and Ra'" (*Vayigash*, 47:9). The first 130 years of his life were lived in the place of רע / *Ra* / bad, as in broken, disjointed details (רע is related to the word רעוע / *Ra'u'ah* / broken, unstable: *Kelim*, 3:5). And the remaining seventeen years of his life in Egypt are *Tov* / good. So Ra is the first 130 years, and *Tov* the final seventeen years (*Tov* is also numerically 17).

Ra is connected to the word *Re'u'ah* / broken, unstable. In the language of *Chazal* / our sages, *Re'u'ah* means 'uncertain'. *Tov* also means a condition of wholeness (טוב היינו דאין צריך שום תיקון / "*Tov* means something that does not need perfecting": *Tzafnas Paneach*, Devarim, 6:11. Yerushalmi, *Shevi'is*, 6:1).

Towards the end of Ya'akov's life, all the pieces of Ra come together in Tov, wholeness.

His first 130 years of life are a parallel and Tikkun for the 130 years in which Adam was separated from Chavah after they ate from the Tree of Separation, the Tree of Knowledge, of Tov and Ra. Ya'akov needed to serve Hashem within broken relationships with his older brother, Eisav, his father-in-law, and then among his sons. Finally, all this familial separation and Ra resolved into the Tov of life.

We can have 'big picture' and 'small picture' vision. Very often, we find ourselves stuck in the 'small picture'. We see only the immediate details of our story — what is currently happening to us, what we are involved with at this moment or our emotional state at this time. We see the trees and not the forest, as it were.

It is possible to get so bogged down by the small picture vision of life that we veer off course and forget the big picture vision. We lose ourselves in minutiae: "That person offends me... I'm feeling overwhelmed... I am struggling with my studies.... It is only when looking backward that we catch a glimpse of the bigger picture.

We live forward but only understand backward.

VAYECHI

Energy of the Week:
Big Picture Vision

This week's Torah reading infuses us with the power and vision to observe the 'big picture' of life, to attain clarity of vision, and the ability to step back from the details and recognize all our experiences as integral parts of a whole. This way, we can keep sight of our greater goals, purpose and life trajectory, and free ourselves if we have been bogged down by the minutia.

Look back over your entire life until now as one greater whole. Recognize that even the Ra in the past was driving you to greater Tov. See, also, all the Mitzvos, kind deeds, prayers and studies you have engaged, and understand the hidden power of those deeds to bring Tikkun to you and your family, and to bring the world a step closer to its ultimate unified state.

PRACTICE OF THE WEEK:

Recognize the Overarching Theme of Your Life

BOOK TWO:
Shemos

Shemos
The Loss and Regaining of Name & Voice

T HIS WEEK'S TORAH READING OPENS WITH THE children of Ya'akov's descent into the exile of Egypt, and the beginning of our collective story of enslavement and eventual redemption.

The correct title of 'the Book of Exodus', this second book of the Torah, is *Shemos* / 'Names'. Although the name *Shemos* is simply drawn from the second word in the first sentence of this book, the Hebrew titles have a deeper significance that pertains to the entire book. As such, *Shemos* suggests that this book is primarily about 'names'.

Indeed, the narrative of *Shemos* begins when Klal Yisrael are still free, and proudly lists the names of the families who came down to Egypt: ואלה שמות בני ישראל הבאים מצרימה...ראובן שמעון

לוי... / "These are the names of the children of Yisrael who came to Egypt...Reuvein, Shimon, Levi (and continues to list the rest of the names of the twelve *Shevatim* / tribes)." This demonstrates how Klal Yisrael is entering Egypt as a dignified people, each individual with a stated name, and thus a distinct identity.

Klal Yisrael's names remind them of their past and of the patriarch of their particular tribe, empowering them in their present mission, and strengthening them with a vision of their glorious future (*Medrash Rabbah*, Shemos, 1:3–5).

However, immediately after naming them, the Torah continues, "*They* multiplied, *they* increased, the land was full of them..." (*Shemos*, 1:7). They are no longer named. It does not say, 'And Reuvein became a huge tribe, and Shimon multiplied,' rather, they are referred to with the impersonal 'they'. They are now descending into exile, and Torah begins to refer to the children of Ya'akov without names, rather with mere pronouns.

ובני ישראל פרו וישרצו וירבו ויעצמו במאד מאד ותמלא הארץ אתם / "But the Children of Israel were fertile and prolific, they multiplied and increased very greatly, and the land was filled with them." The root of the phrase וישרצו, usually translated as 'prolific,' actually means שרץ / 'swarmed', like insects. The analogy of insects suggests that they propagated like insects do: in abundance, with as many as six offspring per birth (In fact, according to the deeper teachings of the Torah [*Galei Raza*, see *Yalkut Reuveini* on the Pasuk], the souls of the Jews in Egypt were transmigrated souls from the sheep of Lavan, who in turn were the souls of the 974 generations before the Creation of our world: *Chagigah*, 13b).

The Seforno (16th Century Italian commentator) gives us an alternative meaning of "swarmed": נטו לדרכי שרצים / "(The people) veered into the ways of *Sheratzim* / creeping insects." While the Torah is certainly hinting at their multiplying like insects, the term וישרצו can also be understood to mean that the people first reduced themselves, acting and feeling like lowly insects, and then they were reduced by their oppressors to being nameless, expendable creatures, disgusting creepy crawly things that swarmed the terrain. They first diminished themselves from being a proud, distinct, named people to regarding themselves as like roaches and pests. This self-degradation opened them up to being further diminished by their overlords as unworthy creatures, insects upon which to trample and exterminate.

They were then compelled by external forces into a complete state of slavery and *Tumah* / impurity and stuckness. Finally, they reach the lowest point, with no name or sense of identity, debased and crushed.

People may name their cats or dogs, but no one names the roaches that swarm their basement. To be viewed as a roach is to be reduced to nothing, with not even the respect given to a stray cat.

Over time, Klal Yisrael becomes so deeply entrenched in the wretched world of slavery, that they are not just physically enslaved but also mentally and emotionally, their mentality, their very *Da'as* / consciousness is enslaved. In such a demoralized condition, their humanity and freedom have become such a distant memory, that they have come to expect the worst for themselves. At this point, there is a total eclipse of their humanity and selfhood. Exiled in a place of traumatic paralysis and silence, they cannot even speak, even to complain.

Even when they have been enslaved for many decades, we do not even hear of them groaning, crying, or demanding their freedom. They have no voice to speak truth to power, no voice to call out to the Master of the Universe in prayer. They are completely mute.

The Zohar teaches that in Egypt, the notion of "speech" was in exile (*Zohar*, 2:25b). This exile of speech, the inability to voice, even to oneself, one's wants, needs, and desires is the deepest exile possible. To be human is to be a *Medaber* / a 'speaking being' (Rashi, *Bereishis*, 2:7). When we cannot express our thoughts and feelings outwardly nor even inwardly, we are exiled from our own humanity. To take away someone's ability to speak robs them of their capacity for meaningful relationship with other humans and even relationship to themselves.

Speech also implies choice; through language, we define, contextualize, and navigate our world and our needs (Dibbur is connected with *De'ah* / awareness: Rashi, *Bereishis*, 2:7. And without De'ah or Da'as there is no discernment and choice: Yerushalmi, *Berachos*, 5:2). A slave does not have the choice to articulate or reveal who they really are, for their reality is imposed upon them. Nor can a slave listen to another, nor even hear the possibility that their circumstances may change.

A slave has no story to tell. Their inner life, their dreams, aspirations, desires, and longings are devastatingly eclipsed. A slave has nothing meaningful to share or even think about. A slave is subjugated not only physically but emotionally, intellectually, and spiritually.

When, Heaven forbid, any human being is reduced to a statistic until they accept it, they can cease to have an inner life. This is what occurred to Klal Yisrael in Egypt. They stopped dreaming and even believing that an alternative was possible. It seemed as if this state would remain forever: "No slave ever escaped from Egypt" (*Yalkut Shimoni,* Yisro 269).

Their shift toward freedom was utterly miraculous; however, it began with the following apparently 'natural' events: "Now it came to pass in those many days that the king of Egypt died, and the children of Israel sighed from the labor, and they cried out, and their cry ascended to Hashem from the labor" (*Shemos,* 2:23). When the King of Egypt finally died, the 'wallpaper' of their lives changed slightly, triggering a very subtle moment of self-reflection. The Chizkuni writes that at this moment, they realized that they might get an opportunity to rest briefly from their labors. Only when they imagined even the possibility of at least a few minutes of rest, their consciousness opened enough to register the reality of their exhaustion and trauma.

When there was, in fact, no opportunity to rest, and the slavery continued, a 'sigh' or groan finally emitted from their throats (כל זמן שאותו מלך חי היו מצפין שמא יתבטלו זה כשימות גזרותיו... וכשמת זה לא נתבטלו) גזרותיו אמרו מעתה אין לדבר סוף לפיכך ויאנחו / "As long as the old king had been alive, they had hope that with his death the harsh decrees against them would 'die' also. When they found out that they had hoped in vain, they groaned").

Perhaps when the king died, all the Egyptians were busy with the funeral. If so, it may have been the first day in many years that there was a day off for even the taskmasters, as surely they did not show up to work (*Imrei Shefer*, VaNitzak) And perhaps the fact that they were not whipped and beaten and insulted on that day triggered a small awakening in the deadened minds of the slaves. Or, perhaps the slaves were explicitly given a day off (*HaAmek Davar*, Shemos, 2:23), creating enough dissonance to jolt them into an awareness of their trauma.

In any case, somehow they realized that day or that moment could be different. And then they had the faintest glimmer of an insight: slavery was not really their ontological or permanent condition. Trembling slightly and dropping their tools, a buried, distant memory began to arise: there was something called freedom. They were in fact human beings and slavery had been imposed upon them from the outside! With this, their knees buckled and they collapsed, groaning and crying out in convulsive grief.

In extreme trauma, even grief can be suppressed from awareness. Yet, once there is a pause in the oppressive conditions, a person can begin to wake up from their dreamlike stupor and listlessness, and grief is released. In its wake, a yearning to be free can become palpable.

The Torah says, "And they groaned…and Hashem heard their groan…" (*Shemos*, 2:23–24). The Ohr HaChayim on this *Pasuk* / verse notes that the "groan" was not an utterance of *Tefilah* / prayer, nor a cry to Hashem for help; it was simply a visceral, primal cry of pain (Although, later on, the Torah does say, ונצעק אל ה' / "we cried to Hashem" [*Devarim*, 26:7], this refers to the groans of the Tzadikim, who in fact did pray — ותפלת קצתם שהתפללו אז מצדיקי הדור: *Seforno*, Shemos, 2:24).

Similarly, Hashem tells Moshe at the Burning Bush, "I have seen their plight, ואת־צעקתם שמעתי מפני נגשיו / and I have heard their cries because of their taskmasters" (*Shemos*, 3:7). This Pasuk clearly says that their cries were not a form of prayer, rather an involuntary reaction to their state, an instinctual, wordless scream erupting from the realization that they had been abused and dehumanized. This is very different from a cry 'to' Hashem, a cry of intention. Yet because their bodies were softened and opened up enough for their voices to vibrate, Hashem 'heard' and received their groans and screams *as* prayers. Hashem received and interpreted their groaning as reaching out, yearning 'to', longing 'for' — as a prayer.

In a sense, though, their groans did carry an intention: they expressed a gut rejection of their sickening, miserable situation. Even without words or intellect, their cries were cries for change. And in merely allowing this primal response to move through them, they initiated the process of liberation.

The light of pre-dawn began to glow on the horizon of their being when they acknowledged that their state of enslavement was inherently wrong for them and that they did not belong there, and that they could withstand their abuse no more. Their dawn of freedom began to break when they began to think, dream, and speak about freedom, when they began to consider their former greatness instead of their current smallness.

SHEMOS

Energy of the Week:
'Rejecting' Our Slavery to Self-Limitations

This week's Torah reading imbues us with the inner strength and spiritual power to demand positivity and blessing, and to reject our self-imposed limitation, our self-denigration and enslavement to narrow, shallow states of being. As long as we are in any form of exile, we must demand a better reality for ourselves and our world, and give our demands a voice in prayer.

The first step to personal freedom and empowerment is simply to stop accepting slavery to our surroundings, upbringing, genetics, or our inner sensory and emotional environment. We must clearly realize that slavery is not our natural state. Life can be different; we can be the master of our life, be a 'creator' or cause, not merely a 'creation' or effect of our life.

Just by realizing this, we are already beginning to turn away from our narrative of smallness and open ourselves to the possibility of freedom.

When you expect more depth out of life, more depth of life becomes available. Your demand itself broadens your vessel to receive more Light. Demand depth from yourself, and your behavior, as well. Stop serving limited concepts of who you are and what you can be, and argue on behalf of your essential greatness. Then, you will begin to sense that greatness expanding within, strengthening you to achieve ever deeper levels of greatness in action. Convince yourself that success is impossible — and it will be possible.

PRACTICE OF THE WEEK:

Argue for Your Greatness

Va'era

Knowing That Miracles Are Possible

THIS WEEK'S TORAH READING OPENS WITH THE words, "Elokim (G-d) spoke to Moshe, and said to him, '*Ani Hashem* / I am Hashem"; I appeared to [your ancestors]…but [with] My name 'Hashem' I did not become known to them…Say to the children of Israel, '*Ani Hashem*…I will take you to Me as a people, and I will be Elokim to you, and you will know that I am Hashem your Elokim"' (6:2–7).

There are two primary names, modes of expression of the Creator, 'Elokim' and 'Hashem', although of course, there is only One, and thus, וידבר אלקים אל־משה ויאמר אליו אני י־ה־ו־ה / "Elokim spoke to Moshe and said to him *Ani Hashem*."

אלקים / *Elokim* in numerical value is 86, plus 1 for the unit of the word itself, it is 87. Eighty seven is also the sum of אני / *Ani* (61), plus יה־ו־ה / *Hashem* (26). By saying *Ani Hashem,* the Creator is saying, 'My names Elokim and Hashem refer to the One that I am.' Elokim says, 'I am Hashem; there is only One, although this Light of Oneness appears to you, in various colors, shades, attributes and manifestations.

At this revelation, Moshe internalizes three basic truths:

'Elokim',

'Hashem',

and 'Hashem is Elokim.'

These correspond to three Divine utterances:

a) "I am Hashem."

b) "I will be to you Elokim."

c) "I am Hashem your Elokim."

'Elokim' is the 'dimension' of Divinity that creates Heaven and earth and vests Itself in nature. The Hebrew word הטבע / *HaTeva* / 'nature' has the same numerical value as the Name *Elokim* (86). And thus, when the Torah describes the process of creation, it says, "In the beginning, Elokim created the Heaven and earth."

'Hashem' (the four letter name, the Yud-Hei-Vav-Hei, י־ה־ו־ה) refers to the Infinite, the transcendent Divine that is beyond nature. The four letters that comprise the name Hashem (י־ה־ו־ה), when rearranged, spells the Hebrew words 'was-is-will be': היה / *Hayah* / 'It was,' הוה / *Hoveh* / 'It is,' and יהיה / *Yihiyeh* / 'It will be.' Hashem is the aspect of Transcendence beyond time.

Elokim is connected with time and nature, whereas Hashem is miraculous, beyond time and nature.

We sense the presence of Elokim in our life when we feel that we are being guided, or that the details of our experiences are forming an interconnected and meaningful whole, or that we are living according to our deeper purpose. When we contemplate all the details in our life, big and small, we realize that everything is 'providential'; sometimes, there are coincidences that can only be described as 'Divinely planned'.

For instance, let's say several weeks ago, you were walking on your normal route through city streets when your path was diverted to a more unfamiliar area. You just happened to walk by a certain apartment you had never noticed before. A week later, that apartment went on the market, it happened to fit your needs, and now you are moving into that apartment. Or, say you were trying to make a difficult decision, when you took a break from thinking about it, opened a holy book, and began to study. Suddenly, you realized that a viable solution was suggested on that very page. In this way, the experience of the

Name 'Elokim' can include sensing the hand of the Creator working within our natural, unfolding life.

We become aware of the Name 'Hashem' in our lives when we feel as if something completely miraculous and extraordinary has occurred to us — not just unexpected or providential, but actually 'impossible' in terms of the laws of nature. For instance, a person has a condition that is scientifically deemed 'incurable', yet upon receiving a blessing from a *Tzadik* / illumined righteous figure, praying intensely, or doing a remarkable act of charity, that person is spontaneously cured.

These are two basic dimensions of higher awareness: being open to sense the Creator's guiding hand within nature and time, and witnesssing completely 'supernatural' acts of the Creator.

There is also a third and even greater dimension; that of the unity of the Names Elokim and Hashem. To witness the fact that Elokim is Hashem is to live with the recognition that every moment of life (the world of Elokim) is truly an extraordinary miracle (Hashem), and nothing at all is expected, routine, or mundane. This is to perceive as a child, with a sense of wonderment and amazement at every moment.

'Hashem is Elokim' means Elokim is the 'finite' container that is able to hold the Infinite revelation of the *Ein Sof* / the Infinite Light of Hashem. Thus, *Elokim* (numerically 86) is the כלי / *Kli* / vessel (numerically 60) of יהוה / Hashem (26)

(60+26=86). Elokim, 'Divine Presence in this finite world', is the vessel that contains Hashem, 'the Infinite'.

The Divine Names on an Experiential Level

Elokim — Experiencing purpose and guidance within the ordinary world

Hashem — Experiencing the Extraordinary

Hashem is Elokim — Experiencing the fact that nothing is ordinary; everything is miraculous.

At this place of deep awareness we recognize that there is no fundamental distinction between what we call 'natural phenomena' and what we call 'supernatural miracles'. Both are mere expressions of the Creator. Some events manifest through the Name Elokim and some through the Name Hashem, but there is only One Source and Essence of these manifestations. Synchronicity and providential events, as well as the miraculous beauty and intelligence of nature and all of Creation, are all really lightly veiled revelations of Hashem.

"You will know that *I* am Hashem your Elokim...." In general, only Elokim can be *Elokeinu* / 'our Elokim'. This is because we are finite Creations, and the only Divine emanation we can relate to or 'know' is Elokim — the 'finite' dimension of *HaKadosh Baruch Hu* / the Holy One. G-d as manifest within the workings of 'our world' is 'our G-d'. How could we ever relate to 'Hashem', an Infinity completely transcending our very frame of reference? Yet, in the Pasuk, *Elokim* is telling us, 'Know that *Ani Hashem* — "your G-d" is the all-transcendent Infinite One, Hashem. And that's because *Ani*, "I", am both. Those Names may be different, but they are both just names for Me.'

We are rooted in miracles. Each of our births is 'miraculous', we trace our lineage to Yitzchak, whose birth was a miracle, and we were collectively born through our miraculous Exodus from Egypt. Miracles have sustained us throughout history, against all odds. Our mere survival as a people is arguably the greatest miracle of all of history. This is because 'our G-d' is 'Hashem', The Infinite Source of all Life.

When we internalize this knowledge, we open ourselves even more to draw miracles — and the clear perception of miracles — into our day-to-day life.

VA'ERA

Energy of the Week:
Knowing That Miracles Are Possible

Last week's Torah reading brought us to the first step in personal liberation: 'non-acceptance' of a situation that enslaves us, and rejecting our self-imposed limitations. This week's reading infuses us with the power to take the next step: actively believing in the possibility of a better reality — believing in miracles. This means knowing that the harmonious workings of nature are a manifestation of Infinite Light. Life can be better, no matter how it may look right now.

When we simply believe in the possibility of manifesting a state of freedom or thriving — even if it still seems beyond the realm of natural law — our belief and conviction help draw it into existence. To see that the mundane world is one and the same as the world of miracles is to create miracles.

When we live within our human nature and yet recognize that nothing is limited by nature and everything is a continuously recreated miracle, we open ourselves to see miracles.

When we step beyond our natural limits and learn an extra page of Torah each day, or spend the extra minute in prayer, or give charity more consistently, we show the plasticity of our assumed 'limits'. Then we ourselves take on a 'miraculous' quality and unify with the Source of all Miracles, the Infinite Light of Hashem. In this way, we demonstrate to ourselves that our very human nature is miraculous — our Elokim is Hashem — and thus, we can draw down tremendous miracles into our lives.

PRACTICE OF THE WEEK:

Be the Miracle You Want to See

Bo

Holy Imagination

A S THE NARRATIVE OF REDEMPTION CONTINUES, Klal Yisrael is still tightly bound in the constraints of their Egyptian bondage. Yet, in the depths of their exile, they now receive their first Mitzvah — their first nation-wide invitation to connect with the Infinite One: "This month shall be to you the head of the months, to you it shall be the first of the months of the year" (*Shemos*, 12:2). This introduces the Mitzvah of sanctifying the new moon and the beginning of counting time through lunar patterns.

Virtually every calendar in the world tells the story of the earth's correspondence with the sun or the moon, as these majestic celestial characters sail across the sky. Most cultures use a solar (or luni-solar) calendar, based on the seasons, while a smaller number have used a lunar calendar, based on the 12 monthly cycles of the moon.

There is a profound distinction between 'solar time' and 'lu-nar time'. Sun-time is rigid, dictated by an easily predictable, set pattern of movement. The sun rises and sets day in and day out; the sun is always in the sky, even when it is behind clouds. With the completion of each cycle of seasons, the exact same cycle is repeated. In the Book of Koheles, it is written, "There is nothing new under the sun" (*Koheles,* 1:9). In a rigid, predictable universe, there is no newness. The sun represents all rigid linear structures and inevitability.

The ancient Egyptians worshiped a pagan deity called *Ra,* the Sun deity (note that רע / *Ra* is also the word for evil in the Torah). Those living under this deity imagined that there was no possibility of breaking out of the natural order, and this was reflected in their strict, static societal hierarchy. A person who was born a slave would remain a slave forever. "No slave was ever freed from Egypt," our sages tell us. A slave's life, too, was rigidly predictable; there was no room for any real change in his life, no renewal and no hope.

Regarding the statement "There is nothing new under the sun," the Zohar adds, "While under the 'sun' there is no new-ness, the moon *is* new; the moon is in fact a 'newness' that is under the sun" (*Zohar* 1, 123b). *Bnei Yisrael* / the Children of Is-rael, when receiving the Mitzvah to sanctify the months, were initiated into a different paradigm, a paradigm in which there could be newness, change, and eventually, liberation.

The word *Chodesh* / month comes from the word *Chidush* / new. The moon waxes and wanes; sometimes it is observable and sometimes not. The moon represents a paradigm of renewal and the potential for novelty that breaks the monotony of linear time. Renewal is possible because of fluctuation and movement.

In a rigid, predictable universe, there is no newness as there is no fluctuation, waxing, or waning. Yet, in the constant fluctuation of the moon, there is an element of unpredictability. Sometime, it seems that it has disappeared, but soon it will be full once again. Sometimes a people seems to be enslaved, but 'soon' they will be free.

Sunlight is an expression of the empirical, the observable and immediately tangible. Everything can be seen clearly in the light of day. The Hebrew word for sun is *Shemesh*, which comes from the Hebrew word *Mash* / tangible (see *Shemos*, 10:21), the world of 'manifest being'. Moonlight, on the other hand, is dim and fleeting. It represents the world of dreams, night, and imagination. The word *Levanah* / moon comes from the word *Lavan* / white or transparent, connected to elusiveness, intangibility, and a perpetual process of 'becoming'. One day the moon is seen, the next day it disappears; it is in a process of perpetual becoming, beyond what can be seen in the moment, and an openness to new possibilities.

As it follows a yearly cycle, the sun represents slow development over time. The moon represents that which comes in 'haste', from 'beyond' the normal course of space and time.

Commenting on the verse, "The sun knows its setting" (*Tehil-im*, 104:19), our Sages say, "The sun knows its setting and its movement, whereas the moon does not know" (*Rosh Hashanah*, 25a. Rambam, *Hilchos Kiddush HaChodesh*, 17:23). The moon represents a reality beyond knowing, beyond predictability, beyond what can be seen clearly in space or measured accurately in time.

To attain freedom, to leave the paradigm of slavery as an eternal, ontological status, we needed to break free from the grip of the strictly solar reality. We first needed to believe in the possibility of freedom, and that Hashem, the Source of all Life, the source of every status and position, could uplift us into a new vantage point at any moment. Thus, even while we were still slaves in Egypt, we received the *Mitzvah* / Divine mandate to sanctify the new moon, and to view time, and our lives, from a 'lunar' perspective.

We needed to be infused with the Divine promise of re-demption, allowing us to believe in an 'impossible' possibility. Hashem told us, 'Let go of your sun perception, and begin connecting to the world of night, of moon, of possibility, of the miraculous.'

Just being charged to begin counting time was a novelty, as slaves do not own their time. When we began to count lunar months, we were empowered even to imagine ourselves be-ing freed. The more we believed in the Infinite One's infinite power of renewal, the freer and less fearful we became of our taskmasters, and eventually were able to be freed.

BO

Energy of the Week:
Holy Imagination

This week's Torah reading imbues us with power to creatively visualize ourselves in a better state, a freer, less fearful state, and in that way, offers us a direct link to that reality.

This is the third stage in attaining greater inner freedom. The first was to reject our self-limitations and our 'acceptance' of the current situation as permanent. The second was to believe in the possibility of change, to accept the possibility of miracles. The third and final stage is visualizing our new reality and creatively imagining yourself already in that new state. Whatever reality you wish for yourself is within your reach.

Vividly imagine and visualize yourself living in the reality that you desire to live in. With true Emunah and Bitachon, everything is possible. Emunah means having faith that Hashem *can* give you this blessing; Bitachon means trusting that Hashem *will* provide it.

When we place ourselves in the picture of that place, we begin to co-create that reality. By fully imagining ourselves 'into' this new reality, we can truly be liberated from all constrictions and limitations, both those externally and internally imposed. We begin to live with less fear and more openness to life and open possibility.

PRACTICE OF THE WEEK:

Creative Visualization

Beshalach

Stepping Into Your Dreams

THIS WEEK'S TORAH READING OPENS WITH THE fourth and final part of the Exodus narrative, in which Klal Yisrael are finally, actually, leaving Egypt and their enslavement: "It came to pass when Pharaoh let the people go…" (13:17).

Klal Yisrael leaves Egypt in great haste, and then unexpectedly and anticlimactically, encounters before them the raging waters of the sea. Chased by their Egyptian oppressors, who were approaching behind them, and having no means of escape, a spirit of hopelessness enters them and they cry out to Moshe, "Is it because there are no graves in Egypt that you have taken us to die in the desert? What is this that you have done to us to take us out of Egypt!" (14:11)

Hashem responds and says to Moshe, "Why do you cry out to Me? Speak to the Children of Israel and let them travel forward" (14:15).

Hearing this striking message, they realize that even the time for crying has passed. Of course, through the power of crying out, Hashem had heard their prayers and the process of redemption had begun: "and they groaned...and Hashem heard their groan..." (*Shemos*, 2:23–24). However, as they stand there, already a liberated people, HaKadosh Baruch Hu tells them that even their work of praying is complete (they have reached the inner level of Atik, as the Zohar (2, 48a) says, which is beyond all *Avodah* / work). Now, they are instructed to take an actual physical step into their freedom.

When they do take that first step forward into the raging sea, it miraculously parts. The pangs of birth, beginning with the Ten Plagues, are over, and Klal Yisrael can finally be pushed through this watery birth canal. They can finally be birthed as a people, and they can prepare to receive the Torah and begin their journey toward the Promised Land.

"In every generation, a person must regard himself as if he himself had gone out of Egypt" (*Pesachim*, 116b). On one level, this means that when recalling the Exodus from Egypt thousands of years ago, we should envision our own lives as if *HaKadosh Baruch Hu* / the Holy One, has taken us, in *our* generation, out of Egypt. Remembering Yetzias Mitzrayim focuses our attention on all the multitude of redemptions of Klal Yisrael from exiles and *Gezeiros Ra'os* / negative decrees throughout history.

On a more inward level, *Mitzrayim* / Egypt represents any and all *Meitzarim* / constrictions and limitations that suppress or silence our spirit. Here, "every generation" means not only every generation but every *day* (*Tanya*, 47); on each day, it should be as if you had personally left Egypt on that very day.*

Even when faced with an obstacle that seems insurmountable, take that step towards your destination. The 'waters' will part; the doors will open, and the path towards your freedom will be paved for you.

We need to dream, aspire, imagine, and yearn to reach higher and deeper levels of spirituality and also material success. Yet, at some point, we must begin to start living as if our spiritual and physical goals have been reached. We should begin

---

* Rashi, *Shemos*, 13:4, as explained by the Chasam Sofer, *Derashos l' Pesach*, p. 521: We are taken out of our inner Egypt each and every *moment*. The Alter Rebbe teaches (in *Tanya*, above) in the name of Chazal (although Chazal only mention 'in every generation'), that each *day*, a person must regard himself as if he had come out of Mitzrayim. הנה בכל נפש ישראל צ"ל בכל יום בחי' יצ"מ וקי"ס כמ"ש כמו"ס למען תזכר את יום צאתך מארץ מצרים וגו'. וכמארז"ל בכל יום יהיה בעיניך כאלו היום יצאת ממא"צ: *Torah Ohr*, Beshalach, 64a. See also *Likutei Torah*, Emor. The Rebbe adds, although not quoting Chazal, that this means every *moment* of every day: *Sefer haSichos*, 5751, Shemos.

living as if the miracle we are praying for has already occurred.

Step into the bigger possibility. Act and speak as if you have already arrived. And then make it real by stepping into it.

These, then, are the four stages to becoming free:

• First, one needs to turn away from their negative story, whatever it may be. Do not view the current situation of constriction or confinement as fixed or permanent.

• Second, one needs to believe in the possibility of change, accept the possibility of a miracle, and generate faith in their ability to become part of that miracle.

• Third, one should visualize their new reality and imagine how it will feel to be in that new state.

• Fourth, one must take initiative, make that first move, and plunge into positive action. Take a step forward into the sea.

BESHALACH

Energy of the Week:
Stepping Into Your Dreams

This week's Torah reading imbues us with the power to take action and make our liberation happen. We receive the spiritual power this week to take the first step forward into our dream. Rather than looking for ways around the situation, we can take a step forward and go right through it.

The forward momentum that we have cultivated in the previous weeks gives us courage to transcend seemingly insurmountable issues, and creates the vessels for our dream to actualize. Now, we can live our dream as if it is already a reality. Rather than thinking, "One day I will reach a higher spiritual level," think, speak, and act 'as if' you are now on that level. Rather than thinking, "One day I will be wealthy," think: "I *am* already wealthy." Then, we need to take the courageous steps which will trigger our redemption or growth.

Because of one's inner anxieties, expectations, inse-curities, or a fear of being let down — whatever the reason may be — one might hold back and not allow the birthing of our dream. This week's Torah reading gives us the strength to act as if our dream is already fulfilled. If we actually start living that way, perhaps even celebrating as if it has already happened, we can make the *Kli* / vessel for Hashem's blessing to man-ifest.

PRACTICE OF THE WEEK:

Live the Fulfillment of Your Dreams, Now.

Yisro

Receiving Higher Wisdom

T HE TORAH READING OF YISRO FEATURES *Matan Torah* / the Giving of the Torah, the earth-shattering Divine revelation at Mount Sinai. Yet, the name comes from the opening story of Yisro, originally a non-Jew (who later converted: Sifri, Rashi, 18:1), and his suggestion to Moshe to set up a system of judgment. Already as the father-in-law of Moshe, Yisro comes to speak with Moshe as Klal Yisrael are encamped and preparing themselves for the revelation on Mount Sinai (Our sages debate if Yisro came before or after Matan Torah: *Zevachim*, 116a). The reading opens with these words, "Yisro, the chieftain of Midian...heard all that Hashem had done... Now... Yisro...came to Moshe, to the desert where he was encamped" (18:1–5).

When Yisro arrived at the encampment, he noticed how overworked and overburdened Moshe was. He observed him as "he judged the people from morning until evening." Yisro says to Moshe, "The thing you are doing is not good... You will surely wear yourself out...you cannot do it alone..." and so he suggests establishing a judicial hierarchy, wherein only the most difficult issues will be brought to Moshe (18:13–23). This suggestion is accepted and established, and the next episode in the Torah is the revelation at Mount Sinai and the Giving of the Torah.

Everything in life is precisely sequenced, certainly in the Torah (Although אין מוקדם ומאוחר בתורה / "There is no earlier or later in the Torah," it is unusual for the Torah to break the actual sequence. Indeed, the Ramban's opinion is that whenever possible, we should try to understand the Torah as relating events in their chronological order). Yisro's appearance in the Torah before the revelation at Mount Sinai is clearly essential to that revelation. It appears as if the "chieftain of Midian" needed to offer his advice and 'reveal' lower wisdom — before the revelation of Higher Wisdom could occur.

Indeed, the Zohar explains that it was crucial for Yisro, whose name is derived from the root word *Yeser* / added, to arrive and 'add' human wisdom to the Children of Yisrael before Divine Torah wisdom could be revealed. In this way, not only does he happen to meet with Moshe just before Matan Torah, but according to the Zohar, this meeting triggered the possibility for Matan Torah itself.

Lower wisdom is a *Kli* / vessel by means of which 'Higher' or Transcendent Wisdom can become revealed and also understood, internalized, and assimilated. Without the limitations inherent in worldly wisdom, Transcendent Wisdom would be inaccessible and overwhelming. Furthermore, an inter-inclusion of human and Divine wisdom creates the spiritual and psychological conditions that allow Transcendent Divine wisdom to transform us.

At first, Yisro comes as an outsider to Klal Yisrael,* from another land and foreign culture, as an 'extra' or 'outsider' (as his name *Yisro* / 'additional' suggests). This symbolizes the limitation and 'externality' of his wisdom. The Torah reading of Matan Torah is named after him since Torah can only be fully 'received' through contact by the inclusion of the lower or outer wisdom.

---

* The Name Yisro suggests an outsider, someone from an exterior public domain, who is entering into the domain of Klal Yisrael, into their *Reshus HaYachid* / private domain, which is the place where the *Yechidah shel Olam* rests. יתרו the first and last letters are ו - י , numerically 16, corresponding to the (minimum) width for a *Reshus HaRabim* / public domain. The middle letters are numerically 600, corresponding to the 600,000 people who need to pass through an area daily in order to qualify it as a Reshus HaRabim, according to many opinions. See Rashi, and Tosefos, *Shabbos*, 6b: קצת משמע דאינה ר"ה אלא א"כ מצויין שם ששים רבוא כמו במדבר. Although Rambam disagrees — אי זו היא רשות הרבים מדברות ועירות ושוקים ודרכים המפלשין להן ובלבד שיהיה רחב הדרך שש עשרה אמה ולא יהיה עליו תקרה: *Hilchos Shabbos*, 14:1. As such, his name suggests someone who is coming from the outside, from the world of separation into the world of Unity.

Yisro comes not only to trigger a revelation of the harmony and unity between the lower and Higher wisdoms but also to create a *Tikkun* / rectification and unification between two brothers. When he first arrives at the camp in the desert, he declares, אני חתנך יתרו / "I am your father-in-law, Yisro" (*Shemos*, 18:6). The first letters of these three words spell אחי / *Achi* / brother (*Sefer HaLikutim*, Yisro). Yisro is hinting to Moshe that they are actually 'brothers' and he has come to meet him to complete the rectification of the tragedy that occurred between the first set of brothers in the Torah: Kayin and Hevel. These archetypal brothers were separated when Kayin struck and killed Hevel.

This rectification was not only upon 'brothers' — rather, all souls are rooted either in that of Kayin or that of Hevel (*Sha'ar Gilgulim*, Hakdamah 36 and 38. *Pri Etz Chayim*, Shar Krias Shema, 39b). These two root souls are the prototypes of two basic kinds of people. Kayin, the Torah tells us, was a 'farmer' and landowner, very rooted in the ground and not very mobile. Hevel, by contrast, was a shepherd, living a nomadic lifestyle, a highly mobile, creative personality.

Kayin means 'acquisition', which is the concept of 'land'. Kayin thus works the land and is rooted there. Hevel literally means 'breath', representing someone who is more ephemeral and detached, a suitable character trait for a shepherd. A shepherd can move about like the wind, like breath. *Hevel* also means 'empty', in this case lacking all *Kinyan* 'land' or worldliness (*Sisrei Torah*, Abulafia, Orach Chaim, p. 24).

Those whose soul root is in Kayin are physically stronger (*Pri Eitz Chayim*, 39b) than those whose soul root is in Hevel. For this reason, souls from Kayin need to be more careful about the effects of their actions. Souls from Hevel need to be careful about the effects of their words, their externalized 'breath'.

Souls that are rooted and connected with Hevel, feel a heightened sense of love and aliveness when close to or immersed in water (*Sha'ar haGilgulim*, Hakdamah 36. *Pri Eitz Chayim*, Sha'ar Kerias Shema, 3). By inference, those whose root soul is with Kayin are perhaps irrationally frightened by water, especially by deep water and the darkness of the depths.

Despite all differing traits, the unitive meta-root of all souls is the 'head' of *Adam Kadmon* / Primordial Humanity, as embodied in Adam *HaRishon* / 'the First Human Being' (*Sha'ar HaGilgulim*, Hakdamah, 12. Ramak, *Shiur Komah*, 2. See also *Medrash Rabbah*, Shemos, 40:3. *Tanchuma*, Ki Sisa, 12. *Tanya*, Igeres HaKodesh, 7). As they descend from the head of Adam, souls begin to differentiate and flow into his arms and legs, as it were. Hevel is the right shoulder, arm, and leg, and Kayin is the left shoulder, arm, and leg.

Kayin represents action and physicality; an earthly person is connected with the work of his hands. Kayin has a lot of *Gevurah* / power or 'fire' energy, which is from the left column of the Sefiros, and he is an extrovert. Hevel represents speech and thought, and is a more cerebral, thoughtful, gentle, introverted person. He has more *Chesed* / kindness, which flows like water

(Kayin souls tend to roll their Tallis neatly on their shoulders, and because of their Gevurah, they are not allowed to recite the blessing after meals with a knife on the table).

Yisro is rooted in the soul of Kayin, and Moshe is rooted in Hevel. Moshe is a shepherd by trade, and an ephemeral prophet, a receiver of Divine Wisdom. He lives in the transcendental worlds more than in the lower worlds; he is more 'Hevel', detached and abstract. This is why Moshe leaves his wife. Practical and worldly, Yisro brings Moshe back to his wife and children, and he tells Moshe, "*Lo Tov* / it is not good" for you to judge from morning to evening. In this statement, he is also subtly hinting to the *Lo Tov* in the story of creation, when the Creator, after creating Adam alone, says, *Lo Tov* / "It is not good" for man to be alone.

In suggesting a system of judgment, Yisro is lobbying for the practical execution of Torah law. He asserts the need for healthy boundaries, 'vessels' of lower, practical wisdom. These vessels allow the ethereal, transcendent wisdom of the Torah to be received in an integrated way, even by Moshe himself. Thus, Yisro must meet Moshe before Matan Torah can occur.

YISRO

Energy of the Week:
Receiving Wisdom

This Torah reading imbues us with the power to bridge the physical and spiritual, the transcendental and the worldly. It allows us to bring Heaven down to earth and elevate the earth to Heaven, in our own lives. To be open to receive the Transcendental Wisdom of the Torah, our minds and hearts need to be open also to its practical guidance for day-to-day life on earth. We need to ground our 'breath' in the 'land'.

"Who is wise? One who learns from every person," says the Mishnah. Every person and situation we meet is there to teach us something new about ourselves and how to live. There is wisdom to be found within everything and everyone.

Every human being expresses another face of the Infinite faces of our Creator. The Creator is talking to us with every encounter, with hints at Higher Wisdom nested within practical information. This week, we are energized with the ability to become aware of these messages and to 'receive the Torah' reflected within every experience.

PRACTICE OF THE WEEK:

Be Receptive to Learn Wisdom From All of Life

Mishpatim
Resetting Our Moral Compass

"And these are the Mishpatim / ordinances that you shall set before them" (21:1).

MISHPATIM ARE THE ETHICAL AND CIVIL LAWS that govern our behavior towards our fellow human beings; details of a social contract, as it were.

At Mount Sinai, we had a collective mystical and transcendental experience in which all of Klal Yisrael experienced the Oneness of Hashem. Immediately after the Torah depicts our total realization of *Ein Od Milvado* / "There is nothing else but Hashem," the text launches into basic civil laws, the ordinances governing the interactions between man and man. For example, what is the rule if you dig a pit or place an obstacle in a public domain and a passerby is hurt by it? What do you need to do if your animal hurts another person?

One might not expect, following such a transcendental experience, to abruptly turn to a long list of laws dealing with damages and disagreements. Perhaps an appropriate next section would be an unfolding of the Torah's mystical teachings, or contemplative Mitzvos such as study or prayer.

Yet, there is a direct correlation between the exalted experience of witnessing the absolute Oneness of Hashem and living our day to day mundane life. This is what the Torah is pointing out. Experiencing Oneness is translated into treating every human being, and their property, with respect. As Hashem is One, everything and everyone belongs to Hashem.

If our spiritual experiences of revelation, or of praying or studying Torah, do not translate into refined day-to-day behavior, it shows that there was a disconnect. Only by living Torah in real time do we demonstrate that we have really accepted the Torah's revelation of the Oneness of Hashem, and prove that its truth has truly infused us. This is why Mishpatim comes right after Mount Sinai.

Interestingly, the Zohar chooses the beginning of this portion, from among all other Torah readings, to explore mystical teachings on the reincarnation of souls.

Generally, our souls incarnate to reach our fullest actualization. Each reincarnation articulates another element of our soul. Each incarnation is a different person with a different

Tikkun — a rectification of the particular element of the soul revealed in that incarnation.

We are all born with an individual soul and a particular soul 'type'. Imagine a blank sheet of paper, symbolizing the beginning of life. It is empty, life experiences have not yet been written on it. On the other hand, this blank sheet already has a hue, texture, and weight. Some sheets of paper have a subtle yellow tint, others have more of a blue tint, and others are gray. Some are matte, and some are glossy.

We all have natural inclinations and ways of being, even before our distinct story of life begins to unfold. One person is more inclined to be open and generous, and another person is more inclined to be restrained. Such are the particular tints in the background of our story, informing how the story will be seen and understood. Every day and every moment, we are 'writing' our story. Our thoughts, deeds, and experiences are being imprinted on our paper, our particular soul.

Different personalities will experience the same event differently, according to their background 'tint' or type of soul. All souls are rooted in different parts of the soul of *Adam Kadmon* / the Primordial Human Being. Some souls are rooted in the 'head' of this being, and some stem from its 'hands', 'heart', or 'feet'.

'Head' souls may gravitate toward intellectual pursuits, whereas 'hand' souls may tend to work with manual dexterity.

'Heart' souls may brim with emotion or devotion, and 'feet' souls may be oriented toward active lifestyles and movement. The genetic patterns of our physical body, together with our upbringing, conditioning, and environment, are all providential expressions of our soul-type.

Each image of soul is holographic; a 'head' soul is not without heart, and a 'heart' soul has some 'head' attributes. Each distinct expression of the primordial soul possesses all the capacities to think, feel, work, and move. Yet, one born with a 'head' soul who decides to occupy himself with 'hand' soul activities and concerns, is acting counter to his true nature. This will prevent the person from fully realizing himself. To be a fully realized and actualized human being, we need to articulate who we really are, our distinct expression of soul needs to be fully expressed. This is our Tikkun or perfecting.

Our conscious selves, including our actions, words, thoughts, experiences, and memories, are expressions of our personal soul. This is who our soul is for all eternity.

As a general principle, our special brilliance, that part of our soul which already manifested as our uniqueness or gift, does not reincarnate. It does not need to return to earth because through its development, challenges, and successes, it has already attained full Tikkun in this life. The parts of us that need to be reincarnated, rectified, and completed are the aspects of our soul that we have had little experience with in life.

The soul reconfigures itself in the afterlife as well as during life. As our unique personality is rendered in this life there are sparks of our soul that we connect to, and there are other sparks that remain dormant. After consciousness separates from the body, the sparks that made up our individual configuration in this life remain with our soul for eternity. The sparks that had been dormant throughout our life reincarnate and gradually become components in the individual souls of others. In each human life, we are attempting to live out another 'hue' until we have lived out the complete spectrum of the soul.

There is one form of reincarnation, however, in which the *totality* of who you were in the past will reincarnate to create a Tikkun for that past life (*Sha'ar HaGilgulim*, Hakdamah 8, 11. *Reshis Chochmah*, Sha'ar HaYirah, 13. *Medrash Talpiyos*, Gimel). This generally occurs for the sake of a Tikkun on issues between people, such as unfinished monetary issues. Various unethical dealings between people require the totality of self to return and hopefully achieve rectification (*Mishlei*, Gra, 14:25. *Even Shelomo*, 3:8).

Rebbe DovBer, the Maggid of Mezritch, once requested his teacher, the Baal Shem Tov, to reveal to him the secret of reincarnation. The Baal Shem Tov encouraged him to travel to a certain location and told him that when he will reach a tree with a stream nearby, he should rest there until the evening, observe what will transpire, and then return. He was clearly instructed not to interfere or participate in what would happen there but only to observe.

That is exactly what he did. He traveled to that particular location, sat down and noticed a traveler passing by. The traveler put down his bags, rested for a bit, and ate something before continuing on his way. When the traveler left, the Maggid saw that his wallet was accidentally left behind. The Maggid also remembered that he had been instructed to observe and not to participate.

Soon, along came another traveler who rested in the very same place. While lying there, the second traveler noticed the unmarked wallet, picked it up, put it into his pocket, and left. A few moments later, a third man came along. He had just sat down to rest his tired body when along came the first person, the one who had lost his wallet. Assuming this third man had found and pocketed his wallet, he asked him for it back. When the man honestly denied any wrongdoing, the first traveler lost his temper and beat him.

Puzzled, the Maggid returned to the Baal Shem Tov and told the story. The Baal Shem Tov explained: in a previous life, the first person owed the second one the amount of money that was found in the wallet but refused to pay him. When they went to their rabbi, who was the third person in this event, the Rabbi carelessly ruled incorrectly and did not demand the first person to pay up. Each one was now repaid appropriately (*Devarim Areivim*, Mishpatim, 18. *Baal Shem Tov al HaTorah*, Mishpatim, 1. *Degel Machaneh Ephrayim*, Mishpatim. Note a similar version of this story is found in an earlier Medrashic source. See *Torah Sheleimah*, Mishpatim).

Our goal in our present life is to fully articulate our particular aspect of soul within our lifetime, and not incur a reincarnation of this unique self in the process.

To this end, it is of utmost importance to rectify all negative patterns of unethical behavior that we might have expressed in our lives. In our business dealings, and all other relationships, we must be cautious to be moral and honest and repair any unscrupulous behaviors.

Certainly, we may not wrongly take money from others. If money was taken from us, and we were wronged, we are allowed to do everything we can to ethically retrieve that money. Once we realize that it may be impossible to do so, we need to recognize that, while the other person might be a reincarnation of the thief, and the effects of his actions will catch up to him in his current life or his next — yet in terms of our perspective, that money no longer belongs to us and we need to let it go.

MISHPATIM

Energy of the Week:

Resetting Our Moral Compass

This week's Torah reading imbues us with the power to effect repair, or Tikkun, for interpersonal issues, particularly in regard to monetary dealings and any dishonorable behaviors.

Throughout the week, it is important to be extra mindful when it comes to ethical dealings with others. Try to recognize your negative patterns and mistakes with regard to business, financial dealings, or damages, and receive the power of this Parshah as an impetus to break out of these behaviors.

Rectifying our negative or unethical patterns will ensure a complete Tikkun in our current lifetime and an ability for our soul to move forward in this world the next without the need to 'come back' to be rechallenged and complete our soul's journey.

PRACTICE OF THE WEEK:
Reevaluate Your Monetary Dealings

Terumah
Rooting 'Highs' in Proper Vessels

F OLLOWING KLAL YISRAEL'S EXODUS FROM EGYPT
and the receiving of the Torah at Mount Sinai, they
were instructed to build a *Mishkan* / Sanctuary, a
'dwelling place' in which they could encounter the Presence of
the Creator:

"Hashem spoke to Moshe saying: 'Speak to the Children of
Israel, and have them take for Me an offering... And they shall
make Me a sanctuary and I will dwell in their midst.'" (25:1:8)

Klal Yisrael needed a method for encountering the Divine
Presence, and they needed to know that Hashem was dwelling
in their midst.

But why, precisely, was a *Mishkan* necessary to accomplish this? Perhaps some other method or idea could have communicated the Divine Presence — why an actual structure?

To answer this, we need to know what 'precipitated' this command, as it were. This is the essence of an important debate between the great medieval scholars of France and Catalonia, Rashi and the Ramban, regarding *when* this commandment was given (Rashi, *Shemos*, 31:18. Ramban, 25:2). Were they told to construct the Mishkan directly after the revelation at Mount Sinai? Or is the text out of chronological order here, and they were commanded to build the Mishkan directly after the episode of the Golden Calf? (The latter is the opinion of Rashi)

First, let us consider the Zohar, which interprets the events in chronological order and understands this to be a logical sequel to the events at Mount Sinai. In this way, the Mishkan is a re-creation of the spiritual, transcendental Sinai experience in real-time, in tangible and physical space. This means the Mishkan served to recreate Matan Torah within space. In this way, they were able to carry with them the experience of Matan Torah, wherever they traveled. And this is Ramban's opinion as well; the transcendent experience of Mount Sinai precipitated the need for a mobile vehicle of Sinai in this world of space ("And the secret of / וסוד המשכן הוא, שיהיה הכבוד אשר שכן על הר סיני עליו שוכן בנסתר) the Mishkan is that the Glory (of Hashem) that rested on Mount Sinai now rested upon the Mishkan, in a more hidden way": Ramban, *Shemos*, 25:1).

Klal Yisrael experienced a tremendous spiritual awakening when they received the Torah and its laws, a transformative mystical experience, and they now required a vessel to contain that which they had received. Through this receptacle, the inspiration would be retained and kept alive.

The Mishkan served as a place in which all that they had received could be contained, and in that way, the initial spiritual high coupled with their emotions and thoughts of Sinai would stay with them throughout their journeys in the Desert.

A simple example of this idea in our own lives is with regard to our emotions. An emotion that is felt, however strongly in the moment, can easily be lost and forgotten with time. If something tangible is produced or acquired, as a "vessel" to preserve the memory, then even when the initial excitement has passed, that feeling can always be accessed through the tangible object. For example, when someone feels an intense stirring of love and then purchases a piece of jewelry, photo, or keepsake, for their loved one to provide a tangible expression, that gift will have the power to reawaken and re-establish that feeling much later in time.

In the same way, the Mishkan, being the gift-object borne of our affection, became a vessel for our love and commitment to *HaKadosh Baruch Hu* / the Holy One. It was a physical embodiment of the spiritual experience of Sinai, able to reawaken that Divine self-revelation as long as it existed.

From another vantage point, the rooting of spiritual and mystical experiences in the creation of the Mishkan ensures that the 'high' of the Sinai experience was directed into a proper and holy vessel. The energy of that heightened experience needed an outlet, and since it was not channeled immediately into enthusiastically building a holy vessel, it was channeled into enthusiastically fashioning an idol. This is Rashi's answer to the debate with the Ramban; the Mishkan was precipitated by the episode of the Golden Calf. Thus, the sequence of events was that the Golden Calf episode occurred right after Mount Sinai, and the Mishkan came after the Golden Calf.

In our own lives, it works the same way. Any high that is not channeled for the positive will inevitably be channeled to the negative. We have a choice; the intense energy will need to go 'somewhere', and we need to direct it into an appropriate vessel, and by all means not into a 'idol', whether metaphorical or real. For example, when a person who was in debt wins a lottery, in their euphoria, they often over-spend and within a short time they are back in debt. An appropriate 'vessel', in this case, could be committing to the direction of a financial advisor or trustee.

The Baal Shem Tov teaches that some people pray with great fervor and intention, only to direct their spiritual energy-high into anger or frivolity later on (*Degel Machaneh Ephrayim, Ki Sisa*). Anger and frivolity are both likened to idol worship, and represent the devastating fall into worshiping the Golden Calf.

In our society, one has to be vigilant not only around the af-
ter-effects of spiritual highs in intense prayer, prolonged study,
fasting or deep contemplation or meditation, but also the effects of other 'highs' such as engaging in sports or exercise,
earning or investing money, drinking alcohol, playing music
or dancing, having philosophical epiphanies, taking vacations,
moving to a foreign country, 'acing' exams, making art, creating
an invention or technological or social advance, speaking or
performing publicly, becoming an authority or a famous figure,
or just changing your mode of dress.

Whatever gives you a very heightened sense of aliveness,
bliss or ecstasy, an adrenaline or dopamine rush, or even very
deep relaxation, freedom or silence, has a powerful after-effect.
When the body and soul are energized or uplifted, we need
to contain that energetic influx and direct it into productive
and positive action, and ultimately, in the service of the Divine
Presence that "dwells in the midst" of Creation and human
beings.

TERUMAH

Energy of the Week:

Making a Vessel to Contain & Direct the Highs of Life

This week's Torah reading imbues us with the power and motivation to root each of our expansive experiences, emotions, thoughts, ideas, and creative energies into a practical *Kli* / vessel. The good that we contain, we can maintain. If we don't harness it, it remains transient, intangible, and ultimately dissatisfying. We will continue to feel empty or depleted and seek that stimulus again. Such a cycle of gaining spiritual highs and then losing them cannot be redemptive; the transformational potential is never assimilated and put into action.

We are empowered this week to create firm, positive, life-affirming *Kelim* / vessels of action so that our highs can be integrated into this world and body, and be truly transformative.

PRACTICE OF THE WEEK:
Put Spirituality Into Action

Tetzaveh

Refining our Spiritual 'Wardrobe'

F OLLOWING THE INSTRUCTION TO BUILD THE *Mish-kan* / temporary Divine sanctuary in the desert, Moshe is now told to instruct the *Kohanim* / Priests, and his brother Aharon the High Priest, to properly attire themselves for their service.

The Torah reading begins with the words, "And you (Moshe) shall command...And bring near to yourself your brother Aharon, and his sons with him...You shall make holy garments for your brother Aharon, לכבוד ולתפארת / "for honor and beauty" (27:20–21, 28:1–2).

In general, there are four human purposes for garments: 1) physical protection, warmth and wellbeing, 2) psychological protection and wellbeing, 3) honoring one's status or role, and 4) expressing beauty and honor.

1) On the most basic, physical level, garments fill our need to protect the body and keep it warm, like the protective shells and coats of animals which protect them from the elements. This utilitarian purpose is connected to the Nefesh level of soul, the animating, enlivening force of the body.

2) The psychological purpose of garments is to cover and alleviate one's sense of shame. This is a more 'internal' level of protection, which is found only among human beings, as the emotion of shame is connected to the higher level of the human soul, the level of *Ruach* / emotions. Among all the living creatures, only humans appear to feel shame and to blush (*Orchos Tzadikim*, Sha'ar HaBusha, 3. *Migdal Oz*, Aliyas HaBusha).

Shame arises when we feel judged by an 'outside' source, be it other people, or a more external part of ourselves. Animals are integrated creatures whose behavior is congruent with their inner beings; they *do* what they *are*, and there is never an inconsistency between their internal world and their external behavior. Humans, however, have free choice and can thus come into conflict with their inner nature, which may then bring them to feel shame. The physical manifestation of shame, blush, occurs because, in addition to our freedom of choice, we also possess a strong sense of self-awareness. The former gives us the ability to be at odds with ourselves, the latter causes us to be aware of it and, consequently, to feel shame and blush.

"And they (Adam and Chava) were both naked…and were not ashamed" (*Bereishis*, 2:25). Shame is an emotion that can only exist when there is awareness of an 'other'. Since they did not yet eat from the *Eitz haDaas* / 'the Tree of Knowledge', and they had not yet tasted the worldview of duality and conflicting interests, they did not have a strong sense of a separate 'other'. Thus, they were not ashamed to be in their childlike, natural state.

Ever since we lost our innocence, both historically and personally, we cover ourselves in garments to hide or heal our shame. As such, the word לבוש / *Levush* / garment comes from the words לא בושה / *Lo Busha* / without shame (*Shabbos*, 77b: לבושה, לא בושה), as a garment helps to free us from shame and begin to recover our innocence and oneness.

3) The intellectual purpose (the inner world of Neshamah): On this level, a garment is worn to bring attention to the social status or 'honor' of the wearer. This is a higher objective than the utilitarian and psychological objectives of garments, as it is not merely for one's own protection.

An official's uniform honors their particular expertise or role in serving others. On the occasion of a wedding ritual, a white gown can help create כבוד / *Kavod* / honor for the bride, uplifting and empowering her transition into married life (Note *Ta'anis*, 26b). A judge may put on a black robe to create an atmosphere of seriousness so that those entering the courthouse respect the process of judgment and the court's decision.

When a person wears a garment of Kavod, it also invites their self-respect. The mere act of donning a special garment compels the individual to become attentive to the task they are assuming. In all these examples, the garment helps create a proper mindset, awakening the power of the Neshamah, the intellectual level of soul, within that context.

4) The 'pleasure' purpose (the inner world of Chayah and Yechidah). Here a garment is worn to bring joy and pleasure. It expresses one's pre-existing inner beauty — not in order to fill a psychological need, but just for the sake of the 'beauty' of life itself.

At the subtlest level, garments have no 'value' in themselves; rather, they are an expression of soul, and wearing them is an act of embodying תפארת / Divine beauty. The value of beauty is in itself; it brings pleasure not as a means to another end but rather simply to bring appreciation for the Divine beauty. This is the level of pure *Ta'anug* / pleasure, connected to the soul level of Chayah and Yechidah.

There can be a 'hollow' perception of beauty, and one that is utilitarian in nature, i.e., 'what can I get' from this beauty, and how can I come to possess it. And there is deeper 'inner' perception, which beholds all beauty as a manifestation of the ultimate beauty, the beauty of the Divine attribute of Beauty. In this deeper perception, one can see beauty without feeling a need to control, take hold of it, or use it as an end in itself. Here, the outer beauty is a true reflection of the inner beauty of the soul.

'Hollow' perception is not only a condition of the eyes of the beholder, but it can be because the person projecting that form of beauty is also doing so in a superficial manner, beauty of the body and to attract attention to self, and thus as a utilitarian objective, how to 'get' something out of the beauty.

The beauty and splendor of the garments of the Kohanim aroused in them a deeper longing and yearning to connect and unify with the Ultimate Source of Beauty. They wore them not to beautify or honor themselves nor create a sense of self-importance. Rather, they wore them as a Mitzvah, an instruction revealed by Moshe, the humblest of men, who lived with total *Bitul* / selfless transparency to HaKadosh Baruch Hu. On the highest level, that of the Yechidah, these garments were simply an expression of one's essential transparency to Hashem's 'beauty' and 'honor', so-to-speak, within this world.

Besides literal garments, we wear 'garments of the soul', which are our thoughts, words, and actions. While literal garments conceal the body, they can also reveal a person's innermost psyche. Similarly, the garments of thoughts, words, and actions can conceal or reveal our soul.

Another Hebrew word for garment is בגד / *Beged*, which can also be read as '*Bagad*' / treason or betrayal (ותנח בגדו אצלה, ולא לבושו, דבוגדים בגדו (ישעיה כד) אלא בגדו, לישנא :אלא בגדו *Zohar, Raya Mehemnah*, Ki Seitzei, 276a. See also *Kidushin*, 18b). In fact, the first time the Torah uses the word *Beged* to refer to a garment is in a story of "betrayal" — when Rivkah puts the clothes of Eisav on Ya'akov, so that their blind father Yitzchak will think that Ya'akov is Eisav and give him the blessing of the firstborn. While the idea of clothing is found in the story of Adam and Chavah, the term *Beged* is not used there.

As such, a Beged can serve to betray or hide the truth. A person could disguise himself in a certain garment and others would mistake him for a different type of person. Another term for clothing is לבוש / *Levush*, the rearranged letters of which phonetically suggest שביל / *Shvil* / passageway. Garments can be used as a blockage of self-revelation or as a passageway to self-revelation. On the highest level, garments reveal inner qualities to the outside world in such a way that observers gain a passageway to recognition of the Divine Presence.

Like regular clothing, the garments of thought, speech, and action, are interfaces between observer and observed. To enter into another person's internal world, we first need to enter the space of their 'garments', the interface of their projected self, their words and actions. Then we can gradually begin to understand their thoughts, and ultimately know them on a soul level.

For example, when you meet a person for the first time, and you feel an affinity and want to get to know them better on a more inner level, it can nevertheless be hard to begin a conversation. Yet, even if you feel intimidated or nervous, you may be able to enter dialogue via 'garments', more external levels of connection. In some contexts, this could mean making a joke, as a shared laugh is where both sets of 'garments' meet and relax. When your speech and action thus create a 'passageway', you may connect on the level of thought and even contact their soul in a deep conversation.

On the other hand, people can also put on a facade or inappropriate 'garment' just so that they can feel they fit in socially. For example, one may laugh at a joke that they do not understand so people might think that they are quick and witty. When someone says something intelligent or in another language, one might make an outer display of understanding it just to make people think that they are learned or sophisticated.

All of this is also true in terms of interfacing with different spiritual realms and becoming closer with our Creator, as the Zohar (2, 229a–b) teaches: "The soul does not ascend to be seen before the Holy King before it is worthy of donning the garments of Above so that it may be seen there. In the same way, the soul does not descend below until it wears the clothes of this world...." In order to interface and become unified with the Divine King, the Kohanim needed to wear garments of great sanctity and light, beauty, and honor. On Shabbos and Yom Tov, we, too, should wear our most honorable and refined clothing to express our unification with the holiness of the day.

TETZAVEH

Energy of the Week:

Aligning Our Outer Expressions With Our Inner Self

This week's Torah reading imbues us with the power to create 'garments' of honor and beauty. It gives us an ability to express our soul through the way we dress, speak, behave, and think. We are empowered to realign any untrue expressions of who and what we really are, and allow our inner truth to be reflected consistently through our outer self.

This Torah reading is often read on the week of Purim, a day when one might dress up as some version or representation of their soul, such as a king or queen, or they might dress themselves as another person and seemingly conceal their true identity. On a deeper level, wearing an external mask allows a person to reveal their internal light; the mask is not there to conceal, but rather, paradoxically, reveal.

In either case, during Purim, one should at some point remove their mask and reveal and feel their true soul identity without crutches or coverings. You are already a child of the Infinite King, and full of spiritual beauty and honor, just as you are.

This week gives us the Ko'ach and the Kavanah to let go of clinging to our false *Levushim* / garments. When our *Beged*, our interface of thought, speech, and action, reflects self-honor and expresses our inner beauty, it is no longer *Bagad* / 'deceitful', rather, it reveals our deeper reality and allows us to connect to others on a more profound level as well. When we 'dress' in a way that reflects our truth, and speak and behave in aligned ways, we are able to express ourselves authentically and form honest relationships.

This week, we are also given the gift of wisdom to know how to interface with another person's garments. For instance, we receive the wisdom to say the right words at the right time to the right person, and how to truly connect with them.

PRACTICE OF THE WEEK:
Reveal & Enter Your Inner Self

Ki Sisa

Going Beyond the Image &
Connecting With the Ideal

" **H**ashem spoke to Moshe saying, when you take the sum of the children of Israel according to their numbers, let each one give to Hashem atonement for his soul when they are counted." The Torah continues: ‫זה יתנו כל־‬ ‫העבר על־הפקדים מחצית השקל בשקל הקדש עשרים גרה השקל מחצית השקל‬ ‫תרומה לה‬ / "They shall give, everyone who goes through the counting: half a Shekel according to the holy Shekel. Twenty Gerah equal one Shekel, half of [such] a Shekel shall be an offering to Hashem."

Simply put, every person should give a half a Shekel for the upkeep of the *Mishkan* / Divine Sanctuary in the Desert. The question is, why does the Torah reiterate the message through a seemingly circuitous way: "Twenty Gerah equal one Shekel, and half of [such] a Shekel shall be an offering to Hashem...."

Even if the value of the offering needs to be clarified, why not simply say, "Give a half Shekel, which is 10 Gerah?"*

* The Rambam rules (*Hilchos Shekalim*, 1:1) that we give these 10 Gerah, this half Shekel, in a single act of giving: ואינו נותן בפעמים. בפעמים רבות היום מעט ולמחר מעט אלא כלו נותנו כאחת בפעם אחת / "The half Shekel should not be given in several partial payments, today a portion, tomorrow a portion. Instead, it is to be given all at once." This ruling does not seem to come from the Gemara, so then, what is the source of this Halachah? Also, what is the exact meaning of this *Sevara* / logic that we must give all 10 Gerah at one time? The Rogatchover writes that the 10 Gerah are not a *Shiur Mitztaref* / 'combined amount' of 10 separate Gerah, rather they are a single *Etzem* / essence, one *Metziyus* / 'reality' of giving. The Torah's enumeration of 10 Gerah is not actually 'quantitative', rather it is 'qualitative' — the idea is the quality of *half* of a Shekel HaKodesh. So the Shiur is 'half a Shiur', as it were. However, this does not imply that it is less than a Shiur, rather, the Shiur *is* a half Shekel. (Note the opinion of the Maharam Chalvah, who writes that according to the opinion that *Chatzi Shiur* / 'a half measurement' of non-Kosher food is prohibited according to Torah law, not merely Rabbinic law, yet, this is only if its literally a half of Shiur, but if it is less than a *Chatzi* / half of a Shiur, then it is not prohibited according to Torah law. This suggests the idea that a 'half' is considered a 'whole' entity.)

The Ramban writes, והדל לא ימעיט והנראה מן הכתוב הזה שאם הביא הדל הדל בשקלו פחות ממחצית השקל שהוא עובר בלאו הזה. In other words, if a person gives 5 Gerah, not only has he not fulfilled his obligation of giving a half Shekel, which is 10 Gerah, but he is violating a *Lav* / Torah prohibition. But the obvious question is: true, he is giving less than 10 Gerah, but a person who does not give *at all* merely does not fulfill the Mitzvah of half a Shekel — he does not transgress a Lav. Why, then, if he gives only 5 Gerah, is it 'worse' than giving nothing, and he has transgressed a Lav? (Not that this would be a transgression of *Lo Tigra* / 'do not diminish the details of a Torah law,' which is a separate Lav, rather perhaps it is a Lav connected with not giving exactly a half Shekel.)

The Brisker Rav answers that the Ramban is talking about a person who does, in fact, ultimately give the half Shekel, but he gives in increments, let's say, two Gerah at a time, and over time he gives 10 Gerah. One who does this is Over the Lav because the Torah clearly implies that the half Shekel has to be given as a single unit. Although the Ramban does not quote the

There must be some hidden message in the mention of "20 Gerah."

In the course of this week's Torah reading, we learn of Klal Yisrael creating, and eventually worshiping, a Golden Calf. The half Shekel was given as an atonement for this drastic transgression and spiritual deviation.

An obvious question is, how, after the revelation at Mount Sinai and the awesome recognition of the Oneness of Hashem that illuminated all of Klal Yisrael, did they suddenly fall into the devastating spiritual blunder of idol worship? How was such a dramatic descent, from such an elevated state of consciousness, even possible?

The answer is that Klal Yisrael did not wish (originally) to serve an actual idol, rather they craved an *image*, a form through which to connect to the Transcendent and Imageless Infinite Creator. They initially desired, as the Kuzari and the Even Ezra write, a צורה מורגשת / "a tangible form" to connect to the Formless Source (*Kuzari*, Ma'amar 1, 91–117).

Having such a desire is actually completely normal. A human is, in part, a physical, three-dimensional form. The objective of going out of Egypt and receiving the Torah was to con-

---

Rambam, this is exactly what the Rambam rules; one needs to give the half Shekel in one giving. The Chidush of the Ramban is that if one did not, one is actually *Over* a *Lav* / transgressing.

nect this form to Hashem, Who is utterly transcendent and non-corporeal *Ein Sof* / Infinity. However, it is difficult for a form to have a real relationship with the Formless. We instinctively seek out tools and intermediaries, such as images, words, and concepts, that will hopefully allow us to grasp and sense even just a glimpse of the Unknowable, Ineffable Mystery, the Hidden Ein Sof.

In addition to this human tendency, the people anxiously assumed that Moshe was no longer with them, and that he had ascended to Heaven. This is because Moshe told them that he would be on the mountain for 40 days, and they miscalculated by a day. They approached Aharon and demanded: "Make us a leader who will go before us, for the 'person Moshe'… is no longer." Note that they asked for another Moshe; they did not ask for an idol (as the Ramban, 32:1, writes: אבל היו מבקשין משה אחר). What they thought they needed was a tangible, physical object that would allow them, just as the 'person Moshe' had allowed them, to access the intangible, non-objective Creator. They wanted an image to allow them to have access to the Imageless, a form to allow them to connect to the Formless.

Let's assume for a moment that a physical object could connect them to the Infinite Creator in the way Moshe did. However, when they gathered around that object, they lost their spiritual balance. Instead of using the object, the form, to direct their focus toward the Formless Creator, they began focusing on, and then worshiping, the object itself: אלה אלהיך ישראל / "*This* is the G-d of Israel" (32:4).

What began as a natural desire for an intermediary ended up as devotion toward the form itself. The transgression occurred when the 'finger' pointing toward Hashem itself became regarded as Hashem.

Many of us, sadly, also worship a subtle 'image', such as money, power, physical objects, or even a person. They initially pursue financial gain or positions of power in order to provide benefit to their loved ones and the world around them. They have real altruistic motives, and they are aware that the money or power is just an intermediary. And not only can they use it to nourish and shelter their family, but it helps them to give charity and do acts of *Chesed* / kindness. The money is an 'image' with a higher purpose. Over time, however, without maintaining clarity and *Kavanah* / intention, and without engaging in frequent self-evaluation to confirm that their original motivation is intact, the money or object can become an end in itself.

Here, the pursuit begins with an ideal; however, ideals can easily be lost in the image. The means can subtly become the end, and the pursuit becomes 'idolatrous'. The emotions or anxieties driving idealism can drown out the actual ideal. We can become so involved with the 'tools' of our virtuous pursuits that we begin to look upon the tool as desirable, even to the point of 'bowing' to the tool in veneration.

Let's return to our original questions. Why were we commanded to give a half Shekel and not a whole one? And why does the Torah go out of its way to tell us that the worth of a whole Shekel is 20 Gerah? Also, how is this donation a *Kaparah* / atonement for the *Chet HaEgel* / transgression of the Golden Calf?

The 'half' Shekel alludes to the fact that the physical Shekel is only 'half of the story', and there is another half to consider.

A physical image or 'tool' is part of the external, physical world created with the *Asarah Ma'amaros* / Ten Utterances of Creation. However, the Ten Utterances are meant to correspond to the true 'ideal', inner spiritual world of the *Aseres HaDibros* / Ten Divine Commandments. When we place our life in service to the Divine Oneness, we effect a *Yichud* / unity between the two 'halves': the Ten Utterances of the Physical world and the Ten Commandments of the Spiritual World. When we use our 'tool', our physical money, in service of the 'Mishkan' our spiritual ideal, we are connecting the 10 of Creation with the 10 of Revelation.

Ten is the numerical value of the letter Yud. Yet, when Yud is spelled out, the value becomes 20 (Yud/10, Vav/6, Dalet/4 = 20). The way to live in the physical world with proper intention is to fix our ideals on the spiritual Light represented by the Ten Commandments. Then we are living with 20 — the unity of the Ten Utterances of Creation and the Ten Commandments of Revelation.

The word עשרים / twenty, is numerically 620, which is the

word כתר / *Keser*, which means the 'crown' or purpose of Creation. The purpose of Creation is to create a unity between the physical world (10) and spiritual world (10) — between Heaven and earth, body and soul, and create a dwelling place for the Transcendent One here in the material plane (620 is also the sum of the 613 Mitzvos of the Torah, plus the seven Mitzvos of the Sages — which are the path of unifying Heaven and earth).

This is the deeper reason why everyone had to give a "half Shekel," as it was a *Tikkun* / rectification and healing of the sin of the Golden Calf.[*] Giving a 'half' suggests that the 'physical' coin, the 'tool', is merely half of the story — the physical object, the coin that we can grasp, needs to be consciously associated with the Mitzvah, with the spiritual world that it represents. If not, the half Shekel coin represents only the Ten Utterances of Creation, without the Ten Commandments of Revelation. It is only 10 without being part of the 20.[**]

[*] The words *Nefesh* and *Shekel* both have a value of 430, illustrating the fact that the half Shekel is an atonement for our *Nefesh* / soul. And a 'half Shekel', i.e., half of 430 is 215, which is the same value as *Ruach* / spirit, our emotions (with 1 for the *Kollel* / the word itself), as the Koznitzer Maggid teaches (*Avodas Yisrael*). Thus, in the giving of a half Shekel, we are making a Tikkun on our *Ruach* / spiritual level of soul, emotional level, as well as our *Nefesh* / physical level of soul.

[**] The Half Shekel is an atonement for the Golden Calf, as Rashi writes: *Kofer Nafsho* / "an atonement for his soul." The *Yerushalmi, Shekalim,* 2:3 unfolds this idea: רבי יודה ורבי נחמיה. חד אמר, מפני שחטאו במחצית היום יתנו מחצית השקל. וחרנה אמר, לפי שחטאו בשש שעות יתנו מחצית השקל דעבד שיתא גרמסין. רבי יהושע בירבי נחמיה בשם רבן יוחנן בן זכיי. לפי שעיברו על עשרת הדיברות יהא נותן כל-אחד ואחד עשרה גרה / "Rebbe Yehudah and Rebbe Nechemiah (were expounding on the meaning of the Halachah). One said, 'Because they sinned in the middle of the day (between the first half and the second half), they shall give

half a Shekel.' The other said, 'Because they sinned in the sixth hour, they shall give half a Shekel, which is worth six grams.' Rebbe Yehoshua the son of Rebbe Nechemiah, in the name of Rebbe Yochanan ben Zakkai said, 'Because they transgressed the Ten Commandments, each of them shall give 10 Gerah.'" The Half Shekel was a Tikkun for the Golden Calf, because the Calf (also a young / 'half' bull) was only a 'half' of reality, just the Ten Utterances of physical Creation, without the 10 Commands of Divine Revelation; the world without Transcendence.

Avodah Zarah / 'idolatry' (and even *Shituf* / 'ascribing Divinity to an intermediary in "combination" with Hashem's Divinity', as we will shortly explore), is mistaking a part for the Whole. In fact, everything is merely a 'part' or aspect of reality, while the Wholeness of reality is Hashem — transcendent and yet immanent within Creation, in other words, inseparable.

The Medrash (*Tanchuma*, Ki Sisa. *Yerushalmi*, Shekalim, 2, *ibid.*) teaches that we need to offer a half Shekel of 10 Gerah because we violated the Ten Dibros (committing idolatry is equal to violating all the commandments of the Torah, and all the commandments are encoded in the Ten Dibros): 10 Gerah to atone for the Ten Dibros. But if so, then why does the Torah need to say, 20 Gerah is a full Shekel?

It must be that while we need to rectify the Ten Dibros, these Ten are also connected to the number 20, and the half Shekel, too, is connected to the twenty. How so?

The Arizal (*Mavo She'arim*, p. 305) explains that the word *Shekel* is related to the word *Mishkal* / weight, as the Torah itself says, "the Shekel's 'weight' is 20 Gerah." To verify something's weight, a scale is needed. A scale has two pans with a rod in the middle to balance them. The two pans are related to the two Heis (ה) in Hashem's name. The rod itself, the line in the middle is the letter Vav (ו), and the Shekel coin is the Yud (י). The above is based on the Zohar in *Raya Mehemna*. The Zohar also teaches (2, 187b) that the inner meaning of giving a half Shekel is related to the two Hei letters, and the letter Vav balances these two Hei letters. The weight of the Shekel coin, held in one Hei (representing one *Caf* / 'hand', or one 'giving'), is 20 Gerah. How can this full Shekel coin represent the Yud, which is only 10? Although Yud is 10, when the word *Yud* is 'filled' it is 20 (Yud/10, Vav/6, Dalet/4=20). In this sense, when we give just half a Shekel (Yud, 10 Gerah), we are mystically giving a 'filled' or whole entity (as if it has a 'weight' or value of 20 Gerah). By giving a Yud (10), we have reconstituted the 'fullness' of reality (reuniting the Ten Ma'amaros of physical Creation with the Ten Dibros of spiritual Revelation).

The letter Yud (10) is both Chochmah (the tenth and highest Sefirah above the other nine Sefiros, from the perspective of the physical world below), and it is also, in its fullest expression 20, Keser (which is the tenth and highest Sefirah from the 'perspective' of the Above). Keser unites the upper and lower perspectives from Above.

The word עשרים / *Esrim* / twenty is numerically 620, which is also the value of the word כתר / *Keser*. As mentioned, Yud is 10, and its fullness is 20, which is Keser. Ten is the world of Creation; the physical universe is 10, created from the Ten Ma'amaros. Yet, the Ten Ma'amaros is a reflection of the Ten Dibros. The Sefirah of Keser (20) is the power that can unite the 'Ten' of the physical world and the 'Ten' of the spiritual world. The Ten of this world is really a *Kli* / vessel for the Ten of Divinity.

Matan Torah was the revealing of אנכי / *Anochi* / the essential Divine "I". The word *Anochi* stands for כ[תר]-אני / *Keser-Ani* (Anochi is spelled as *Ani* with a letter Chof inserted in the middle — Chof symbolizing Keser.) Creation and the Transcendent Light of Hashem were revealed as united at Mount Sinai. This unity is symbolized by 20, as it is a unification of the Ten of Creation and the Ten of the transcendent Dibros. The Torah gives us the ability to recognize the Oneness of Hashem reflected in the Ten Dibros as they are rooted in the Ten Utterances.

If we speak of a 'half' of something, it is understood as the half of a whole — we are silently speaking of the 'whole' as well. So, although we only give half (10), the whole point of the giving is to remember that there is a full Shekel, Keser (20).

The word עשרים / *Esrim* / twenty has the same letters that spell רשעים / *Reshaim* / sinners, and שערים / *She'arim* / gates. Through the giving of the Shekel we create a שער/ *Sha'ar* / 'gate' of entry and a Tikkun even for those who are, at this point, in a low state, such as a רשע / *Rasha* / 'sinner' or an *Oved Avodah Zarah* / idolator, who sees only a half of the image of reality.

This is why we need to 'give' a *Metziyus* / existence of a half Shekel, the 10 of this world. In this act, we recognize that this world, the Ten Utterances of Creation, is not complete without the spirituality of the Ten Dibros of

Just as the half Shekel is but the physical representative of a deeper spiritual reality, every created thing that we use to accomplish our purpose in life is only half of the story. Our purpose is the Divine 'command' of our life. A life lived without purpose, meaning, intention, and direction would be merely 'half' a story. Only by marrying our life story to our inner purpose can we be complete and true to ourselves.

On an interpersonal level, this is also the case; to live fully, we need to secure a healthy awareness that we are only 'half' without our loved ones. To live deeply, we need to create *Yichud* / unity with our family, all of Klal Yisrael, and the world at large — and we need to actively help others by revealing the Divine soul, the spark of Moshiach, and the truth of Yichud, within all of us.

Revelation. Involvement with physicality without a predominant spiritual focus is engaging only half of the image of reality, and it becomes 'Avodah Zarah'. When we complete the 'fullness' of the image, humanity is healed and this lower world can be a dwelling place for the Divine Presence, as a vast 'Mishkan'.

KI SISA

Energy of the Week:

Getting Beyond the Image

This week's Torah reading imbues us with the power and mindset to see past the 'tools' and intermediaries we use and fix our intention onto our ideal, goal, or life mission. We might sometimes get distracted by the trappings and forget the bigger picture and ultimate purpose of our pursuits.

This week's contemplation provides the strength to reconnect with our original intentions. It gives us the Ko'ach to take a personal inventory and return to the real intent behind our projects. It gives us the ability to look beyond the immediate 'imagery' and reclaim our connection with the Imageless One, the Absolutely Whole One.

When our work in this world 'below' is unified with its aspect in *Avodas Hashem* / Service of Hashem, we become open to receiving the Infinite blessings from Above, as HaKadosh Baruch Hu is Unity, and Unity rests upon unity.

PRACTICE OF THE WEEK:

Reconnect With Your True Ideals

Vayakhel

Our Being Is Reflected in Our Doing

MOSHE GATHERS TOGETHER THE ENTIRE COM-
MUNITY and instructs them regarding the build-
ing of the Mishkan, the temporary and moveable
Temple in the Desert:

ויקהל משה את־כל־עדת בני ישראל ויאמר אלהם אלה הדברים אשר־צוה ה'
לעשת אתם / "Moshe called עדת בני ישראל / the whole community
of the children of Israel to assemble and said, these are the
things that Hashem commanded to make... on the seventh
day (Shabbos) you shall have sanctity (rest from work)."

Moshe then lists the offerings that could be donated to build
the Mishkan: "Every generous hearted person shall bring...
gold, silver, and copper" (35:1–5).

Moshe had already received the detailed instructions for building the Mishkan, even before the sin of the Golden Calf occurred, as the Zohar understands the events. Now, following the episode of the Golden Calf and procuring atonement for the people, Moshe assembles the entire community and relays to them the construction plans.

Before he begins, however, he first tells all the assembled about the day of Shabbos: "On the seventh day (Shabbos), you shall have sanctity, a day of complete rest." Then, after this, he says, "Every generous-hearted person shall bring...gold, silver, and copper." 'Shabbos' comes before the 'building the Mishkan' — and in this way, the Mishkan needed to be constructed from within a paradigm of Shabbos.

Shabbos After Work or Shabbos Before Work

Shabbos can be a place *to go to*, after a long, hard work week; it can be a day to rest from work. And it can also be a place *to come from*, a perspective of restfulness and inner peace that allows you to work with strength and focus during the coming week.

In the Creation story, first come the Six Days of 'creative' work, and they conclude with the seventh day, a Shabbos of rest. Yet, from the perspective of Adam and Chavah / Eve, who were created on Friday on the cusp of Shabbos, their reality *begins* with Shabbos and the work week comes afterward. For them, the six days of the week flow from Shabbos.*

We can experience Shabbos as the culmination of the work week, where we go to, or as the source and foundation of the coming work week, where we come from. At the beginning of this week's Torah reading, Moshe is imparting a deep truth to the assembled people: in order to go out into the world and work and create properly, we must come from a place of Shabbos.

Shabbos Is Our State of 'Being' Versus Our State of 'Doing'

Shabbos is an oasis in time where we can rest into simply 'existing'. Shabbos is a time to reveal our innermost self, unrelated to our work, titles, functions, or job descriptions. It is a time in which we can more easily identify ourselves with who we are, rather than our external expressions or labels based on what we do. It is a day of 'who' rather than 'what'.

---

* *Shabbos*, 69b. אמר רב הונא: היה מהלך בדרך או במדבר ואינו יודע אימתי שבת, מונה ששה ימים ומשמר יום אחד. חייא בר רב אומר: משמר יום אחד, ומונה ששה. במאי קמיפלגי — מר סבר כברייתו של עולם, ומר סבר כאדם הראשון / "Rav Huna said: 'One who was walking along the way or in the desert, and he does not know when Shabbos occurs, he counts six days from the day that he realized that he lost track of the days, and then observes one day as Shabbos.' Chiya bar Rav says: 'He first observes one day as Shabbos and then he counts six weekdays.' With regard to what do they disagree? One Sage held: 'It is like the creation of the world, weekdays followed by Shabbos.' And one Sage held: 'It is like Adam, the first man, who was created on the sixth day. He observed Shabbos followed by the six days of the week.'"

'Building the Mishkan' represents the work that each of us does throughout the week. In fact, the forms of 'work' that we are not allowed to do on Shabbos are the 39 types of work that were done to construct and prepare the Mishkan.* By extension, our work during the six days is, in a sense, rooted in the work of constructing the Mishkan.

The creation of the Mishkan required human participation — and the input of every capable man and woman of Klal Yisrael. It took the unique gifts and creativity of each person.

In the world of doing, we are all different from each other. One person can do a certain job better than someone else; one person can draw better, and one person can sculpt better. For this reason, while expressing our individual creativity and prowess, we run the risk of arrogance, perhaps coming to the conclusion that 'my work is more important than yours', or even 'I am more important than you.'

Thus, before Moshe relays to them the instructions for building the Mishkan, he "gathers together the entire com-

---

* *Shabbos*, 49b. And perhaps the 39 Melachos of Shabbos are rooted in the 39 forms of service that were performed *in* the Mishkan: *Medrash HaGadol*. See *Torah Sheleimah*, 23, Pekudei, pp.118–119. According to the *Yerushalmi*, this includes all the Melachos performed when offering an actual Korban: *Shabbos*, 10:3 And from the opening words of this week's Torah reading, אלה הדברים / "These are *the things...*," our sages find an allusion to the 39 Melachos / creative actions that are prohibited on Shabbos. אלה / "these" is numerically 36, and it is plural, thus another 2. *Ha* / 'the' is another 1, thus 39: *Shabbos*, 70a.

munity" and "assembles" them. 'Gathering them together' is symbolic, not just collecting everyone together in one area so he can speak to them. Rather, Moshe is teaching them about unity within a group, about how when they are gathered together, they are "assembled" in a unity.

Gathered With Da'as

Moshe gathers them as an עדת / *Adas* / 'community', a term which is related to the word דעת / *Da'as* / awareness. He gathers them and shows them how to be aware. Moshe is the *Bechinah* / paradigm and embodiment of Da'as (*Pri Eitz Chayim*, Sha'ar Chag haMatzos, 1), the one who brings Torah, Divine wisdom and higher awareness to Klal Yisrael.

Earlier, when Klal Yisrael "gathered" around Aharon and asked him to fashion for them an idol, the Torah says, ויקהל העם על־אהרן / "The *Am* / nation gathered to Aharon" (*Shemos*, 32:1). Here the Pasuk says ויקהל משה את־כל־עדת בני ישראל / "Moshe gathered the entire *Adas* of the children of Israel...." Whereas before, they gathered as one 'nation' to create an idol, here Moshe is creating a Tikkun for that negative gathering and gathering them together as a 'community' to create the Mishkan (*Likutei Torah*, Arizal, Vaykahel).

They gathered to Aharon as one 'mass', in a 'mass hysteria', and now Moshe (who is Da'as) gathers them with Da'as, with conscious awareness, calmly showing them the purpose and intention of why they are gathered.

Around Aharon, they gathered in a tumult and hurriedly threw their individual 'contributions' of gold into the fire. Now they are gathering mindfully as one, and when they go and bring their individual creative contributions to the Mishkan, their foundation will be 'Shabbos'; the source of their actions will be their 'being'. Moshe rectified their previous behavior by showing them to root their 'doing' in a state of 'being'.

Doing / Individuality vs. Non-Doing / Equality

In the process of creating and producing, we are all different. Everyone has something unique to contribute, and one person may 'do' better than another. Yet, everyone is equal in 'being'. In a 'non-doing' state of rest, we recognize that at our essence we are different yet equal.

Tzimtzum to Reveal Finitude,
Our Tzimtzum to Reveal Infinity

Hashem is *Ein Sof* / Infinite. In order to make the 'space' to create a world, the Ein Sof went through a *Tzimtzum* / metaphorical 'self-contraction and withdrawal' from that space. Infinity concealed itself, withheld its manifest Light to give room for finitude to appear.

'Doing' for the Creator is an expression of infinity, while 'not-doing', as in a 'Tzimtzum of doing', allows the Creator to express finitude. We, who are created in the Divine 'mirror-image', have the exact opposite experience. For us, doing is an expression of our finite self, our measured contributions to the world. Yet, when we practice Tzimtzum, not-doing, withholding, resting, or Shabbos, we reveal our infinite essence and our equality with all human beings.

This then, is the Da'as that Moshe imparts. He tells them, 'You are about to build a Mishkan. Each person will contribute their individual creative talent, yet the foundation of your 'doing', your construction of the *Mishkan* — a place where the Infinite Creator can 'rest' in this world — must be founded on the principle of non-doing. You need to source your contributions in Shabbos, the equalizing state of infinite 'being'.

We, too, must act and create out of a rootedness in our infinite being, for 'what' we do in the world needs to be founded on 'who' we essentially are.

VAYAKHEL

Energy of the Week:

Creativity Rooted in Being

This week's Torah reading imbues us with the power of 'beingness', staying in touch with our essence, our stillness, our inwardness, who we deeply are — even while we project, create and express our individuality in a multitude of ways. We can take the energy of Shabbos, of our essential state of 'being', and draw it into our life's work.

By hearing Moshe's public lesson, we are empowered to recognize ourselves as part of a collective of equals, each having our own unique abilities and life path. Therefore, we can contribute to Creation while remaining rooted and humble.

After this Shabbos, as we move into the 'doing' and the creativity of the coming week, we can take the stillness and beingness of Shabbos with us. We can then imbue all our accomplishments with the flavor of our true self, and source our doing in our deepest level of 'being'.

PRACTICE OF THE WEEK:
Doing From a Place of Being

Pekudei
Every Individual Counts

"These are the Pekudei / numbers of the Mishkan, the Mishkan of the Testimony, which were counted at Moshe's command" *(38:21).*

Thus begins this final portion in the Book of Shemos and its narration of the Exodus. The second half of the Book of Shemos speaks of the Mishkan, beginning with the instruction to Moshe to build it. After describing its construction and completion, the Torah gives a detailed accounting of all the individual contributions and the various materials that were given toward the construction.

Following this accounting, the Pasuk says, "A cloud covered the Tent of Meeting, and the glory of Hashem filled the Mishkan" (40:34). Apparently, the Presence of Hashem could not fill the Mishkan before this detailed review of each individual contribution that went into its creation.

Upon its completion, the Mishkan shone as a composite of Klal Yisrael's creativity and generosity. The building project united the 12 *Shevatim* / Tribes of Israel as they came together with a common goal, solidifying them as a nation. Yet, the emphasis in this portion is on the *individual* within the group and collective.

Since the gifts and talents of each individual contributor were acknowledged before the Divine Presence could rest in the Mishkan, the message was clear. Klal Yisrael was not to be viewed as a homogenous mass of humanity, a nation where the individual disappears into the collective.

"They shall make Me a *Mishkan* / sanctuary (singular) and I will dwell among them (plural)" (*Shemos*, 25:1:8). 'Plurality in singularity' is the vision statement of the Mishkan and what it could achieve. *V'Shachanti B'Socham* / "I will dwell among *them*" — the singular Mishkan would also serve to reveal Hashem's Presence to "them," dwelling or 'resting' upon each individual person in their own life and on their own level.

For the Oneness of Hashem to rest within this world of duality and multiplicity, we need a proper vessel: human unity.

When we are truly unified below, we can receive Unity from Above. Yet, unity is not 'sameness' nor the eclipse of unique selves — on the contrary.

Hashem is infinite Unity, and true infinity must include expressions of finitude; otherwise, it would be paradoxically finite. Likewise, true unity must include multiplicity; otherwise, it is exclusionary and paradoxically divisive. In the words of a *Rebbe* / teacher of the Ramban, "The Infinite One is perfect completeness with no detraction, and if you say Hashem only has power with the unrestricted, the Infinite, but does not have power with the restricted, the finite, you are detracting from his perfect completeness" (כשם שיש לו כח בבלתי בעל גבול כך יש לו כח בגבול, שאם תאמר יש לו כח בבלתי בעל גבול ואין לו כח בגבול הרי אתה מחסר שלימותו :Rebbe Azriel of Gerona, *Biur Eser Sefiros*. Quoted later by Rebbe Meir ben Gabbai, *Avodas HaKodesh*, 1, 8. *Derech Emunah*, Chap 2). The Unlimited One thus incorporates an unlimited range of possibilities, including even limitations.

In the same way, Hashem's Infinity "rests among us" and *in* us personally, and thus we too need to embody this paradox of 'unlimited and limited'. We too need to create a singular Mishkan in 'unlimited' unity with others, yet simultaneously ensure that our limited individuality is always present, in service to that Unity.

A large, beautiful puzzle, seen from a distance, may appear as a glorious whole, a seamless, undivided photograph. Upon closer examination, one will find that it is formed of thousands of distinct shapes, each containing its own boundaries, colors, and 'contribution' to the whole. While each one is different from the next, all are crucial to the complete picture. Were even one of these pieces to go missing, the puzzle would appear glaringly incomplete. Such is the individual within the collective. Each person needs to retain their uniqueness and relate harmoniously with the individuality of others, or the bigger picture will be impossible to construct. There will just be a pile of monochrome pieces.

To create a beautiful space worthy of Hashem's Infinite presence, there must be unity, and true unity can never come at the expense of individual expression. Sadly, many people may think that in order to fit in as a part of a community or collective, they need to give up their individuality and uniqueness. But here, the Torah is saying just the opposite. If you do not know who you are as distinct from others, what is your personal calling and contribution, then you cannot become part of the collective. Then, unfortunately, "I" cannot "dwell among them."

'I need you,' says Hashem, 'to make Me a Mishkan' composed of your personal qualities. I need you to embrace 'yourself', so that the multidimensional puzzle can be complete — and then My Glory can shine within each one of you, and all together as one.'

PEKUDEI

Energy of the Week:
Honoring Individuality

This week's Torah reading awakens the power in us to express our unique individuality within the greater Klal of Yisrael. We are called to contribute our G-d-given talents, strengths and abilities in our personal relationships, our spiritual community and our workplace.

Even as we are a part of a whole that is bigger than ourselves, we must remain true to our own self to actualize both our potential and the potential of the collective.

And honoring your individuality will allow you to honor the people within our sphere. It will ensure that the 'you' that Hashem fashioned in His Infinite Creativity is present in and contributing to the power of the whole.

PRACTICE OF THE WEEK:
Be Yourself in Harmony With Others

BOOK THREE:
Vayikra

Vayikra

Re-scripting the Future

S *efer Vayikra /* THE BOOK OF LEVITICUS BEGINS IN THIS
way: "And Hashem called to Moshe...saying, 'Speak to
the children of Israel, and say to them: When a man
from [among] you brings an offering...'" (1:1–2).

In general, the theme of the Book of Vayikra is living with
Kedushah / sacredness; sanctity in marriage, other relationships,
and in eating. It teaches us how to live as a nation of *Kohanim*
/ priests, by practicing 'holiness' or separation from eating
non-Kosher foods, marrying certain people and staying separate from others, and within one's marriage, separating from
intimacy at certain times. Yet, the most pronounced theme in
this Torah reading is that of the various *Korbanos /* offerings
that were brought during the times of the Beis HaMikdash.

Many of the offerings that were brought were offered to atone for past negative actions, whether intentional or unintentional, to bring a person to a state of greater purity, or to allow him to untangle himself from a web of negativity and begin life anew, in the present.

There is a tradition that when a *Katan* / small child is ready intellectually and emotionally to begin learning and living intentionally and responsibly, we should begin by teaching them this third book of the Torah, the Book of Vayikra (*Shach*, Yoreh De'ah, 245:8). An allusion to this idea is found in the fact that the Aleph (*Aleph* also means 'teach') in the first word of this book, *Vayikra* / ויקרא, is smaller than the other letters. *Aleph Katan* / 'small Aleph' also means 'Teach a small child' (Rabbeinu Yoel, *Sefer HaRemazim*, Vayikra). This is also based on a Medrash that says, "Let the pure (child) come and study (the laws of) purity" (*Vayikra Rabbah* 7:3). This practice emphasizes that the idea of offerings is a type of 'reset button' allowing any individual to begin again and be like a child who is just beginning to learn Torah, purity, responsibility, and intentionality.

In the times of the Beis HaMikdash, offerings were used to achieve atonement, and as such, they represent a state of purity and beginning again. How so? The Pasuk says, אדם כי־יקריב מכם / *Adam, Ki Yakriv Mikem*, which is commonly translated as "When a man from among you brings an offering..." A more literal translation would be, 'When a person offers *of himself...*' (*Likutei Torah*, Vayikra).

One who wished to create atonement would bring or sponsor an offering with the intention that they were *giving of their very own self.* When they gave of their own earnings, they took money that could have been used for their own physical benefit, such as for food or clothes, and instead purchased or brought an animal to offer to Hashem. By thus relinquishing their personal desires or 'ego' and transcending their instinct to self-preservation, they connected to a deeper reality, a heightened sense of purity.

Atonement Is Re-alignment

Every action creates a reaction. Positive actions have positive effects and harmonious or 'balanced' energetic qualities, while negative actions create negative effects and chaotic or 'imbalanced' energies. A negative action done in the past, based on the laws of cause and effect, will create a negative consequence in the present. To undo this consequence and wrest oneself free of the cycle of negativity, what is needed is a powerful shift, a rebalancing in the present, that *retroactively*, so-to-speak affects the quality of past action. This is a recontextualization of the past, and hence, it has a different effect within the present and the future.

During the times of the Beis HaMikdash, such a recontextualization was made by bringing an offering, while intending to offer oneself. This act restored the equilibrium and allowed a new beginning for the person. These offerings brought the giver a tangible sense of purity, of being unsoiled, refreshed, and empowered to change the trajectory of their life.

Time as Yesh, Time as Ayin

Creation is a *Yesh* / form that has arisen from *Ayin* / no-thing-ness, formless Presence. Creation is the world manifest form of time, space, and personhood, but it is rooted in pure, formless Divine Presence.

Within the rhythm of time, there are two paradigms. From a perspective of Yesh and form, time appears to flow in a lin-ear fashion, from a past to a present and future. On a personal level, our perception of time and relationship to time is based on the prism of our ego, our 'separate' Yesh. Therefore, what happened in a separate past moment indelibly imprints the separate present moment, and gives birth to a separate future time. Identified as a Yesh, we sense that 'cause and effect' have a real, solid Yesh quality.

Yet, time, as all created forms, is rooted in Ayin. From the perspective of Ayin, all time, space, and personhood is unified as one pure potential, empty of rigid form and some-thing-ness; time is always only now. Tapping into the Ayin of time gives us an ability to instantaneously refresh our lives. As we enter into the lightness, fluidity, and formlessness of total pres-ence, as into a *Mikvah* / ritual pool, we unburden ourselves of all past experiences.

How do we come into the 'Mikvah' of total presence, Ay-in-consciousness? By 'offering' our *Yesh* / ego. When we offer ourselves in selfless giving, we leave behind the world of ego and enter into the world of timeless freedom and newness. From this detachment from the concept of a 'separate past', we can begin again, as a child, a wide-eyed, innocent Katan beginning to learn *Vayikra*.

Through our *Tikkun* / repairing the fabric of our lives and starting over again, we find ourselves unjaded and excited like a *Tinok* / child. תיקון / *Tikkun* has the same letters that spell the word תינוק / *Tinok*, as well as ניתוק / *Nitok* / cutting away. In a state of childlike presence, we cut away our jaded past. We repair our sense of wonder and openness to the 'now', free to be recreated, in purity, in the world of form and time.

VAYKIRA

Energy of the Week:
Re-scripting the Future

In order to reverse the 'inevitable' effects of negative deeds in our past, we need to go inward to a place inside us that is beyond the paradigm of cause and effect.

In a world of strict natural order, there is no way to reverse the laws of cause and effect.

Going beyond our natural state of being, beyond our comfort zone, and sacrificing ourselves by placing our ego needs in the hands of the Creator, we can create a new reality for ourselves and rewrite the script of our future.

If you are an introvert, one way to 'bring an offering' is to say good morning to the people you meet on the street. Be present in the 'now' in front of them and listen to what they have to say or tell them something that may make them feel alive and hopeful.

If you are an extrovert, spend a little more time today praying, with deep presence in front of Hashem, and with inner intention and focus.

This Torah reading gives us the power to undo the negative consequences of our past actions. It gives us the strength to perform deeds in the present that reverse the effects of the past. Through 'self-sacrifice' in egoless acts, we can start over like a child, break our negative patterns, and re-enter life with pure, positive potential.

PRACTICE OF THE WEEK:
Push Your Assumed Limits

Tzav
Consistency & Perseverance

THIS WEEK'S TORAH READING CONTINUES ON THE theme of offerings, and begins with the word צו / *Tzav* / 'command': "And Hashem spoke to Moshe, saying, *Tzav Es Aharon* / command Aharon..." (6:1–2). Rather than more oft-used words in the Torah — *Daber* / 'speak' to the people of Israel, or *Emor* / 'say' to the people of Israel — the word *Tzav* is used, standing out as offering some unique insight.

When a person is merely 'told' something, they often forget overtime who told it to them. As the idea becomes absorbed and 'owned' by the hearer, the origin of the idea becomes lost.

However, when a person is acting on another's explicit 'command', the action that they are doing is continuously rooted in an awareness of the 'Commander'.

The word *Mitzvos* / מצות comes from the word *Tzav* / צו / 'command'. The word is also associated with the Aramaic word צוותא / *Tzavta* / 'together' or 'bind'. In this sense, a Mitzvah or Tzav binds the recipient with the speaker; the commanded one remains consistently connected with the Commander.

Parshas Tzav speaks of a continuous and lasting connection between the Eternal Being and temporal beings, between the Creator and humanity, between the world beyond time and the world of time.

While the *Beis HaMikdash* / Temple (and the Mishkan) stood, it was a common practice to bring an offering for a special occasion, such as an offering of gratitude. For example, a person who had been healed from sickness or saved from imminent danger gave a *Korban Todah* / thanksgiving offering. In need of atonement, one would bring an offering called a *Korban Chatas*. These were occasional offerings and offered on the initiation of the individual with a desire to draw closer. However, there were also routine offerings that were brought on a daily basis, "The first in the morning…the second in the evening". All of these offerings were placed on the same altar, using the same fire, the *Aish Tamid* / the Eternal Flame that continuously burned on the altar.

Both the offerings that were offered on special occasions, times when a person felt grateful for example, and offerings that were offered daily, were both consumed by the same Eternal Flame: "An eternal flame shall burn upon the altar, it shall not be extinguished" (6:6).

This verse seems repetitious, "An eternal flame…shall not be extinguished." Either one of these phrases would make it clear that the fire should remain lit constantly, why the redundancy? It is to make clear the message of consistency. It shall be eternal, and we also need to make sure that it is consistent and never extinguished. This comes on the heels of the opening of the Torah reading, the 'Tzav', which forces us to accept a constant awareness of our 'Commander', and to forge an eternal connection with Him by bringing these offerings.

The Eternal Flame represents a world beyond time, beyond memory and past, a world that is forever new and fresh, a world of constant renewal. This 'eternity' is felt in our excitement and passion when we experience something new. And the more unusual and extraordinary the experience, the greater our sense of eternality.

Today, when prayer takes the place of animal offerings, 'bringing an offering' is accomplished through praying for atonement or thanking Hashem for the kindness that has been shown to us. When we feel overwhelmingly grateful for having been released from bondage or saved from mortal danger, the Eternal Flame within is already aroused, and we are filled with great passion, excitement, and enthusiasm as we bring our offering.

To bring a special offering in a time of inspiration, when one is overwhelmed with remorse or gratitude, requires little effort. To bring a routine daily offering, day in and day out, with that sense of excitement and inspiration is where hard work comes in. Yet all offerings, both special and routine, needed to be offered upon that same Eternal Flame, that same enthusiasm.

The sages of old debated on what is the most important verse in the entire Torah; which verse expresses the very essence of the Torah? (*Toras Kohanim*, 4:12. *Nesivos Olam*, Nesiv Ahavas Re'a)

Several verses are suggested, which are easily understandable as to why they were chosen. For example, "Love your fellow man as yourself" (*Vayikra*, 19:18), said the great Rebbe Akiva. Indeed, loving and giving is a foundation of the entire Torah. Ben Azai posits the verse, "This is the book of the generations of Adam — on the day that Hashem created man, He made him in His Image" (*Bereishis*, 5:1). Indeed, the idea of mankind being created in the Divine image could easily be considered the most essential verse in the Torah, as the root of all ethics and spiritual responsibility is the awareness of the unique Divinity within all human beings (חביב אדם שנברא בצלם / "Beloved is man for he was created in the Divine image": *Avos*, 3:14. ובכל אדם. Tosefos Yom Tov, ad loc). Ben Zoma declared, "Hear O Israel, Hashem is our

G-d, Hashem is One." The awareness of absolute Monotheism is surely a foundation of the entire project of the Torah. But then one of the sages, Shimon Ben Pazi offered, "The first... you shall offer in the morning and the second...you shall offer in the evening" (referring to the daily offering: *Bamidbar*, 28:4). 'Rabbi so and so' stood up and declared that the ruling was in accordance with the opinion of Ben Pazi.

How can these words, "The first...you shall offer in the morning and the second...you shall offer in the evening," be the most essential passage in the entire Torah? It seems quite mundane in comparison to the powerful passages that speak of love, responsibility, and Monotheism. The answer lies in this verse's message of consistency. Consistency is the essential key to all attainments.

Yes, "Love your fellow man as yourself" is certainly a foundation of the Torah, and treating others, because they too are created in the Image of the Creator, is essential for human behavior, and clearly the oneness of Hashem is a fundamental of faith. However, consistency and perseverance is the essential key to putting each of those foundations into practice.

Consistency is everything. As mentioned earlier, "One who reviews his studies one hundred times is not comparable to one who reviews his studies one hundred and one times" (*Chagigah*, 9b). Working on any given project for 10,000 hours surely will make a person successful and an expert. Indeed, success is reached when we push forward even when we are not feeling inspired by it. And yet, through doing so with perseverance, we *imbue ourselves* with *Aish Tamid* / a perpetual flame, allowing us to find passion even within the routine. This is called *Isarusa d'leSata* / awakening from below, from consistent effort, as distinct from *Isarusa d'leEila* / awakening and inspiration that comes from Above, without human effort.

How do we awaken ourselves when we are not already feeling inspired? Of course, we need to receive the fire of the poets and prophets and rebbes, but we also need to adopt the order and structure of the Kohen's daily *Avodah* / service. Our work should never become automatic or regarded as a 'routine'; rather, we need to ignite ourselves with consistency and perseverance and actively see our work as new. We need to actively illuminate ourselves with the Eternal Flame, to repeatedly renew our freshness, awakeness, enthusiasm, and vigor, day to day and moment to moment. And we need to ensure, by all means necessary, not to let our light be extinguished.

TZAV

Energy of the Week:
Consistency & Perseverance

This week imbues us with the power of constancy and an ability to persevere — with passion and excitement. The key to lasting success in whatever our Avodah is, is keeping at it, continuously, through the easy times and the hard.

To do this we need to keep our inner flame burning bright. When we begin something, it is easy to find the passion and excitement to get started. Everyone is good at starting new projects. A week later, a month later, years later, is when we may need to reawaken our enthusiasm and keep up our momentum.

All of us have a purpose and various projects which need constant attention, passion, and perseverance to see them through.

This week, we receive an infusion of Ko'ach to actively keep our fire alive, to fan the flame, to add more fuel, and to continue marching toward success. Thus, we will come back to our projects again and again, day in and day out, with the brightness of entering them for the very first time.

PRACTICE OF THE WEEK:

Repetition Without Rote

Shemini
The Unity of Striving & Complacency

T HE TORAH READING OF THIS WEEK OPENS WITH the words, "And it was on the Eighth Day, that Moshe summoned Aharon / Aaron and his children..." (9:1). For seven days, Moshe was preparing and dedicating the *Mishkan* / Sanctuary in the Desert for its purpose, and on the Eighth day it was fully dedicated. Moshe then summoned Aharon and installed him as the *Kohen Gadol* / High Priest.

Every morning during the seven days of preparation, Moshe constructed the Mishkan, served in it as the Kohen Gadol throughout the day, and in the evening dismantled it. On the eighth morning, he constructed in such a way that it would remain standing, and summoned Aharon to begin serving as the Kohen Gadol.

In this way, the idea of 'seven days' symbolizes Moshe, and 'eight' symbolizes Aharon and his descendants throughout time. On the other hand, Moshe actually served as the Kohen Gadol up until a certain point at the beginning of the eighth day, and Aharon then continued. That is, until "Moshe summoned Aharon," Moshe was the only Kohen Gadol. In this way, the 'eighth day' embodies a quality of unity, a unification of Moshe (seven) and Aharon.

What do these ideas represent, Moshe, Aharon, seven and eight? There are essentially two opposite movements in life:

We are either moving outward or inward.

We are externalizing or internalizing.

We are either exhaling or inhaling life.

We are either desiring what is outside of us or drawing inward to what is already inside.

We are striving or we are satisfied.

We are yearning for the future or being present.

We either feel want or we feel full and sense completeness.

We can live from a place of passion, movement, growth, ambition, and desire — or from equanimity, stillness, and perfection. The former is the place of *Yesh* / existence, the fullness of life, and the other is the level of *Ayin* / no-thing-ness, the 'self-emptiness' of life.

Moshe / Ayin vs. Aharon / Yesh

Moshe embodies the level of *Ayin*, detachment from physicality. This is a place of self-emptiness and higher intellect (*Da'as*), in which reality is perceived as always perfect. In this state of equanimity, there is no desire, as desires come from a place of lack, a sense of something missing and desiring to be filled.* Desire and other emotions are based on perceiving one-

* Moshe comes from the water, representing the state of Ayin. The three letters in Moshe are Mem-Shin-Hei. Mem is spelled Mem-Mem (the additional letter when thus 'filled' is Mem). Shin is spelled Shin-Yud-Nun (the added filling letters here are Yud and Nun). Hei is spelled Hei-Aleph (the filling letter here is Aleph). All of these filling letters — Mem, Yud, Nun and Aleph — can be arranged to spell the word מאין / *Me'ayin*: Rebbe Menachem *Tziyoni*, v'Zos haBeracha. Also cited by the *Shaloh*, Shemos, 2.

Moshe is detached from the world of desire, hence he separates from his wife, and he cannot understand the need for 'meat' (and all that meat or 'flesh' represents). When the people complain to him that they want meat, Moshe responds, מאין לי בשר / *Me'ayin Li Basar* / "From where can I produce meat?" (*Bamidbar*, 11:13). These words can also mean, "I am Ayin, so how can meat (desire) come through me?"

It is for this reason that Moshe does not understand why Aharon makes distinctions between the various offerings, and also why he allows his personal mourning and grief (when his two children die) to interfere with the eating of the offerings.

Aharon, on the other hand, represents the realm of emotions, he thus kindles the Menorah with the seven branches, symbolic of the seven emotions. He is the counselor and healer who elevates and directs the emotions of Klal

self as a separate, limited 'self', a 'someone' who is lacking. However, Moshe transcends all sense of separation and limitation, and thus of all natural desire.

Aharon is a man of the people, a lover of humanity, and hence a paradigm of emotions. His life's purpose is serving in the Mishkan, a place where people who feel distant desire to become closer and offer a *Korban* / offering, from the word *Korev* / drawing closer. Aharon is the paradigm of *Aish* / fire that consumes the offering. This is a process of engaging and rectifying the Yesh, the 'self' in people.

Six / Seven / Eight
From a slightly different perspective, Aharon is connected to the six days of the week, which symbolize the place of Yesh and emotions,* and Moshe is connected to Shabbos, the seventh, the Ayin.

Yisrael: *Likutei Torah*, Behaalosecha. Indeed, the two sons of Aharon have 'too much passion' and thus expire in ecstasy and are consumed by the *Aish* / the fire that descended upon their incense offerings. Their Tikun and reincarnation are into Shimson / Samson, the passionate prophet and leader of Klal Yisrael, and into Pinchas, who is Eliyahu haNavi, both of whom were *Kana'im* / 'zealots' who used passionate emotion to fuel their interventions that saved Klal Yisrael.

* The six 'emotional' *Midos* or *Sefiros* are: *Chesed* / kindness, *Gevurah* / strength, *Tiferes* / beauty, *Hod* / humble gratitude, *Yesod* / intimacy, and *Malchus* / nobility.

For six days of the week, we work hard, we aspire, we want, we are identified with our outwardly projected selves, and we continually try to fill the nagging emptiness we feel. This is the paradigm of 'six'. It is the drive for movement, progress, and growth. There is a perceived *Cheser* / lack, which is the etymological root of the word *Chol* / weekday. The six weekdays are, in a sense, empty, like a tube, and we naturally wish to fill that sense of emptiness.

After the six days comes the Seventh Day. Moshe is the seventh Tzadik to significantly draw the *Shechinah* / revealed Divine Presence back into the world after Adam and Chavah ate from the 'Tree of Knowledge of Separation' (In this map, the seven are: Avraham, Yitzchak, Ya'akov, Levi, Kehos, Amram and Moshe). He is born, and also passes away, on the seventh of the month of Adar and on Shabbos (Tur, *Orach Chayim*, 292. See *Bach*, ad loc). Thus Moshe is symbolic of the day of Shabbos. Shabbos is the day of rest, and being still, of feeling yourself already *Shaleim* / complete and whole. Shabbos is *Shalom* / wholeness, completion, and basking in the light of the Shechinah.

When the seventh day of the week comes along, we ought to feel "as if all our work is done" (*Mechilta d'Rebbe Yishmael*, Yisro, 7. Rashi, Shemos, 20:9). There is nothing else to do, physically, financially, mentally, emotionally, and even spiritually (*Meor Einayim*, Miketz, Ki Sisa. *Sheim M'shemuel*, Bamidbar, Chasuna. See also: *Likkutei Torah*, Balak, p. 71). There is no longer any desire, as we have arrived. We are perfect. Everything is perfect, just the way it is.

In this dynamic, 'six' and 'seven' are polar opposites from each other. In 'six' we are creating, building, striving, lacking, and desiring. In the seventh, we cease to build and create, and we experience stillness, wholeness, rest, and completion.

This dual dynamic of 'six days' vs. 'the Seventh Day' can produce two extreme outcomes:

1) The dominant force in the week can be a 'six days' paradigm, in such a way that the Seventh Day of rest merely creates greater longing and desire to return to work and effort. This can feel like a tease; the restfulness of Shabbos lingers for a fleeting day, but then it disappears, creating an even greater yearning and longing to attain it. In this sense, the ceasing from work, from growth, from desire and want, produces an overall sense of the *absence* of Shabbos. The predominant feeling is like pulling back a bow to make the arrow fly higher, or crouching down in order to leap further.

2) The dominant force in the week can be Shabbos, suffusing even the six work days with wholeness, perfection, relaxation, and equanimity. In this paradigm, while a person works and is involved in progress, movement, and ambition, the Shabbos element is felt, decreasing the tension of ambition, desires, and the longing to progress. This can create a subtle sense of 'quietism' or even complacency; when we have a foreground sense of completion every day of the week, it is more difficult to summon up the tension of yearning and striving.

On the surface, the first outcome characterizes both Aharon and Moshe. Aharon's duty was to work constantly; he needed to bring Korbanos even on Shabbos. Moshe was engaged in constant work, constructing and deconstructing the Mishkan and serving in it, for seven days straight. Moshe did this because he wanted to awaken the quality of 'seven' within the work of building the Mishkan, as the Mishkan should be the embodiment of all our work that needs to be done in this world. Thus, even on Shabbos, when one may not light a fire, a fire was nonetheless commanded to be lit within the Mishkan, and later in the Beis haMikdash.

On a deeper level, during these seven days, while assembling and disassembling the Mishkan, Moshe was also serving as the Kohen Gadol with the Mishkan. Moshe embodies the quality of being one with the complete Presence of Hashem, even when there is no physical Mishkan (See also *Ye'aras Devash*, 1:13: this is the reason that the second Beis haMikdash began to be destroyed on Motzei Shabbos, right after Shabbos (*Ta'anis*, 29a, *Erchin*, 11b), or was destroyed on Shabbos itself. According to the *Yerushalmi* [*Ta'anis*, 4:5], it was destroyed on Rosh Chodesh, and we know that the 9th of Av that year was on Sunday). This is because Moshe is the embodiment of Ayin, the state of eternal Shabbos, in which the Mishkan is always present, even when physically (on the level of Yesh), it is not. He was in a state of rest and wholeness even while constantly laboring during those seven days. This alludes to a level above the polarity of six workdays and a Seventh Day of rest.

Eight

While Moshe is basically connected with 'seven' and Aharon is basically connected with 'six', they meet in a place beyond 'seven' and 'six'. The number eight represents the unity of Moshe and Aharon, and a unification of rest and work, completion and yearning, wholeness and progress, creation and ceasing from creating. The number 6 is enfolded within the number 7, and both are enfolded within 8. In this way, 'eight' is the light that permeates both the paradigms of seven and six.

There are two major mentions of 'eight' in the Torah. One is in reference to the eighth day of a baby boy's life, when he receives the *Bris* / circumcision. In the act of circumcision, a human being works to complete the boy's body; Hashem created the body 'lacking' one detail, and then asks us to participate in our own 'creation' — to do an act of 'six'. The other mention of 'eight' is in reference to the building of the Mishkan, where Hashem says, "Make for me a sanctuary, and I will dwell within them." Again, it refers to our efforts and participation.

Eight: Feeling Full & Restful Within Yearning

Many people walk through life feeling a devastating emptiness. They tirelessly seek to fill that emotional and spiritual 'hole' with various objects, such as money, power, fame, and even knowledge. The problem is that trying to fill an internal emptiness with external things ultimately leaves one feeling even more unsatisfied. The reason one feels emptier the more one attempts to fill oneself with objects is that through the fulfillment of a desire, one's vessel of desire expands. As the vessel expands, so does the emptiness of the vessel, the feeling of craving or yearning. This is accompanied by a growing existential frustration with the sense that one's appetite can never be quenched or pacified since bigger, more extreme, more stimulating or more expensive objects are always required to attain the fleeting sense of satisfaction that one seeks.

Only by tapping into and revealing the wholeness and rest that already always exists within us can striving, desiring, and attaining come from a healthy place. Only internally produced satisfaction comes without exacerbating anxiety, insatiable desires and addictions, depletion, grief, and emptiness.

Additionally, when we have established internal or unconditional satiation, we can be inwardly restful and whole even while part of us is yearning for more. This is the paradigm of 'eight', in which two apparently opposite emotions ('six' and 'seven') are unified as one.

SHEMINI

Energy of the Week:
Balancing Striving & Complacency

Within each of us, there are two seemingly opposing states: yearning and completeness. The empowerment we receive this week is the power to unify these
qualities.

Healthy desire does not come from a place of insatiability. If I am insatiable in my desires for more and
more, it demonstrates that I am not focusing on my
inner wholeness or on the wholeness and content-
ment that I have been given — even in the simplest
gifts of life. If my desire is free of insatiability, it is
coming from a place of wholeness and completeness.
I desire something because I 'want to' attain it, not
because I 'have to' attain it *in order to be* whole.

This week, we are given the ability to transcend the pettiness of our limited self and narrative, and simultaneously enjoy the fullness of this Divinely created, animated and infused world. We are gifted with the Ko'ach to attain a healthy balance of work and rest, of inhaling and exhaling, of desire and satisfaction, of yearning and presence, of wanting and completeness, in such a way that this balance persists throughout the entire year.

PRACTICE FOR THE WEEK:

**Yearn for a Better Life & World,
While Staying in Touch With
Your Inner Wholeness**

Tazria
Healthy Transitions

T HIS WEEK'S TORAH READING OPENS WITH THE laws of *Tumah* / ritual impurity and *Taharah* / ritual purity. It is important to keep in mind that these concepts are utterly unrelated to personal hygiene, disease, or value as a person. 'Impurity' does not connote an unworthiness. In fact, Tumah and Taharah usually relate to an inability or ability to perform certain acts, such as bringing an offering to the Beis HaMikdash.

All forms of Tumah are connected to some type of severance or ending — a literal or metaphorical form of death. The Torah's definition of Tumah is that which is connected with death and separation, both in a literal sense (coming into contact with a corpse) but also figuratively, such as certain skin pigmentations that demand separation from other people. Taharah is defined as anything that is associated with life, aliveness, and connectivity with others. Water, and particularly fresh "living" water, is the main medium that allows one to return to basic Taharah.

Tumah is related to the idea of סתום / *Sasum*, closed off, as in the word טימטום / *Timtum* / shut off (*Yuma*, 39a). The root letters of Tumah are Tes-Mem. These two letters in sequence suggest something that is hidden, as in טמון / *Tamun* / concealed, or טומטום / *Tumtum* / a person whose gender is anatomically concealed.

Tumah is thus an experience of concealment, a closing off, stopping, or a recent ending. In the terminology of the Zohar, "A foreign (negative) force is hidden and does not bear fruit" (2, 103a). In the state of Tumah, there is a sense of stoppage. In Tumah, we experience rigidity, stuckness, and a stunting of progress. There is a general closing off and shutting down of productivity and fruition.

By contrast, to be טהור / *Tahor* / literally 'pure' also means to be 'revealed' or 'open' (see *Yuma*, 59a: מאי טהרו אמר רבה בר רב שילא: פלוגיה דמזבח, כדאמרי אינשי טהר טיהרא והוי פלוגיה דיומא *Likutei Torah*, Yom Kippur, p. 69a). *Tahor* connotes clarity and transparency, as the Pasuk says, וכעצם השמים לטהר / "like the appearance of the Heavens in terms of *clarity*" (*Shemos*, 24:10).

Tahor is related to the word צוהר / *Tzohar* / brilliant, illuminated, as Noach is told that "A *Tzohar* / window you shall make for the Ark." This verse is interpreted as meaning that Noach should make a skylight, or affix a brilliant stone, to illuminate the Ark. In this way, *Tahor* also alludes to something like a window opening to the outside, suggesting transparency and illumination. Indeed, in the languaging of our Sages, Tahor is used specifically in reference to *light* and *day* (*Chulin*, 60b).

Purity Means Life / Movement / Hope. Impurity Means Death / Stagnation / Hopelessness:
Whereas Tumah means ending, Taharah means a connection to life and continuation. In addition to 'closed off', Tumah implies shut down, depressed, or despondent, and Taharah implies illumination, hope, and possibility.

Purity is fluidity and openness. Impurity is being cut off and stagnant. Life is fluid and moving. So long as there is life, there is hope and the possibility for improvement. Death is a sense of ending.

Inwardly, we experience a subtle form of 'death' when we are in a state of stagnation or immovability. As such, all forms of impurity are related to 'death'. Any form of cutting off from life is fundamentally 'impure'. That which is alive, expanding, growing, and teeming with possibility is 'pure'.

This week's Torah reading begins with the words, "And Hashem spoke... Speak to the children of Israel...If a woman conceives and gives birth...she shall be impure for seven days..." (12:1–2).

It can be argued that the mother becomes impure because the process of childbirth is, by its very nature, life-threatening.

Until relatively recently, the mortality rate in childbirth was quite high. In any case, as the mother bumps up against a symbolic or real possibility of death, she is energetically impacted and becomes ritually 'impure'.

From a deeper psychological perspective as well, it can be said that the birth itself is intimately related to death and separation, and hence Tumah. No new beginning comes without marking an end to something else. Every birth comes along with the 'death' or end of the previous stage of life. For the duration of a pregnancy, the mother may feel as one with the fetus. With the dramatic event of birth, this unified life ceases and the child is physically separated from the mother. As a result, she may have ambivalent feelings related to the experience of birth. This may, in fact, be part of the phenomenon of 'postpartum depression', which can be understood as a psycho-physical expression of 'Tumah'.

A man can be called 'a father' at the moment the mother conceives a child, whereas the mother might not be considered 'a mother' until she gives birth. In other words, from the perspective of the father, the moment there is a child in the womb, he has fathered a 'separate being' that is now residing within his wife's womb (Rebbe Yoseph Engel, Beis HaOtzer, Av. Maharal, Ohr Chadash). From the mother's perspective, the child within her is not yet a separate being. Prior to birth, the Torah considers an unborn a Yerech / 'limb' of the mother, as the child exists and lives only within the mother. (Baba Kamah, 47a. Tosefos, ad loc).

Whereas birth is the 'beginning of life' for the child, for the mother, it is an experience of 'death'. When the baby emerges as an individual being, the cord is cut and there is an intense sense of separation. Prior to this physical severance, the mother's food was the child's food, and the mother's wellbeing was the child's wellbeing; they were one on all levels. The mother's experience of total union with the child is abruptly ended, and because of this, she enters a state of Tumah.

Similarly, a woman waits 'seven clean days' following menstruation before immersing in the waters of a Mikvah. These days are established in response to the loss of a potential pregnancy and new life, which is a minor symbolic death, engendering a state of Tumah.

These seven days mirror the seven days of *Shivah* / mourning for a close relative. They allow her time to grieve for losing the feeling of a potential new child within her body. And like the laws of Shivah, by which the mourner is allowed to be quiet and not engage in conversation, during these seven days, the woman has a quiet time and does not engage in intimacy with her husband.

Once the seven days are complete, she then immerses herself in the purifying waters of a Mikvah and returns to her regular state of Taharah.

TAZRIA

Energy of the Week:
Mindfully Releasing the Past and Being Present With Endings

Every beginning comes with the ending of a past era. Even a joyous 'rebirth' ends a previous chapter, and can bring a sense of separation.

We experience cycles of birth and death continuously; one door closes and another one opens. We cannot move forward without marking the end of a completed phase of life (See *Zohar* 3, p. 88a). Attachment to a past place of residence, a past relationship or job, or era in one's life must be released and 'buried' in order for a new one to be birthed and to flourish.

While the birth of a new reality is to be celebrated, we still need to be mindful of the 'death' and separation that comes along with it.

We need to let any grief or abandoned hope flow through us with the cleansing waters of time. If we merely suppress grief, it eventually suppresses joy as well.

A healthy life transition includes consciously and respectfully marking the past, and feeling all of our feelings, before rushing forward joyfully into the new era or stage.

This week, we are given the Ko'ach to stop and acknowledge the meaning of endings. We are empowered to turn over a new leaf and let go of a limited state of being which needs to flow on by in the waters of life.

PRACTICE OF THE WEEK:

Mindfully Acknowledge Endings

Metzora
Letting Go of What Is Beyond Your Control

T HE TORAH READING THIS WEEK BEGINS WITH THE
words, "And Hashem spoke to Moshe…This shall be
the law of the person afflicted with Tzara'as, on the
day of his cleansing, he shall be brought to the *Kohen* / Priest"
(14:1–2).

Tzara'as is an ancient (and no longer existing) miraculous
spiritual affliction that manifested as a specific skin pigmen-
tation (אינו ממנהגו של עולם אלא אות ופלא היה בישראל / "It is not a natural occurrence, rather a sign and a wonder that once existed…" Rambam, *Hilchos
Tumas Tzara'as*, 16:10). An individual diagnosed with Tzara'as was
considered to be *Tamei* / impure.

As previously noted, in order to understand this teaching, it is essential to keep in mind that 'impurity' in the Torah has nothing to do with physical hygiene, the 'valuation' of a person, nor their social class or gender. Also, Tzara'as was not a form of leprosy, psoriasis, or any other physical condition. 'Impurity' and Tzara'as refer to spiritual conditions which had temporary implications in ritual law.

The skin of the *Metzora* / person afflicted with Tzara'as, turned white or colorless, indicating an absence of the redness of blood. The color red is a sign of life and vitality, and inwardly of passion and aliveness, of hope and power. In this way, Tzara'as symbolizes the absence of life: כי הדם הוא הנפש / "for blood is one's *Nefesh* / embodied level of soul." When skin loses its coloring, it is a symptom of an imbalance or deadness, connected with the ideas of apathy, hopelessness, depression, or powerlessness.

Being in a condition of 'impurity' means being connected with death in some way, whether actually or figuratively. Personal stagnancy, lack of movement, loss of hope, despondency, and certainly depression are all subtle forms of 'death' and 'impurity'. Conversely, purity is defined as being connected with life, growth, passion, and hope.

Purity Is Hope; Impurity Is Hopelessness
'Purity' is life, enthusiasm, and optimism;

'Impurity' is lifelessness, indifference, and pessimism.

'Purity' is *Tikvah* / Hope;

'Impurity' is *Yei'ush* / despair and giving up hope.

A highly pure person, a *Tzadik* / righteous, illumined person, is one who is living with unconditional hope. A *Rasha* / 'wicked' or deeply stuck person is one who is not living up to his or her mental, emotional, and spiritual potential because they actively reject hope. *Ra* / 'negativity' is essentially living without any hope.

These are the two extreme prototypes: those who are full of hope and optimism, and those who reject hope and optimism. But the truth is, most people fluctuate; one moment, a person could be on the level of a Rasha, and the next moment, on the level of a Tzadik. Someone whose baseline belief is that what has been done is done and nothing can or will ever change, lives with *Yei'ush* / despair, is in that moment a *Rasha* / 'conduit of negativity'. Regarding the Rasha, the Book of Tehilim says, "Distant from the Rasha is salvation" (*Tehilim*, 119:155). Such a person has actively distanced *himself* from salvation in that moment of pessimism. By contrast, someone who expresses hope, and lives with hope, is in that moment a Tzadik and a 'conduit of righteousness and blessing'. With reference to the Tzadik, the Prophet says, "My salvation is soon to come" (*Yeshayahu*, 56:1), as he has actively brought himself toward a condition of 'salvation' from negativity.

Again, 'Rasha' and 'Tzadik' are not permanent statuses. Even if we have fallen into negativity and are at that moment a 'Rasha', we can do *Teshuvah* / 'turn ourselves around' and become a 'Tzadik' in the next moment. As our Sages teach us, "Do not consider yourself a Rasha." Never despair, for 'Tzadik' is the identity of someone who gets up again after falling — and then again and again.

The Two Birds: One in Our Control, and One Not in Our Control

The Torah describes the purification process for the Metzorah: "Then the Kohen shall give the order, and the person to be cleansed shall take two live, clean birds...and he shall slaughter the one bird over *Mayim Chayim* / pure, non-stagnant, 'living waters'.... He shall then send away the other live bird into the open field" (14:4–7). These two birds illustrate the process of allowing an individual to move from a state of stagnancy to a place of purity and flow, or from a place of deadness and hopelessness to life, freedom, and hope.

Today, we do not, sadly, have a physical *Beis haMikdash* / Temple to perform this purification with two physical birds, yet, everything in Torah is eternal. When something cannot be performed through physical acts, they can still be performed inwardly or symbolically. As such, we need to activate this process within our own lives as we move into new realities, and shake ourselves free from our own inner impurities, especially the negativity of deadness, hopelessness, and despair.

The Mitzvah and ritual of the two birds references what brings us to a state of *Tumah* / impurity and *Yei'ush* / despair and despondency in the first place. It makes us realize that if we attempt to control everything in our life, and yet we find that there are things that are beyond our control, we are at risk of falling into a state of Yei'ush and Tumah. We need to understand deeply that there are some things in life we can control, and others will just fly free into the 'open field'.

Many people give up hope because first they try to control 'everything', and when that does not work out, they surrender 'everything' and then just live with total helplessness. But if we understand that some things can be controlled and other things are out of our hands, we gain one of the keys of life and can return to the 'purity' and 'righteousness' of faith, optimism, life, and hope.

The two birds are given different fates; one is offered and the other is sent free. The first bird we hold onto, we 'control' and offer it up. After it is ritually slaughtered, it needs to be buried in front of the person, as the Mishnah (*Negaim*, 14:1) says, "A hole was dug and it was buried in his presence." In the words of the Rambam (*Hilchos Tumas Tzara'as*, 11:1) וחופר וקובר הצפור השחוטה בפניו / "And we dig and bury the slaughtered bird in front of him."

In our lives, we need to mark the ending of our past state of 'impurity', and mindfully acknowledge that we have felt hopeless in our struggle to wield control over life. We need to remove the life force we have actively given to this Yei'ush, offer it up to Hashem, and bury our habit of grasping. This means we need to offer to Hashem even the things that we can control and hold in our hands, and acknowledge Hashem as the ultimate Controller of all events.

The other bird, representing those things that are definitely beyond our control, we must release and set free. These things have a life of their own and will always elude our grasp. Only when we release our attempts to grab them can we regain our hope.

By acknowledging the distinction between what we can control and what we cannot, we begin to emerge from stuckness and Yi'ush into purity, aliveness, and reengagement with life.

'Offering up' even our realistic sense of control instills in us the recognition that *HaKadosh Baruch Hu* / the Holy One is the ultimate Controller. It also gives us better control of what is truly in our domain; we gain mastery over our responses to what life throws at us, and this also gives us hope.

Letting go of that which we can never control and releasing these issues into the 'open field' not only brings relief from despondency, but it also allows us to resume confident control in the areas of life that HaKadosh Baruch Hu places in our hands.

METZORA

Energy of The Week:
Relinquishing Control

This week's *Ko'ach* / power and energy is that of purity, clarity, and the ability to regain hope and aliveness, by knowing what we can control and what we cannot. We are encouraged by the Torah's guidance to relinquish what we cannot hold, and to offer our habits of control up to Hashem. We are given an opportunity to vividly feel the freedom and purity that results from letting go.

PRACTICE OF THE WEEK:

**Let Go of Trying to Control What You
Cannot Control & Acknowledge
the One True Controller**

Acharei Mos
Between Love & Reverence

THE TORAH READING THIS WEEK BEGINS WITH THE words, "Hashem spoke to Moshe after the **death** of (his brother's) Aharon's two sons, when they drew near before Hashem, and they **died**. Speak to your brother Aharon, that he should not come at all times into the Holy.... בזאת / 'With this' shall Aharon enter the Holy" (*Vayikra*, 16:1–3).

בזאת / "with this" means that only with this precise procedure, that has been detailed, can Aharon enter into the Holy area, the innermost space within the *Mishkan* / Sanctuary. There is a meticulous regimen of ritual practices to be followed to the letter of the law for Aharon to enter.

After the death of Aharon's two sons, who died "when they drew near before Hashem," i.e., they died of spiritual ecstasy (as the Ohr HaChayim writes), Aharon is instructed in a detailed procedure of entering into the holiest of places. These details are antidotes to the ecstatic behavior of his sons that led to their death.

The Zohar points out that the passage says, "After the **death**...and they **died**" and asks why it mentions twice that they died. This teaches us, says the Zohar, that they 'died' first internally or spiritually, as they had transcended their physical reality. Then, "after" this death, they died externally and physically. As they expired 'twice', there is no redundancy in the text.

The Two Themes of the Torah Reading

This detailed description of the בזאת is the first theme of this week's reading; how Aharon could enter the Holy of Holies, which was done on Yom Kippur. In fact, this elaboration of בזאת is what we read in the public Torah reading every Yom Kippur morning.

The second major theme of this week's reading is the laws of *Arayos* / forbidden physical relations. This is the Torah reading for the *Mincha* / afternoon service on Yom Kippur.

Our sages tell us that ביוה"כ קורין אחרי מות ובמנחה קורין בעריות / on Yom Kippur we read the portion of Acharei Mos and at Mincha we read the portion of the Arayos (*Megilah*, 31a). Rashi comments: שמי שיש עבירות בידו יפרוש מהן לפי שהעריות עבירה מצויה

שנפשו של אדם מחמדתן ויצרו תוקפו / "...Because all who have become guilty should separate themselves from these transgressions. Such violations are widespread since people are continually attracted to these (acts), and their negative inclination
overcomes them" (See also *Tosefos HaRosh*, ad loc).

Yet, from the fact that these two themes are linked together
in the Torah within the same portion and fascinatingly both
read on Yom Kippur, it must be that these two themes are in-
terlinked. Somehow, the "death of the two sons of Aharon" is
linked with the idea of Arayos.

The laws of Arayos are actually repeated a few times in the
Torah, but most prominently in this week's and next week's
Torah reading. In this week's reading, the first thing the Torah
tells us is, איש איש אל-כל-שאר בשרו לא תקרבו לגלות ערוה / "None of
you shall come near anyone of his own flesh to uncover nakedness" (18:6). After this, it continues to describe, over the
course of the next 17 verses, all of the prohibited relationships,
G-d forbid, beginning with incest and continuing through
cross-breeding with animals.

In contrast, next week's portion of Arayos begins with ואיש
אשר ינאף את-אשת איש / "If a man commits adultery with a married woman" (20:12).

Notice that this week's portion begins with the people who
are most physically close to the person, "your own flesh," and
then progresses to more distant people, as in adultery, and fi-

nally to interspecies abominations. In next week's reading, the Torah begins with adultery, prohibited relations with a woman to whom one is not related, and specifically a married woman.

Reasons for the Prohibitions

Regarding the various forms of forbidden familiar relationships — which are universally taboo and seen as disgusting (so that any healthy person would naturally spurn them) — many reasons are offered for these prohibitions. One reason is simply that each of them is a Divine *Chok* / decree (,והנה העריות מכלל החוקים דברים שהם גזירת מלך, והגזירה הוא הדבר העולה על דעת המלך שהוא החכם :Ramban, *Vayikra*, 18:6), and the effect of this Divine decree in the world is the instinctual, absolute, and ubiquitous rejection of these acts by all civilized societies.

Other sources offer that since relatives are in constant contact and proximity to each other, allowing such relationships would only increase a male's craving for more, as "A man has a small body part that when it is starved, it is satisfied, and when it is fed, it is hungry" (*Sukkah*, 52b), and the Torah wants a man to curb his animalistic cravings (Rambam, *Moreh Nevuchim*, 3, 49. *Sefer HaChinuch*, Mitzvah 190. *Even Ezra*, Vayikra, 18:6).

Another reason offered is that when someone's genes intermingle with different genes, healthy and spiritually-aligned children will be born. Also, if people would marry family members, the families of Tzadikim would remain Tzadikim, and families with negative traits would remain that way or become even worse. To blend different families creates greater possibilities for the entire nation and world.

In the words of one of a 'student' of the Ramban, עַל יְדֵי עֵירוּב מִשְׁפָּחוֹת יִתְעָרְבוּ הַכֹּחוֹת וְיִתְעוֹרְרוּ צִנּוֹרוֹת הַגְּאוּלָה / "By means of inter-mingling families, their powers are intermingled, and thus so are the channels of Redemption" (Rebbe Menachem Tziyoni, ad loc).

The Simple Meaning and Reading of the Torah

Another very simple reason can be offered, and if we closely read the words of the Torah, the words themselves reveal this reason: לֹא תְגַלֶּה עֶרְוָתָן כִּי עֶרְוָתְךָ הֵנָּה / "Do not uncover their na-kedness, because their nakedness is yours." At first glance, this verse seems to use circular logic: 'Do not uncover their naked-ness, because they are nakedness to you.' Yet, on a deeper level of the literal meaning, the word כִּי / "because" suggests that this is *the* reason. In other words, the reason we are forbidden to have relationships with our close relatives is "because their nakedness is *yours*" — they are 'naked' to you, meaning 'they are too exposed, revealed, and familiar to you.'

What does this mean? The Torah is conveying a powerful message by enfolding the laws of Arayos, beginning with one's own family, within the context of this portion, which also de-scribes the service of Yom Kippur.

Yom Kippur is a day of utmost intimacy between humans and their Creator. It is the day in which the *Kohen Gadol* / High Priest enters, alone, privately, and quietly, into the inner chamber, the Holy of Holies, what is called "the Chamber of the Bedroom," and encounters the Beloved Creator in deepest intimacy.

Intimacy and expressions of love create familiarity, and sadly, this sometimes comes at the expense of mystery, reverence, respect, and boundaries. Sometimes, the need for love and expressions of love make people possessive, obsessive, or overwhelmed, with no sense of healthy separateness. Love can even devolve into utter selfishness, no longer about the other at all.

The sons of Aharon were madly in love with HaKadosh Baruch Hu. They wanted intimate oneness; they wanted to 'possess' Hashem, as it were. Thus, they became consumed by their spiritual cravings and died in ecstasy.

Healthy love requires healthy *Yirah* / trepidation, awe, respect, discipline, boundaries, and order. Love and awe are the two wings that allow us to fly, says the Zohar. A one-winged bird cannot take flight. Losing a wing in mid-flight causes it to turn circles and then crash to earth.

Marriage is called *Kidushin*, which is the idea of *Kedushah* / 'sacredness', implying being set apart due to awe and respect. In the wedding ceremony, when the groom declares מקודשת לי / *M'kudeshes Li* / "You are 'sacred' to me, it also means מיוחדת לי / *Meyuchedes Li* / 'You are unique to me' (Tosefos, *Kidushin*, 2b). מקודשת / *M'kudeshes* also implies דאסר לה אכולי עלמא כהקדש / *Asar Lah al Kulei Alma k'Hekdesh* / "renders her forbidden to everyone else like something that is consecrated (to the Temple)"

(*Kidushin*, 2b. Or, 7b: וניפשטו לה קידושי בכולה). On a deeper level, this means not only that the couple is excluding any other marriage partners but that there is also a measure of *Hekdesh*, 'forbidden sacredness' of the other partner, even within the marriage itself. There is a sacred space that remains off limits to the other, even in a loving marriage, and each partner needs to honor those limits.

When two people choose to share a life together in unity, there still must always remain a sense of mystery, apartness, and honoring the spouse's space and boundaries. This is true interpersonally as well as between humans and their Creator.

And this requirement for awe, respect, and boundaries is precisely the reason the Torah teaches us about these laws of Arayos within the context of Yom Kippur service and the death of the sons of Aharon. And that is another reason that we read this portion on the afternoon of Yom Kippur.

בזאת / "With this" precise and detailed procedure of show-ing awe and honor, Aharon was permitted to enter into the Holy of Holies. This teaches us that there is a very specific way we, and our representative, the Kohen Gadol, can enter the space of ultimate intimacy on Yom Kippur. This way is un-like that of the sons of Aharon, who were consumed in their rapturous love without awe, their poetry without law, their re-leasing of all boundaries — these were a subtle level of Arayos. The delineated laws of how a Kohen is to serve on Yom Kippur demonstrate the 'spiritual insurance' we need to have in order to ensure balanced intimacy.

Love must be coupled with trepidation and familiarity mitigated by mystery.

We need to interact with our spouse with a respect for their other-ness; not to become too familiar in the sense of 'casual'. This is another reason why "None of you shall come near anyone of his own flesh (his family) to uncover nakedness." Besides its repugnancy and the emotionally traumatic and genetically unhealthy act of relating that way with a family member, it is basically *impossible* to create authentic intimacy with one who is so familiar.

Intimacy paradoxically demands unfamiliarity, distance, and otherness. It requires a certain tension and distance, and the overcoming of this distance, all the while forever remaining 'other', hidden and mysterious to each other.

This is how the two themes of this week's Torah reading are linked. They both speak about intimacy, whether with Hashem or with other people, and how we need to make sure that the wing of love does not overpower the wing of awe. They both teach how to establish closeness founded on both love and awe, closeness and respect for space, passion and equanimity, poetry and prose, ease and trepidation, oneness and otherness, revelation and mystery — and all of these simultaneously.

ACHAREI MOS

Energy of the Week:
Love & Giving With Boundaries

This week imbues us with the Ko'ach to strike a healthy balance between love and admiration, closeness, and reverence.

We have an innate capacity for giving love. Yet, when we want to show our love, we can sometimes overstep the receiver's boundaries. In the excitement of giving, we may give too much. For example, because of our love for our children and our desire to protect them, we may overwhelm them and compromise their need for independence.

Also, if we are giving an extraordinary amount of time, energy, attention, and passion to our job or to a charitable or spiritual cause, we may not have enough time and attention left to nourish our own family. Despite our 'rapturous' love for those causes, it can drive us to overstep our family's boundaries.

Ultimately, our love can be at the expense of respect (*Likutei Sichos*, 7, p. 342). *Kavod* / respect, is related to, and spelled the same as, the word *Kaved* / heavy (see *Targum Unkelus*, Shemos, 17:12). To give respect to another, to revere them or honor them, is to subscribe to them a degree of 'weight' or importance; to take their perspective, boundaries and needs seriously.

Love fully and unconditionally, but always retain a healthy measure of the sacredness of the other.

PRACTICE OF THE WEEK:

Express Love, Honor & Respect to
Each Member of Your Family or Close Friends

Kedoshim

Love Founded on 'We'

THE TORAH READING OF KEDOSHIM BEGINS WITH the words, "And Hashem spoke to Moshe saying, 'Speak to the nation...say to them: You shall be holy... for I am holy'" (Vayikra, 19:1–2).

The Torah reading goes on to illustrate various Mitzvos through which we become holy and elevated; Mitzvos that are performed between us and Hashem, and Mitzvos between ourselves and others. Among them, this Parshah enshrines the Mitzvah of "Love your neighbor as yourself, (for) I am Hashem" (19:18).

This injunction, says the illustrious Second-Century sage Rebbe Akiva, "is a great principle of the Torah" (Sifri, Vayikra, 19:18. Yerushalmi, Nedarim, 9:4). Certainly, "Love your neighbor as yourself" is the 'essential Mitzvah' of this entire Parshah (*Likutei Sichos*, 17, p. 219. And in fact, love is the foundation of the entire Torah, as Hillel teaches, "What is hateful to you do not do to your friend. This is the entire Torah, the rest is commentary." *Shabbos*, 31a).

To love oneself is as natural as breathing. To be precise, loving oneself does not mean 'being in love' with oneself — that is simply narcissistic self-infatuation. Rather, a natural love for oneself is what compels us to eat and sleep properly, to procreate, secure our sustenance, fulfill our psychological needs, and keep ourselves out of harm's way. Self-preservation is innate and healthy. To love another human being "as yourself" is to understand that essentially the other person is one with you. Their needs are your needs. In essence, in loving the other, it is yourself that you are loving.

Our soul is the breath of life the Creator breathed into us: "blew into his nostrils a breath of life." Since this life-force is transmitted from the 'inner dimension' of the Infinite One, our soul is a 'slice' of Infinity. As Infinity is, by definition, One and indivisible, my soul and your soul are both rooted in Divine Oneness, and they are refractions of the Same Light. When we understand this well in our mind and heart, we will naturally love others as our very own self.

Three Levels Deep

Broadly speaking, there are three levels of showing kindness and love towards another. In every relationship, there are three elements, a 'you', a 'me', and a 'we':

1) ME

In this level of love, I am aware of a 'you' and a 'me', and I am showing love to 'you' out of the goodness of my heart. The focus is more on the 'me' — it is me reaching out to you.

2) YOU

In this level of love, the 'me' is lost in the 'you'. An overwhelming love causes my individual existence to merge into the other. The focus here is only on the 'you'; giving 'you' what you want and need, without consideration for 'me.'

3) WE

In this level, 'you' and 'me' are both present and involved in a relationship of giving and receiving. For a relationship to work mutually, there must be two equal, fully involved parties.

'We' relationships are founded on the recognition that I am special and unique, and so are you; we are both expressions of the Divine (שכולן מתאיממות ואב אחד לכלנה / "We are all interconnected and are children of one Father": Tanya, 32).

By concluding the verse "Love your neighbor as yourself" with "...I am Hashem," the Torah guides us to understand that loving another is founded on "Hashem," our common Source. It stems from the fact that at our essence, we are all an indivisible breath of the Divine. The Torah is asking us to love on the level of 'we'.

The Circle of Love

The Torah asks us to love our *Rei'a* / 'neighbor' or 'friend' in the singular; it doesn't say, 'Love everyone.' Rather, we are to expand our circle of love: once we have love and respect for ourselves, we can extend authentic love to others, beginning with those closest to us. Once we can surround our spouse, children, or closest friends with love, we can authentically widen the circumference to include our other acquaintances, our community members, all human beings, and eventually all of Hashem's Creation.

Often, it seems easier to love a total stranger than to love someone you know very well, such as your parents or your in-laws, for example. It is also possible to feel more love for people who share your values and mindset than the people in your life who, in a sense, deserve your love the most yet think differently. Sadly, some people *feel* more love for their pet, or even their garden or their car, than other human beings. But real love begins at home; it begins by first motivating us to care for our family and community before it widens to include strangers — and only then does it include members of the animal, vegetable, and mineral kingdoms. This is why we are asked to love our "neighbor"; it means start with the one closest to us.

Actually, like water, love first fills *you* before it overflows upon the people closest to you and spreads out to cover more 'distant' groups of people. To begin to love others 'as yourself', you must first recognize, honor, and love yourself. True self-love stems from a deep knowing that your life has intrinsic meaning and value, and that you are vested with a Divine purpose. We all have something unique to contribute, both towards our personal *Tikkun* / self-development and towards the ultimate Tikkun, the perfection of the entire world.

True love of another being transcends their physical existence. It also goes beyond what that person can do for you, and even what that person means to you. It is the realization that at our very essence, we are both part of One; we love others because *Ani Hashem* / "for I am Hashem." With this realization, the love that emerges from you is as natural as breathing.

Once our sense of self-love is also founded on the fact of Hashem's Presence, it will automatically then expand to others and not become self-centered. When we see that we are created in the Divine Image, we will see that each person we encounter was created in the Divine Image. And when we truly recognize that the Creator placed us in this world for a specific and unique purpose, and gave us special gifts to attain this purpose, we will recognize the same in others, as well. "Love your neighbor as yourself, for I am Hashem"— for both of you bear My Image.

Not only are we asked to love the Divine Image within ourselves and others, but we are also asked to consciously love people because this love is the foundation of consciously loving Hashem. "One who is careful with the Mitzvos between man and man, in the end will also be scrupulous with the Mitzvos between man and Hashem, for Hashem will have compassion for him, just as he has shown compassion to others, and Hashem will thus draw him closer and open his eyes to see the truth. This is the deeper meaning of the words, "Love your neighbor as yourself; I am Hashem," meaning, if you love your fellow as yourself, then I will be 'Hashem' to you — I will draw you closer" (Rebbe Moshe Dovid Valle, *Kisvei Yad*, 487).

KEDOSHIM

Energy of the Week:

Expanding Love to Embrace All of Hashem's Creations

This week's Torah reading imbues us with the power to love ourselves unconditionally and then extend that inner harmony to envelop our immediate family, siblings, or those who need it most in our lives, and then in ever-widening spheres.

When, in this way, our love becomes increasingly inclusive, it opens us up and allows us to live with expansiveness, a sense of abundance. When our love and care for others is rooted in *Ani Hashem*, it also opens us up to receive Hashem's loving compassion. As our love expands, our hearts become bigger and deeper, and we begin to enjoy *Mochin d'Gadlus* / expansive consciousness. We are gradually drawn 'closer' to the Divine until we enter states of unity or harmony with the will of the Creator.

PRACTICE OF THE WEEK:
Expand Your Circle of Love Stage by Stage

Emor
Protecting Sacred Space

T HE TORAH READING THIS WEEK BEGINS WITH
the words, "And Hashem said to Moshe, 'Speak to
the *Kohanim* / Priests…and say to them: Let none (of
you) defile himself for the sake of a dead body. Except for that
of his relative who is close to him'" (21:1–2).

In the world of 'perfection' and 'unity', there is no decay and
thus no 'death'. In the world of 'imperfection', the world of
'duality', there exists the potential for blemish, defect, decay,
and 'death'.

Throughout the Torah reading this week, we learn of the
boundaries of the *Kohen Gadol* / the High Priest and generally with regards to all *Kohanim* / priests. In the times of the
Beis HaMikdash / Temple, a Kohen lived a transcendent life,

standing apart from the rest of the nation, staying 'above' the noise and movement of worldly life in general. As such, he was commanded to avoid most encounters with death. For this reason, a Kohen is not even allowed to marry a divorcee, as it would involve getting entangled in a web of old dramas and traumas. Nor could the Kohen Gadol marry a widow, so that he could remain detached from the sadness of loss and death, and remain joyful and hopeful, dedicated to his unique role with a clear, objective vision.

By keeping themselves above the world of drama and death, they were able to strongly embody a space of sacredness, transcendence, and 'perfection'. And from this place, they were able to bless, guide, and heal the congregation without interference from the chaos and noise of their own daily struggles. The purpose of their detachment was in order to help those who were dragged down by the attachments of life. Only someone who 'stands above' a certain problem can have the objectivity and strength to bring healing to those who are enmeshed within that problem. A healthy measure of detachment is required to help someone stubbornly holding on to attachments (In the language of Chazal, מוטב יבא זכאי ויכפר על החייב / "It's better for the meritorious to come and bring atonement to the liable": *Shavuos*, 14a. Or, as the Rishonim write, כדי שיבא זכאי ויכפר על החייב / "In order that the meritorious should come and atone for the liable": Tosefos, *Nedarim*, 7b. Rosh, *ad loc*).

This week's reading also speaks of not desecrating the Mishkan (or the Beis HaMikdash). If the Kohen had a 'defect' in his body, as it were, "He shall not profane these places which are sacred to Me, for I, Hashem have sanctified them" (21:23). This is the idea of keeping the Beis HaMikdash 'perfect', separate from all seeming imperfection.

In this week's reading, we are also instructed to observe days of sanctity — Shabbos and the *Yamim Tovim* / Festivals, and thus create a sacred space within our patterns of time. These days are called *Kodesh* / sacred, for they stand apart and function as a retreat from the daily business of making life function well. Shabbos and Yom Tov allow us a respite from the labors of the week, and refresh us so we can focus again on the labors of the week that follows.

Everything in this world is comprised of three elements:

Olam / Space

Shanah / Time

Nefesh / Personal or Individual Consciousness

• Within time, the sacredness of Shabbos and the Festivals shines, and we need to protect this sacredness and not defile these days.

• Within space, there is the Beis HaMikdash, and we need to ensure we do not defile its sacredness.

• Within the world of consciousness, there are the 'Kohanim', who need to live a sacred, transcendent existence and not defile *themselves*.

In order to live a healthy, un-anxious life, fully involved in the worlds of time, space, and consciousness, yet not entangled or enslaved by the drama and trauma of life, we need a healthy dose of separation, sacredness, and detachment.

In order to participate in the daily unfolding of life without becoming overly enmeshed in it, an element of 'apartness' of 'transcendence' of standing 'above' is essential. In the words of Rebbe Mendel of Kotzk, "If you want to be *in* this world, you need to stand one step *higher*."

This is why the Torah speaks about the three dimensions of sacredness — and the human ability to be both 'above' and 'within' time, space, and personal consciousness.

Indeed, within each and every individual, the deepest region of their soul always remains aloof and separate from physicality and the conflicts of life. This level of self is always pure and whole. Tapping into this purity and perfection, free from all narratives, allows us to have a healthy relationship with the objects, people, and even the narratives, in our life.

We all carry within ourselves an 'inner Kohen', an inner greatness, a place of perfection, transcendence, and purity (thus, the Torah could say, ובני דוד כהנים היו / "And David's sons were Kohanim": *Shemuel* 2, 8:18 — although they were actually from the tribe of Yehudah). We also have realities within us called 'Beis HaMikdash' and also 'Shabbos'. The more we live from the quiet, still transcendence of these realms within us, the more we can be involved in daily life in empowered, righteous, and healthy ways. And then, when we encounter someone who is entangled in the dramas of time, space, and individual consciousness, we will be a healing presence for them and lift them up. We will naturally convey blessing to them: blessings of being above the world and within it at the same time, involved but not enmeshed.

EMOR

Energy of the Week:
Protecting Our Sacred Space

Often, we are so busy that we are distracted by life's daily struggles, pains, and dramas, and we become too close to them. When we no longer stand above a problem and observe it objectively, we cannot untangle ourselves from it. No longer do we have an external, objective problem; sadly, we 'are' the problem.

Learning about the Kohen, the Beis HaMikdash, Shabbos, and Yom Tov guides us to reconnect with the place of transcendence in the deeper levels of our own self. To live within and above this world, we need to reveal within ourselves a space that stands apart from conflicts, a time untouched by our struggles, and a level of consciousness that is above the entanglements of personal narratives.

'Death', meaning a state of separation and the absence of life, growth, and potential, is not allowed into this inner sanctuary. This is a 'protected' space.

We can access this place within ourselves 1) at certain times throughout the day, 2) in certain places,
and 3) in certain states of consciousness. For example, 1) during prayer, 2) in the *Shul* / synagogue,
and 3) in the higher consciousness embodied in the
silent Amidah prayer. When we emerge from this
profoundly sacred experience, we draw its reserves
of objectivity and transcendence, clarity, and lucidity
into the world — into the rest of our day, into all the
places we go, and into all our interactions with the
people we encounter.

Revealing this sacred time, place, and state of mind
within ourselves necessitates setting firm boundaries.
For example, the morning prayer should be performed
uninterrupted and at a certain time; the Shul needs
to have a certain level of cleanliness and sanctity, and
in the Amidah prayer, one should not be distracted
by thoughts of personal narratives or problems.

After having dipped into this state of separation
from the world, we are empowered to see our problems as if from 'above.' Practically, this means that
when faced with a challenge, we can either grapple
head-on with the issue — engaging directly with it

in order to overcome it, or we can envision ourselves standing above the challenge, and from this higher position, more easily master the issue at hand.

In order to access this higher consciousness, we also need to craft a sacred space within our relationships and protect the boundaries that ensure its sacredness. This also helps us maintain the sanctity of that part of ourselves that is pure, untouched, and perfect, free of any negativity and doubt.

This week imbues us with the strength to protect our sacred spaces and ensure that they are properly maintained and secured.

PRACTICE OF THE WEEK:

See Your Challenges as if From 'Above'

Behar
Rest & Refocus

"AND HASHEM SPOKE TO MOSHE...WHEN YOU COME to the Land that I am giving you, it shall be a Shabbos for the Land...You shall sow your field for six years...But in the Seventh Year, the Land shall have a complete rest — this is a Shabbos for Hashem..." (25:1–4).

This, the opening of this week's Torah reading, reveals the seven-year agricultural cycle; six years of work and one year of "rest." These six years of work mirror the six workdays of each week, and the seventh year, called Shemitah, is like the seventh day, Shabbos.

There are a total of 52 Shabboses within each yearly cycle. In addition, every year has seven Torah-defined *Yamim Tovim* / holy days (which are one day of Rosh Hashanah, one day of Yom Kippur,

two days for the first and the last day of Sukkos, two days for the first and
the last day of Pesach, and one day of Shavuos) and so there are 59 days
that we need to rest — and to rest the land — within the yearly
cycle. However, in a certain way, *fully* resting on these 59 days
is not possible. There are some conceptual forms of desecrating
'Shabbos rest' that are virtually unavoidable.

For example, say you plowed your field on Friday. Although
you did not plow on Shabbos, nonetheless, you set things into
motion on Friday, and on Shabbos, your field grew as a result.
While this was technically allowed, on a subtle level, it caused
a kind of 'cultivation' of your field to occur on Shabbos — a
desecration of Shabbos on a subtle level.

As such, in the course of six years, there are 354 "days of
rest" that are not *fully* restful (59x6=354). 354 is the number
of days in a lunar year. To compensate for all the days of rest
that were not fully restful over the course of six years, on the
seventh year, the Torah gives us a full year of 'Shabbos', the year
of Shemitah (*Tiferes Yonasan,* Vayikra, 25:2).

The weekly Shabbos and the year of Shemitah are, in essence, one idea.

Rest as the Apex of Work or as Its Foundation
Our sages paint the following dilemma: a person is traveling in the desert and forgets which day of the week it is and
therefore does not know which evening is the beginning of
Shabbos (*Shabbos,* 69b. See also *Shulchan Aruch,* Orach Chayim, 344:1).

How should he keep the Torah commandment of Shabbos as he must? "Rav Huna said, he must count six days (from the day he realized he forgot what day it is) and observe that seventh day as Shabbos. Rav Chiyya bar Rav said, he must observe the first day as Shabbos, and afterward count six 'weekdays' until the next Shabbos." What is the basis of their argument? The first opinion holds that the traveler should follow the sequence of Creation: first there were the Six Days of Creation, and then there was Shabbos. The second opinion holds that the traveler should follow the order of the creation of Adam, who was created on the Sixth Day of Creation, and soon thereafter began the Seventh Day, Shabbos (The Gemara sides with the opinion of Rav Huna: *Ibid*).

In essence, this argument is whether Shabbos is a 'destination', a place to arrive after six days, or a point of 'departure', a place from which to enter the following six days. This dynamic is also reflected in the seven-year cycle.

The Torah begins the passage by saying, "When you come to the Land that I am giving you, it shall be a Shabbos for the Land." This seems to suggest a rest that comes *before* the work, before the six years of working the Land. But then the Torah continues: "…You shall sow your field for six years…but in the Seventh Year, the land shall have a complete rest", which is a rest that comes *after* the six years of labor.

Indeed, the Shemitah year, the 'Shabbos' of the seven-year cycle, is both a place to come *from* (Shabbos "before" the six years of work) and a place to go *to* (the Shabbos "after" the six years of work). Shemitah is both a state of rest that gives rise to our work, and it is the rest that comes after the culmination of our work.

Besides these two perspectives on the Shemitah year, there seems to be a twofold reason for the Mitzvah of Shemitah itself.

The Dual Purpose of Shemitah
When the Land lies fallow for a year, it accomplishes two things. Firstly, the Land *itself* rests and rejuvenates and produces a greater quality and quantity in the following years. This rest is for the purpose of the soil and Land itself (Rambam, *Moreh Nevuchim*, 3:297). Secondly, the person who farms the Land will receive a year to stop working it and reflect on how everything truly belongs to Hashem (*Sefer HaChinuch*, Mitzvah 84). In doing so, the farmer will relax and reflect on his purpose in life, re-centering himself, as it were. As such, letting the Land rest is also for the purpose of human inner rest (These two reasons are related to whether the Mitzvah of Shemitah is for the Land to rest, or for man to rest from working the Land: *Minchas Chinuch*, Mitzvah, 112. MaHari Perlo, *Sefer HaMitzvos Rasag*, Mitzvah 61. *Likutei Sichos* 17, p. 286).

These two reasons for Shemitah can be placed within the frame of the two forms of Shabbos: after six workdays or before six workdays. The *Shemitah / * rest that comes *before* working the land corresponds to the purpose of human rest, just as

Shabbos gives us time to reflect and gain strength and focus for the future week. The Shemitah that comes *after* the Land has been worked for six years is for the purpose of the Land's rest, so that the earth can rejuvenate after working for six straight years, just as Shabbos gives us rejuvenating rest after six days of toil.

The Rest-Work-Rest Paradigm

The above-quoted Pasuk does not merely say *when*, or *if*, you will work for six years, then you shall rest the field in the seventh year — rather, it says, "...you *shall* work the fields." This implies that work is not a suggestion but a *directive*, another Mitzvah of sorts.

"Man is born to toil" (*Iyov*, 5:7). This does not just mean manual labor but rather intellectual and spiritual toil. In any case, it means we are not created to sit idly on the side or to receive from life passively (Spiritual toil should be our ideal — הוי אומר לעמל תורה נברא והיינו דאמר רבא כולהו גופי דרופתקי נינהו טובי לדזכי דהוי דרופתקי דאורייתא / "You must say that one was created for the toil of Torah. And that is the meaning of what Rava said: 'All bodies are like receptacles to store items until use. Happy is one who is privileged, who is a receptacle for Torah'": *Sanhedrin*, 99b).

Our work and toil is where our uniqueness shines; where we can express our individual talents and genius. Through our work, we can create positive change within ourselves and the world. Through our work, we can move Creation forward and become co-creators in the *Tikkun* / perfecting of the world.

Yet, a world and a life without Shabbos or Shemitah is a life of ceaseless toil. Those of us who do not "work the land" still toil with our possessions and our sustenance. Ultimately, work without rest enslaves us to our work and, by extension, to our possessions and sustenance.

From a purely 'natural' and rational perspective, it would seem more productive to work every day. If you are trying to accumulate wealth, for example, why cease your involvement for a day every week? Yet, the Torah says, "Six days you *shall* work — there is a 'Mitzvah' to participate, to be proactive, engaged and ambitious. And on the seventh day, as well as on the seventh year, Hashem commands us to let go of work and 'doing', and just rest in 'being'.

The Divine Seven Day / Year Cycle

Time is patterned with seasons, with varying weather patterns, temperatures, and qualities of light. A full cycle of these seasonal patterns creates a year, and thus, a year is a 'natural' phenomenon.

There is also a 'natural' astrological phenomenon of months. The cycle of the moon, from its inception and waxing through its waning and disappearance, creates a month.

Years and months are both part of the natural order of life; thus, all peoples, throughout all of human history, have counted and marked months and years. Solar calendars follow the objectively experienced cycle of seasons, while lunar calendars follow the more subtle phases of the moon.

One may ask where weeks come from. Why does a week exist at all? And why specifically a seven-day week, which seems to have no astrological nor seasonal reason behind it, nor any basis in a universally observable phenomenon? There is no physical, astrological, or seasonal reason for a seven-day week. In fact, many ancient cultures did not have the construct of weeks, and some had a nine-day week. Similarly, the seven-year cycle of Shemitah does not parallel any objective seasonal, astrological, or natural seven-year cycles.

Weeks actually originate in a Divine mandate, based on a sacred view of time. The only possible reason for our seven-day week is that the narrative of Creation revealed its existence. It is Hashem's conception of time; it is not natural, it is supernatural. And yet, the seven-day week is embedded in human consciousness and psychology, and thus physiology, to the point that all known civilizations now measure time in this way. In this sense, the supernatural has become 'natural'.

Seven Is a Gift from Above

When we rest on the seventh day and seventh year, we consciously contact our higher, deeper self, the dimension of soul that is beyond finitude and 'doing'. This part of us is not defined by what we do or have but by who we *are*. This conscious contact is the gift of Shabbos and the gift of Shemitah.

BEHAR

Energy of the Week:
The Power to Refocus

Shabbos of the weeks and years is a time of rest and renewal — centering us and refocusing us on our purpose in this life, and allowing for a glimpse into a self that is not defined by or enslaved by what we do.

This week imbues us with the *Ko'ach* / power and wisdom to carve out a place for Shabbos rest in our space, in our time, and in our personal consciousness. This applies to Shabbos itself, and also to one's personal schedule, such as taking an occasional 'sabbatical' from one job, and taking time each day to pray and introspect. For example, the time, space, and consciousness we carve out for *Tefilah* / prayer is a manifestation of 'Shabbos' in each and every day (Alter Rebbe, *Torah Ohr*, Noach, 9a).

This week's Torah reading infuses us with the strength to pause and refocus our lives at least once a week, once every several years, and once every day. We are empowered to take time to stop, get off the 'hamster wheel' and refocus, so that we will have strength and clarity to accomplish our work and purpose in this world with mindfulness and intentionality.

PRACTICE OF THE WEEK:

Carve Out Time for Shabbos Rest

Bechukosai
Connecting with Blessings &
Becoming a Blessing

T
HIS WEEK'S TORAH READING BEGINS WITH THE
words, אם־בחקתי תלכו / "If you follow My statutes and
observe My commandments... I will give your rains
in their time... ואולך אתכם קוממיות / and you will walk erect."
And then it says, ואם־לא תשמעו / "But if you do not listen...
I will order upon you...hopeless longing and depression. You
will sow your seed in vain...(and concludes with the phrase)
ביד־משה / "in the hand of Moshe" (26:3–46).

Essentially, the entire Torah reading this week is about
blessings and curses. What is the text's definition of a blessing, and what constitutes a curse? A 'blessing' here is rain and
abundance, and a 'curse' is scarcity and a sense of hopelessness
and despair.

On a deeper level, a blessing is anything that is truly life-giving, life-affirming, moving things forward, meaningful, pur-

poseful, and ultimately creates a sense of unity and wholeness. A curse is something that blocks life-force, lacks any apparent meaning, and ultimately creates a sense of separation and dissension. When something has meaning to us, we are and feel connected to it. When it has no meaning to us, we are and feel separate from it. Meaning creates connection.

Throughout all levels of reality, there are two primordial ingredients: *Ohr* / light and *Kli* / vessel. 'Light' means *Chayus* / life-force (Baal Shem Tov) and *Mochin* / intentionality and meaning (Arizal). Thus, Ohr is a sense of connection and unification, the 'why' of life, the inner purpose of all our experiences. A Kli is something solid or opaque, separating one space from another. It represents that which closed off, implying a sense of alienation, separation, and disconnection from life.

In the world of 'vessels', meaning the empirical world as we observe it, there is great beauty and grandeur, but it is also, in itself, seemingly devoid of meaning. Meaning comes from the light. Experientially speaking, a world of vessels without light is a deafening silence and empty abyss, leaving a person feeling alienated and imprisoned. A world of light, of Divinity, and connectivity is a world flowing with aliveness, meaning, and a sense of belonging and freedom.

Blessing Is Ohr, Light; Curse Is Kli, Vessel

Every experience and every encounter has both a light element and a vessel element. The light is our connection to the experience, our 'aliveness' in it, and its meaningfulness — the 'why' of experience. The vessel is the actual 'body' of the person or object we are encountering, its raw 'data' and description — the 'what' of experience (Empirical knowledge and science are meant to describe the 'what' of the universe, what can be seen with the eyes, while Torah explains the inner reality, the 'why' of our existence. The 'what' and the 'why' should not be confused).

For example, imagine the experience of a precious child sleeping on your shoulder. Their weight on you will feel less than their actual 20 pounds. Because of the aliveness and connectivity of the experience, the 20 pounds may feel more like two pounds. Now imagine you are seated in an airplane, and a stranger has fallen asleep on your shoulder mid-flight. Their head will feel much heavier to you than the few pounds that he is imposing on you. His 10-pound head will oppress you like a 20-pound boulder. The reason for this discrepancy is that the more 'Light', connectivity, purpose, and meaning you feel with the other person, the less 'vessel' there is. And the more that the physical 'vessel' of the experience stands out for you, the less 'Light' will enliven you.

Similarly, our experience of time expands and contracts depending on the 'Light' in the experience. Sitting and speaking to a friend for an hour on a park bench can feel like five minutes, whereas an unpleasant encounter with a rude bank teller that lasts two minutes can feel like an hour.

Consider also a woman in labor who is deeply connected to the baby that she is bringing into the world. This child has been living within her, cradled and cherished by her for the past nine months. She will feel less pain in giving birth than in a less intense and less meaningful experience, for example, removing a splinter. Since the purpose and blessings of birth are obvious, there is less suffering. A pain that feels purposeless will cause more suffering. The more meaningful something is, the more it is experienced as a 'blessing'.

Regarding the 'curses', the Torah repetitively uses the phrase קרי / *Keri*, saying, 'If you act towards Me with *Keri*, you will experience *Keri* in your life.' *Keri* means 'happenstance' as in *Mikra* / 'it happened.' As such, Hashem is saying, 'If you walk in My world asserting that "things just happen," then indeed you will experience life as just happening to you. Your life will seem random and everything left to chance; you yourself will seem to be purposeless and aimless. Ultimately, I will leave you to the world of "chance" that you assert.' This is the Rambam's opinion on *Hashgacha Pratis* / 'Divine providence'. The more we recognize and acknowledge providence and specific Divine intention in history and our own lives, and the more we are conscious that everything is unfolding within intricate Divine attention and intention, the more, in fact, we will experience Divine providence.

Put differently, since everything is *always* Divine provi-dence, as the Baal Shem Tov revealed, the more we live our lives with conscious intention, meaning, and purposefulness, the more life will appear to us as intentional and purposeful. Our experiences and encounters will be revealed as means of connection with self, Hashem, and other people, rather than, G-d forbid, chaotic happenstance and random raw data. The more alive we are, the more alive the world appears to us, and indeed, the more alive the world will be. The more intentionality we bring to our actions, the more our surroundings vibrate (on a revealed level) with a sense of purpose.

On a deeper level, not only do we 'receive' blessings or curses from life, but we can embody these qualities within ourselves. We can *be* a blessing (והיה ברכה / "And you shall be a blessing": *Bereishis*, 12:2).

The Aleph-Beis in Correct or in Backwards Sequence
The blessings in this Parshah begin with the first letter of the Aleph-Beis, Aleph: אם־בחקתי תלכו / "If you follow My statutes," and they conclude with the last letter of the Aleph-Beis, Tav: ואולך אתכם קוממיות / "And you will walk upright." When the Aleph-Beis is sequenced in its proper order, it is a sign of blessing. The forward flow of letters signals a correct, seamless flow, continuity, and progress. The curses in this Parshah begin, as the Medrash points out (*Medrash Rabbah*, Vayikra, 35:1), with a 'lower' or later letter, and end with a 'higher' or earlier letter. They begin with the letter Vav, ואם־לא תשמעו / "But if you do not listen," and conclude with the letter *before* Vav, the letter Hei: ביד־משה / "In the hand of Moshe."

The 22 letters of the Aleph-Beis are grouped into pairs. The first letter in each pair is called the *Mashpia* / 'giver', and the second letter of the pair is called the *Mekabel* / 'receiver'. For example, Aleph 'gives' to Beis, and Beis 'receives' from Aleph. Yet, seemingly paradoxically, in each group, the graphic design of the 'giving' letter is open to the 'receiving' letter, whereas the 'receiver' is always facing with its back to the 'giver', and open to the next receiver.

In the pair 'Aleph and Beis' (ב א), the shape of the Aleph (א) is open towards the Beis (ב), whereas the Beis has its back to the Aleph. In the pair 'Gimel and Dalet' (ד ג), the letter Gimel (ג) is open towards the Dalet (ד), whereas the Dalet has its back to the Gimel. This is true of all possible letter pairings in the sequence of the Aleph-Beis.

This subtle detail in the design of the Aleph-Beis and its letters reflects the very foundational idea that each letter, each building block or 'vessel' of Creation, receives from the one before it, and then 'turns around', so-to-speak, to give to the next in sequence. Initially, the 'receiving' letter of the pair is open to the previous letter in a state of receptivity, and then it 'turns around' in an act of giving. Whenever light is received, it is for the sake of giving.

The letters of the Aleph-Beis are the transmitters of Divine *Shefa* / flow and vitality, as they are the metaphysical conduits upon which the Divine 'vibrations of Creation' travel. The origin of the Shefa is within the *Ohr Ein Sof* / the Infinite Light of the Creator, beyond all 'letters' 'sounds' and 'vibrations'; pure Infinity. Yet, for this uncontextualized unlimited Shefa to be revealed within the limits of Creation, it enters into the letters of the Aleph-Beis, moving from pure, Transcendent Light into defined vessels and then specific expressions.

When the flow is properly aligned, meaning from 'Above' to 'below', from within to without, or from Aleph to Tav, and the movement is 'giving' to the 'receiver', and that 'receiver' turns and becomes a 'giver', the Divine sustaining flow reaches us, and nurtures and nourishes the physical plane of existence. This is the course of 'blessings'.

Blessings manifest when we feel the Light and, thus, the inner reason, purpose, and meaning behind the blessings. When you are fully aware of the Divine Source of your blessings — understanding the purpose for which you have received them and what you are meant to do with them — you can receive life fully and share it with others in a way that truly benefits them. Then, not only are you receiving blessings, but you are *becoming a blessing.*

An occurrence that seems purposeless feels like a curse. We cannot connect to its meaning or process it. We cannot find the good in it, and thus, we cannot pass any goodness from it to others. Occasionally, the 'letters', or transmitters of Divine life flow, are preoccupied with absorbing from Above and do not transmit or 'give'. Fixed on receiving, they cause the Divine flow to stop. Their 'backs' are facing us, and we are left in darkness, emptiness, and disconnection. Like a closed vessel, we are not perceiving Light, meaning, or purpose — we only feel the

Kli. When this occurs, we perceive life as negative, and this is to us a 'curse', G-d forbid.

And yet, if we can connect to what is metaphysically happening when there is darkness and disconnection, then we can understand that what we are receiving is still involved in absorbing Light from Above, and the revealing of that 'blessing' has simply not yet reached us. The vessel, the 'receiving letter', is still in the process of receiving from the *Mashpia* / giver before it and has not yet turned around to give to the 'next letter' so that the Divine flow can move all the way from pure *Ein Sof* / Infinity to our defined reality.

In practical terms, a 'curse' may be perceived when a blessing on its way to us is so great and deep that its transmission is delayed and not yet ready to be relayed to us.

The Alter Rebbe, Rabbi Schneur Zalman of Liadi, would serve as the public reader of the Torah every week. One year, he was out of town on this particular Shabbos, and another person read the Torah. When the reader reached the point that speaks of the 'curses', the Rebbe's son, Rebbe DovBer, fainted and remained ill for quite some time. He explained that his fainting and illness were a reaction to hearing the curses that were read. 'But,' he was asked, 'what was different this year?' For he had heard this reading read by his father every year of his life. He explained to the Chassidim: "When my father reads this Torah portion, I only hear *blessings*."

BECHUKOSAI

Energy of the Week:
Connecting With Blessing

This week's Torah reading imbues us with the ability to connect with the blessings in our lives and to become a blessing.

We should observe and unpack the blessings we receive, finding the meaning, purpose, and Light in them. If, at first, an experience feels like a 'curse', the moment we can find even a small sliver of meaning, purpose, or Light in it — perhaps just a way to grow from the experience — at that moment, its harshness begins to transform into some measure of blessing.

This week's Torah reading empowers us to see and appreciate *Hashgacha Pratis* / Divine providence and governance over every aspect of Creation at every moment. It is only through our actions and constricted awareness that we may experience a concealment of Divine providence.

If we deny providence and assert that life is random, we will not perceive providence, and indeed, the world will seem more and more random and mechanical to us. By contrast, the more we see blessing in our lives and sense the aliveness, intentionality, and exactness of Hashem's guiding Hand in Creation, Divine providence will be revealed to us.

This week, we should ask ourselves, "How did the most important blessings in my life come about?" Trace the cause: did you happen to meet someone or do something at the right time? Perhaps in the past you attributed such occurrences to happenstance, luck, or hard work. The more you contemplate the cause, the harder it will be to assert that your blessings came to you randomly. You will begin to see that there is nothing random; rather, everything is designed with utterly perfect wisdom. And the more you live with this awareness, the more the world shows itself to be Divinely orchestrated, down to every single detail.

May we be open to receive the Ko'ach of this week's Torah reading and begin to see blessings within all the events in our life, and within everyone and everything we see.

May we refine our ability to find meaning and purpose in everything that we receive, and may we transmit this Light to others; may we 'be a blessing'.

PRACTICE OF THE WEEK:

**Open Your Eyes to
See the Blessings in Life**

BOOK FOUR:
Bamidbar

Bamidbar
Raising the Individual

W E START A NEW BOOK OF THE TORAH THIS WEEK, *Bamidbar* / "In the Desert." This book chronicles the passage of Klal Yisrael through the Desert and their growth as a people as they transition into the second generation — those who will at last enter the Land of Israel.

The Torah reading begins with a census, a counting of the people: "Hashem spoke to Moshe in the Sinai Desert...saying, ...*Se'u* / 'take the sum' of all the congregation of the children of Israel... according to the number of their names" (1:1–2).

'Counting' is very prominent in this week's and next week's Torah reading. In fact, the way our sages (*Yuma*, 68b) refer to the book of Bamidbar is חומש הפקודים / "The Book of *Pikudim* / Counting," hence the English name, "*The Book of Numbers.*"

It would appear that the project of counting people, creating a census of a whole population, marginalizes individuals and individuality for the sake of the collective.

Indeed, one way that a tyrant demoralizes people is to give them numbers, referring to them as statistics. Giving a person a number instead of a name reduces them to a 'product', erasing their individuality, unique value, and even their humanity itself. That being the case, we need to delve deeper and discover the purpose of the Torah's counting.

A special blessing that Klal Yisrael received through the prophecy of Hoshea / Hosea (2:1) is, "The number of the People of Israel shall be like that of the sands of the sea, which cannot be measured or counted." On one level, this states that they will not be reduced to numbers because they existentially defy the numbers. Again, we need to ask why they *are* counted in this Parshah.

Upon closer reading, this verse from Hoshea seems to contradict itself. First it gives an estimate of sorts: "(A number) like that of the sands of the sea." True, this indicates an enormous amount, yet the sands of the sea are not infinite, so it must refer to a hidden finite number. Then the verse concludes: "...which cannot be measured or counted." This means there is no number. Say our sages (*Yuma*, 22b), the second statement is referring to when Klal Yisrael fulfills the will of Hashem; then they defy all possible numbers. The first statement is referring to when they do not fulfill the will of Hashem; then they are like the sands of the sea, having some definite number even if they technically cannot be counted. Here again, counting seems to be a negative activity, revealing the limited nature and erroneous ways of the people. There is even a prohibition in the Torah against counting people: כל המונה את ישראל עובר בשני לאוין / "One who counts a group of Jews violates two negative commands" (*Ibid*). Again, what is the purpose of the counting in this Parsha?

Counting as Lifting

When Moshe is told to take the census, the word שאו / *Se'u* — translated as "take the sum" is repeatedly used. This word comes from the root word 'to elevate' or to lift up. This form of counting people is unique in that it also lifts each individual up.

This census, says the Torah, is counting "according to the number of their names." Unlike normal counting — 'one person, two people, three people...', the Torah says we need to count 'names', meaning, to list their names. One's name is intimately connected with the depth of who they are, and to their talents and purpose in life. A listing of names thus honors each individual, the family, and tribe. Additionally, each individual is 'lifted' and mentioned by name in front of Moshe and Aharon. In the words of the Ramban, כי הבא לפני אב הנביאים ואחיו קדוש ה' והוא נודע אליהם בשמו יהיה לו בדבר הזה זכות וחיים / "One who comes before the Father of the Prophets (Moshe), and his brother, the holy one of the Eternal (Aharon), and becomes known to them by name, thereby receives merit and life" (Ramban, *Bamidbar*, 1:45).

By taking each individual person into account and counting them by means of their distinct name, the person is singled out, honored and loved, and lifted higher. As the person's name is mentioned, their uniqueness is revealed. Every person *counts* and has an indispensable role within the total sum. Without individuals, there is no real 'collective'.

The Number 600,000
The total sum of our Parshah's census, the third census in the Torah — as well as that of the previous census (although perhaps the second and third, which have the exact same sum total, are parts of the same census) — is a little over 600,000 (*Bamidbar*, 1:45–46).

Six represents a fully dimensional world, as there are six basic directions from a vantage point within three-dimensional space: right, left, in front, above, below, and behind. The ultimate fullness of six is 600,000 (as 100,000 is the biggest number in the Torah). Thus there were 600,000 counted individuals during the time period of the Exodus and the Giving of the Torah, when we became a people. This number represents the fullness of Klal Yisrael.

As there were 600,000 physical bodies of heads of families at that time, we know that there are 600,000 'root' souls of Klal Yisrael. All other souls, as there were and are many more than 600,000 people in Klal Yisrael, are 'combinations' of these root souls. And just as there are 600,000 'root' souls, there are 600,000 'root' letters in the Torah. Root letters are the small 'letters' that create a regular letter. For example, there are two

Yuds and a Vav within the letter Aleph; a Yud above, a Yud below, and a tilted Vav in the middle (א). Another way of enumerating root letters is by counting the Yuds in each letter. For example, Aleph has two Yuds, while Gimel (ג) has one. The *Milu'im* / 'fillings' of the letters (spelling them out, as in *Aleph*: Aleph, Lamed, Pei) can also be used, as well as the *Targum* / translations of the letters (See *Chesed l'Avraham*, 2. *Pri Tzadik*, Shemos. *P'nei Yehoshua*, Kidushin, 30a. *Likutei Torah*, Behar, 43d).

The word ישראל / Yisrael is an acronym for יש שישים ריבוא אותיות לתורה / "There are six hundred thousand letters (again, meaning 'sub-letters') in the Torah" (*Zohar Chadash*, Shir HaShirim). Deeply, this means that every soul is rooted in a letter, or dimension of a letter, of the Torah (*Megaleh Amukos. P'nei Yehoshua*, ibid).

Much like a Torah scroll, each letter is integral, and the missing or even blurring of one letter renders the entire scroll unusable. This is true of souls as well. There is a totality of souls, a grand 'sum', and yet, each soul is highly unique, with its own special name, energy, and character. The totality of Klal Yisrael is entirely dependent on the individuals within it.

When we perceive ourselves as integral to the big picture and serving a unique purpose within the collective, we are tangibly 'lifted' and our self-worth is revealed.

Being unique but not within a collective, a 'sum', or wholeness is lonely. To be swallowed up within a collective is also not fulfilling, as one is no longer a unique individual. To be uniquely yourself within the context of a greater collective is to find the wholeness of your individual expression.

This is the blessed paradox of being both a full individual and a full member of a people.

BAMIDBAR

Energy of the Week:
Raising Up the Individual

This week's Torah reading imbues us with the ability to lift ourselves up by recognizing the essential importance of our individual contributions to the greater community. We must always recognize that our unique being and gifts are irreplaceable. In this way, we can never be a statistic; we are 'innumerable'. If even one letter in the Torah is even slightly blurred and not individuated, the whole of the Torah is rendered incomplete. The community is likewise incomplete without each and every person in it.

Look into yourself and recognize that which is uniquely you, and how you as an individual contribute to your family, your workplace and your world. Be sure that you are not 'blurring' yourself in order to fit in, or to be a good member of the community or group, for if you are not being you, then the entire world is incomplete.

There is only one you, and you matter completely. Celebrate your individuality and your unique contribution to Hashem's vast universe.

PRACTICE OF THE WEEK:

Be Your Unique Self in Community

Naso
Routine & Passion

THIS WEEK'S TORAH READING BEGINS WITH THE
words, "Hashem spoke to Moshe...take a census..."
(*Bamidbar*, 4:21–22). This is a continuation of the census
that began in last week's reading. This week's census focuses on
the *Levi'im* / Levites and the *Kohanim* / Priests and the unique
services and rituals that were their duty to perform in the Beis
HaMikdash.

Later in the reading, the Torah speaks of the laws of a *Nazir*
/ Nazirite. A Nazir is a person who chooses to separate himself
or herself from the norms of society, not cut their hair, refrain
from wine, and live a life detached from worldliness.

Some of the practices of a Nazir are similar to the laws of
conduct of a Kohen, such as the law of ensuring that the Kohen does not become *Tamei* / 'impure' through contact with a
corpse. As such, these two are grouped together in this week's
Torah reading.

While there are similarities between the Kohen and the Nazir, there is also a marked distinction between the two. Priesthood is a birthright; you must be born a Kohen, and a non-Kohen can never serve as one in the Beis HaMikdash. Anyone at any time can choose to live as a Nazir.

The family transmission of *Kehunah* / priesthood is the reason why the Kohen may not defile himself by becoming impure through contact with the dead, yet may and should become impure by participating in the burial of a close relative, such as a parent. "Speak to the Kohanim, the sons of Aharon, and say to them: 'None shall defile himself for any [dead] person…except for the relatives that are closest to him: his mother, his father…his brother'" (*Vayikra*, 21:1–2). Yet, a Nazir may not become impure even to his or her close blood relatives: "They shall not go in where there is a dead person. Even if their father or mother, or their brother or sister should die, they must not become defiled for any of them" (*Bamidbar*, 6:7).

Becoming a Nazir is a personal choice, and has nothing to do with family, hence, even to family a Nazir is not to defile himself. *Kehuna* / priesthood is inherited from one's family, and a Kohen is instructed to become defiled through burying a close family member.

Another reflection of this dynamic — hereditary versus self-created, birthright, or choice, order versus passion — is also mirrored in the Nazir and the Kohen's relationship with their hair. The Kohen needed to shave his head (*Bamidbar*, 8:7);

his hair needed to be orderly. The *Kohen Gadol* / High Priest would cut his hair once a week, and the other Kohanim would cut their hair once a month (*Ta'anis,* 17b). In contrast, regarding the Nazir, it is written, "No razor shall pass over his head…it shall be sacred, and he shall allow the growth of the hair of his head to grow wild" (*Bamidbar,* 6:5).

Wild, unkempt hair represents passion beyond the bounds of routine and structure, while trimmed or shaven hair represents routine and structure. The inherited Kohen's life was full of order and routine, including his highly structured service in the Beis HaMikdash. As the Kohen embodies the world of boundaries and order, and thus he serves with short, tamed hair. By contrast, the Nazir would go with long, untamed hair, expressing passion and rebelliousness, breaking the boundaries of the status quo for some time. The first way of life expresses the holiness of order, and the other, the holiness of temporary chaos.

Many Nezirim were, in fact, young, single, and full of idealism and passion. In their personal dedication, they would vow to be a Nazir, most often for thirty days and sometimes longer, and live for that period detached and removed from society. After that period had elapsed, they needed to bring an atonement offering before returning to a more orderly, status-quo lifestyle.

A Kohen served as a representative of the community, with the same basic routine each day. He thus represents our own orderliness and organization in life, our ability to function within a somewhat impersonal system. The Nazir represents our non-ordinary and more personal expression and passionate service.

Every endeavor or goal needs 'context' or structure, and 'content' — the way the structure is filled with life-force. To flourish as a human and spiritual being, we need both the structure and impersonal 'container' of day-to-day routines, and moments when we are fully present with the 'content' of our authentic self, without a sense of obligation to 'containers' and norms.

In a marriage, for example, there is an underlying context — the structure and formality of the marriage agreement. Yet within that structure, there must also be passion, personal authenticity, and intimacy, which is by nature 'informal' and personal.

Tefilah / prayer is another example of bringing together 'context' and 'content' in our lives. Every day, we pray a set prayer within a regular set time, mirroring the specific offerings that were offered every day by the Kohanim, in the Beis HaMikdash, in their set time. Yet, within the structure of prayer, there needs to be our personal involvement, manifested in our *Kavanah* / intention, passion, and *Chayus* / life-force.

There is always a delicate balance between maintaining routines and ensuring that they do not become stale. It is sometimes challenging to be personally invested and engaged on all levels of our being in our religious practices, and still flow within the support and consistency of a strong, regular structure.

The Torah reading this week juxtaposes these different parts of ourselves — 'the Kohen' and 'the Nazir' — to teach and inspire us to benefit from both ways of being. In this way, we can maximize the effectiveness and value all of our practices, relationships, and endeavors.

NASO

Energy of the Week:
Routine & Passion

This week's Torah reading imbues us with the strength to maintain the balance between the structure and orderliness of our lives and the passion and personal Ko'ach that we infuse into that structure to bring it alive.

Review the structures and routines in your relationships, lifestyle choices, livelihood, and spiritual practice, etc. Ensure that these structures are well supported and have firm grounding and proper consistency.

Now, look deeper into those structures and be sure that you are inhabiting them with vitality, personal insight, idealism, and enthusiasm. Ensure that your passion is supported within a safe and grounded framework and yet not extinguished by that framework.

PRACTICE OF THE WEEK:
Put Your Passion Into Action

Beha'alosecha
Rejuvenating the Journey

T HIS WEEK'S TORAH READING BEGINS WITH THE
words, "Hashem spoke…saying…When you kindle the
lights facing the face of the Menorah, seven lamps shall
give light " (8:1–2). The literal translation of the words "When
you will kindle the lights" is 'When you make the lights rise'.

When we feel that there is darkness and we have lost light,
we must actively touch a flame to a wick, and hold it there
until a new flame rises on its own. In order to become inspired
to move forward, we must do a very real action. Sometimes,
our actions flow from our feelings, but our feelings always flow
from our actions. What we do, we eventually feel: "The heart is
drawn after the deed" (*Sefer HaChinuch*). Then, when the heart is
illumined, it can lead to further inspired actions.

The "seven lamps" of our inner 'Menorah' that we need to light are our seven *Midos* / character traits: Kindness, Power, Unification, Perseverance, Humility, Alignment, and Sovereignty. Shelomo HaMelech / King Solomon reveals (*Mishlei,* 24:16), "A righteous person falls seven times and gets up…." This also refers to our seven Midos. The journey of our life often includes setbacks, challenges to our character, and times when we feel our light is weakened. These are points when we need to do something that will help us "get up" and "make our lights rise."

Life as a Journey

Our life journey is reflected in the journey from Egypt to the Promised Land. At first, the journey towards the Promised Land seems to be progressing nicely, when suddenly, it veers off track. Until about the mid-point of this week's Torah reading, the trajectory is clear. First comes the Book of Shemos, which speaks all about the Exodus from Egypt and the receiving of the Torah, then following the Exodus from Egypt is the Book of Vayikra, the laws and customs of the *Kohanim* / Priests and *Levi'im* / Levites who serve in the *Mishkan* / Temporary Temple in the desert, and then comes the Book of *Bamidbar* / Numbers, where everyone is counted, a formation of the positioning of movement is put in order, and they are moving along nicely towards the Promised Land.

This progression continues until this week's Torah reading tells us, "Whenever the ark set out, Moshe would say, 'Arise,

Hashem, may Your enemies be scattered'" (10:35). Moshe
promises that they will find peace in this journey, and then, a
very short time later it says, "The people were looking to complain…" (11:1), and so begins a drama of one complaint after
the next. Things start unraveling, arguments ensue, politics and
war, rebellions and strife abound (the rebellion of Korach, the
misguided spy mission, and so forth), and instead of moving
quickly into the Promised Land, they get stuck in the Desert
for 40 years. Yet, in all this time of hardship, they are continuously moving forward towards their destination.

The Torah comprises five books (See, for example, *Megilah*,
15a–15b. *Nedarim*, 22a. *Sanhedrin*, 44a). As such, the Torah is called
the Chumash, from the word *Chameish* / five. These five books
were 'meant' to describe our journey from the Creation of the
world to our 'destination' and fulfillment in the Promised Land:

Bereishis: Creation

Shemos: Redemption

Vayikra: Living With the Revelation of Divine Law

Bamidbar: Travels Through the Desert

Devarim: Arriving at our Destination*

---

* Another way of putting it, in terms of our relationship with Hashem, is as
follows:

Bereishis explores the relationship between the Creator and Creation.

Shemos is about the relationship between Hashem and us, His people. (In
Shemos, Hashem chooses us as a people and takes us out of Egypt).

Yet, the reality of life is that things don't always go completely smoothly, and there are sometimes stumbling blocks
along the way. We get sidetracked, we lose our way occasionally, and we fall. In a sense, the 'five' books of the Torah no longer
bring us directly to our ultimate destination, so to speak; we
have a need for the paradigm where, in case we fall, we can 're-
kindle' ourselves, get up, and keep moving. Therefore, our sages
teach (*Shabbos*, 116a) that while there are five official books, the
Torah is actually divided into seven parts — seven 'books', as
it were. This is because the Book of *Bamidbar* / "In the Desert"
has three parts.

In the middle of the Book of Bamidbar, there is a distinct
section composed of two verses (10:25–26): *Vayehi BiN'soa
HaAron...* / "When the Ark would travel, Moshe would say:
'Arise, Hashem, May Your enemies be scattered, and may those
who oppose You flee before Your Face!' And when it would
stop, he would say: 'Return, Hashem, You who are Israel's myriad of myriads!'"

Vayikra is about the relationship between Hashem and His servants (the
Kohanim / priests, and indeed all of Klal Yisrael as a priestly nation).

Bamidbar is about the relationship between Hashem as a King and us, his
legions (hence, the census, formations, and encampment).

Devarim is about the relationship between Hashem as a Teacher and us,
His Students. (The idea of the "repetition" of Torah is to secure our knowledge as students, for example of the Mitzvos of writing the Torah, or reading the Torah at Hakhel.)

This short section forms a separation between the first part of Bamidbar, in which we are counted and encamped, ready to 'travel' directly to the Promised Land, and the second half of Bamidbar, in which we experience many spiritual "falls" into rebellion, contention, complaint, and the darkness of unbelief. Because of this, our travel is no longer smooth and direct; what would have been a short process of reaching the Promised Land becomes 40 years of wandering in the Desert, a place of challenges and struggles. Therefore, including the interlude of two verses, the Book of Bamidbar encompasses three distinct 'books' with three distinct themes.

In this way, there are seven books of the Torah, with seven themes and stages of our overall journey. 'Books' five and six are added to address our 'falls': 1) Creation, 2) Redemption, 3) Living with Revelation, 4) Travels in the Desert, 5) Empowerment to Face Setbacks, 6) Re-Alignment, and 7) Destination.

These seven books and themes also correspond to the seven Midos:

1. Bereishis	Creation	*Chesed* / Kindness: *Olam Chesed Yibaneh* / "The world is founded on Chesed"; Hashem created and actively sustained the world with Chesed for the first 26 generations (הגדולה, זו מעשה בראשית: *Berachos,* 58a).
2. Shemos	Redemption	*Gevurah* / Power: going out of Egypt with a *Yad Chazakah* / powerful Hand, and then hearing the Torah *MiPi HaGevurah* / from the Mouth of the All Powerful One (והגבורה, זו יציאת מצרים: *Ibid*).

3. Vayikra	Living with Revelation	*Tiferes* / Unifying the People through the Torah, such as implementing the laws of the Levi'im (והתפארת, זו מתן תורה: *Ibid*).
4. 'Bamidbar A'	Travels in the Desert	*Netzach* / Perseverance: setting out making battle formations and counting the soldiers.
5. 'Bamidbar B', *Vayehi BiN'soa*	Empowerment to Face Setbacks	*Hod* / Humility (in having fallen or experienced setbacks) and gratitude (for Hashem's active protection from inner "enemies," empowering us to get up and rekindle our inner lights).
6. 'Bamidbar C'	Realignment	*Yesod* / Alignment: re-focusing ourselves on the Divine Will.
7. Devarim	Destination	*Malchus* / Sovereignty: preparing to initiate the Kingdom of Israel in the Promised Land. Malchus has nothing of its own, and Devarim is the *Mishneh Torah* / the Repetition of Torah (in this sense, it is not a 'book' of its own). In Moshe's farewell speech, he reviews our entire journey.

'Book' five is this mysterious section of two verses, composed of just 85 letters. This passage is bookended by two outward-facing letter Nuns ( ] … [ ), and as some sources write, these actually indicate parentheses indicating that the passage is 'out of place' (*Maharam Shif*, Shabbos, 115b: ואפשר שכן דרך לעשותו כחצי עיגול כזה): (והוא שאין זה מקומו). The question is, if the Nuns are indeed acting as parentheses, why are they outward-facing or turned 'backwards' away from their contents?

One answer is that this short fifth book is a 'hidden book'; it is not fully revealed. Only two verses of it were revealed (*Medrash Rabbah* (Buber), Mishlei, 24, p. 100. *Sefer HaMefuar*, Rebbe Shelomo Malcho, Beha'alosecha. *Kisei Rachamim* (Chida), Meseches Sofrim, 10:1). And this is because it is a book of 'our own rekindling', the 'book' of our own getting up after we have fallen. It is up to each of us to reveal this book and write it in full. We have been writing this story collectively as a people since the Torah of Moshe was completed, and each one of us has been telling it since our first conscious setback or fall from *Emunah* / faith. This hidden book tells both our personal story and our collective story in the world of exile between the backward letter Nuns. This story will one day, G-d willing, be revealed to be part of the Torah. This book will only be fully revealed and completed in the future, in the Days of Moshiach.

We might not always see how our own story 'fits in' to the greater story of Klal Yisrael in the Torah; how it is part of the glorious revelation of holiness, miracles, and progression toward the Destination of all of history. We might see our story, and particularly our personal setbacks, as 'out of place', inserted between two outward-facing parentheses, not part of the flow of Torah. However, our task is to take practical steps to get up again and to raise up the 'lamps' of our Midos. When we do so, our outward-facing Nuns will turn back toward the center, toward the "face of the Menorah", as it were. Then we will live our lives *Nochach P'nei Hashem* / facing the Face of Hashem, and all energies which attempt to oppose the Divine Light will "flee from before Your Face" (10:35). Then, Hashem will "return the myriad myriads of Israel" (10:36) and the two Nuns will mystically merge in unity forming a final Mem (ם).

When the Prophet Yeshayah / Isaiah speaks of Moshiach, a final Mem appears surprisingly in the middle of a word: לםרבה

המשרה ולשלום אין־קץ / "In token of abundant authority and of peace without limit" (*Yeshayah*, 9:6). This outstanding letter indicates that when the two outward facing Nuns of Klal Yisrael face each other and then unite as one, they will form the letter Mem, indicating the revelation of Moshiach.

Just like us, the Generation of the Desert sometimes lived 'between the parentheses'; sometimes struggling with Emunah, sometimes struggling with each other. Yet, for all the challenges, after their falls and misalignments, they empowered themselves, realigned, and reunited to complete their 40 (Mem) years in the Desert. The number 40 represents genuine transformation. Just as they transformed themselves and finally arrived at their intended destination, so may we. In fact, it is our destiny; we need only to act upon it.

BEHA'ALOSECHA

Energy of the Week:
Rejuvenating the Journey

The journey from Creation to Destination is a metaphor for our own journey through life. While our progression is constant, the way is not always clear. At times, we do not sense inspiration and a way forward, and yet, somehow, we must find a way to act and move forward. In order to reilluminate our lamp, for inspiration to take hold again, we must hold a flame to the wick for some time until it rises on its own.

We must start with some form of forward movement, some deed, no matter how small and insignificant it may feel. This action will become inspiration, and when lit, it will lead to greater light. Even the smallest step forward can get us back on track and heading in the right direction towards our destination.

All true transformation occurs in increments and with setbacks along the way. This week's Torah reading imbues us with the Ko'ach to take small steps forward toward where we need to be in life. That small step will lead to inspiration, which will lead to further steps, which will eventually take us to our transformation.

This week, set your sights on your destination and decide on one baby step that you can take in the right direction. This doesn't need to be some big life-changing act — just a small, mindful movement. When you do this, feel the inspiration take hold and propel you forward. If you seem to fail or fall, you can always return again, relight your lamp, and realign yourself to the Divine Will.

This is the secret of the hidden two-verse book of the Torah. When we fall, there is 'nothing' memorable to record, very little to be written about. Yet, we always have the ability to get up again and take new steps. This is our own story, the Torah's chapter about us.

And we ourselves are writing this story into the Torah; how we are getting up again and making small steps in a beneficial direction, how this is tipping the scales for the good of all the myriad of myriads of Israel, and actively moving all of history in the direction of redemption.

PRACTICE OF THE WEEK:

Get Back Up Again & Again

Shelach

Positive Vision

T HIS WEEK, MOSHE SENDS TWELVE SCOUTS, THE
leaders of the *Shevatim* / tribes, from their encampments in the desert to go observe the current status of
the Holy Land, Eretz Yisrael.

The Torah reading begins with the words, "Hashem spoke
to Moshe saying: Send out men… ויתרו / *VeYasuru* / and they
shall scout out the Land…which I am giving…" (13:1–2). "…
See what the Land is like" (13:18).

Their task was to *see* the Land, to observe with their own
eyes the type of land they were about to enter. They had been
promised that it was a land of milk and honey, yet their task
was to see this truth, not only to believe it, but to see it with
their own eyes. A common misconception is that these noble princes of the Tribes were told to be *Meraglim* / 'spies'.
Looking at the verse carefully, we can see that originally they

were not called 'Meraglim'. Nor were they sent in order to 'spy' out and discern whether or not the Land was conquerable, nor to find the best way to conquer it. These are the two reasons to send 'spies' into enemy territory. Rather, they were merely asked to go and observe the Land.

מרגל / *Meragel* / 'spy' is related to the word רגל / *Regel* / 'foot', representing a spy entering territory on foot to ensure that soldiers can successfully follow. However, the princes were sent to לתור / *Lasur* / to see the Land with their 'eyes'.

On a deeper level, Moshe sends them not only to see for themselves how good the Land is but to effect, through their seeing, a positive elevation of the Land. In this way, these 12 leaders of the entire community — who were spiritually 'impregnated' with the souls of the 12 children of Ya'akov (The leader of each *Sheivet* / tribe became impregnated with the soul of their ancestor. For example, the leader of the tribe of Shimon became impregnated with the soul of Shimon. Yehoshua became impregnated with the soul of Levi, via Moshe) — would 'acquire' the Land, and it would become theirs and transformed into the home of all the 12 Shevatim (including Levi, who was not given a specific area to settle in).

How We See

The ancient philosophers and sages debate how we see things. There are two major theories: 1) in order to see something, the light from the object comes toward us, and we receive it, or 2) our eyes emit a 'light' of vision, which goes out to meet objects. In other words, the question is whether the trajectory of sight is from the object to the subject or from the subject to the object (*Shevilei Emunah, Nesiv* 4, p. 154. *Sha'ar HaShamayim,* Ma'amar 9, p. 53. *Sefer HaBris,* 1, Ma'amar 17:3. *Komtez HaMinchah,* 2).

Today, empirical scientific evidence agrees that images of sense-objects are 'received' in your brain. As you look at the words on this page, for example, rays of light pass from the page to your eyes, and these register as an inverted image of the page in your retina. Light-sensitive cells then cause impulses to pass through your optic nerve, leading to complex electro-chemical patterns in your brain, which you finally interpret as a page with words on it turned right-side-up. This is a one-way path, from the object to the subject.

One thing still remains a mystery in this process, however. Why do we see the image of the page in front of us 'outside' of us, when the image is actually appearing 'within' us, within our brain? Perhaps it would be more accurate to say, 'I am seeing a page in my mind,' rather than 'I am seeing a page two feet away from my face.' Only our projection of the image outward onto an assumed 'outside' world makes objects appear outside of ourselves.

Therefore, in a sense, while light is received by our eyes and nervous system, we can also argue that we project or 'emit' the light of vision outward. Our minds extend to the outside world, so-to-speak (*Likutei Moharan,* 1:76. *Bnei Yissaschar,* Kislev, Ma'amar 4. *Sheim MiShmuel,* Lech L'cha).

Taking this idea further, we enter the realm of basic quantum theory, in which the observer is understood to affect the observed. Biologists and theorists discuss another mystery: some people can, it seems, sense when an unseen person is staring at them. Here, not only does a seer affect the seen, but a 'seer' 'out there' can seem to affect us 'in here'. This is the power of sight.

According to the deep teachings of Torah, the way we see affects the things we are viewing. The viewer affects what is being seen (*Ramban*, Vayikra, 18:19. *Shevilei Emunah, Nesiv haShelishi. Tzeida laDerech*, 2, 1:2. *Nishmas Chayim*, 3:4. *Kav haYashar*, 2). For example, someone with pure intention creates a positive energy when looking at something, and the opposite holds true as well. Our vision emits subtle vibrations into the universe and towards the object or person we are viewing (*Agrah dePerkah*, 160. *Agrah d'Kalah*, Shemos). Looking at something with good intentions and goodwill emanates actual goodness and blessing to that object (*Ben Yehoyada*, Shabbos, 152a. *Zohar* 2, 217b). We impact what we observe (*Magen Avos* [Tashbatz], Avos, 2:16. Arizal, *Sefer HaLikutim*, Parshas Kedoshim).

Coming back to the twelve scouts and the story's unfortunate ending, we find that ten of the twelve failed in their mission. They returned with a negative report, "And there we saw the giants...and we were in our own eyes as grasshoppers, and so were we in their eyes" (13:33).

They had no real way of knowing how they were perceived in the eyes of the inhabitants (although see, *Sotah*, 35a), however, since in their own view they were unfit or not ready to enter the Holy Land, they assumed that the natives were 'giants' and they were mere 'grasshoppers'. They looked from a perspective of negativity and resistance, and therefore, they saw the Land as negative and impossible to enter and inhabit.

We don't see things the way they are. In fact, metaphorically, we see reality 'upside down' — we perceive things the way *we* are. If we are full of *Yesh* / 'existence' or ego, constriction, and materialism, we will see even something holy, such as Eretz Yisrael, as having those qualities. This is the deeper inner meaning of Moshe's question, *HaYesh Bo Eitz, Im Ayin?* / "Does the Land have trees or not?" He was also asking, are you seeing (the trees) from the perspective of Yesh or from the perspective of *Ayin* / selfless transparency?

Four Levels of Seeing: Four Steps in the Journey
There are four levels of consciousness, four perspectives from which one can see, and these are the levels Klal Yisrael needed to traverse in order to see Eretz Yisrael for what it really is, and themselves for who they really are:

1) 'Yesh of *Kelipah* / impurity' is the level of *Mitzrayim* / Biblical Egypt, with all its idolatry and tyranny. This is a complete constriction of vision into coarse physicality and egoism; the light of life is eclipsed by the 'shell' of Kelipah. It is a level of consciousness that creates great negativity; we must imme-

diately free ourselves from this perspective if we ever encounter it.

2) 'Ayin of *Kedushah* / holiness' is the level of the Desert, an "unsown," uninhabitable place. When Klal first broke out of their slavery to Mitzrayim (from the Yesh of Kelipah), they were suddenly lifted to a higher perspective detached from ego and constrictions, a place of holy *Ayin* / no-thing-ness. They saw Divine miracles and felt the Presence of Hashem's Infinite Light surrounding them. However, this state of enlightened seeing was too much to integrate and couldn't be sustained. We need to nurture our capacity to see from this transcendent perspective, but it is not healthy to attempt to live there.

3) 'Ayin of Kelipah' is the level of the spies. They were elevated people (coming from the holy 'Ayin' experience of the Desert) and merited to behold the Holy Land. However, they were entrapped in this state of Ayin and coveted an unhealthy attachment to the holy no-thingnesss of the Desert. Thus, as they scouted out the Land and saw its raw physicality, they were threatened and saw death, the Ayin of Kelipah, wherever they went (דכל היכא דמטו, מת חשיבא דידהו / "For wherever they went, the most important of them died": *Sotah*, 35a).

4) *Yesh Amiti* / 'True Existence' is the perspective of Yehoshua and Kalev, who saw what Eretz Yisrael truly is: a meeting of Heaven and earth, a unification of transcendence and physicality. This is viewing life from the standpoint of who we really are, a transcendent soul engaged in the material world without

being trapped in it. We can see the Divinity in mundane existence when we know ourselves as an embodiment of soul.

The ten scouts, who had become 'spies', had ulterior motives in the way they looked at the Land. They wished to remain spiritually sheltered in the Desert, detached from the world in holy Ayin, led by Moshe, who is Ayin (see above, Torah reading of Shemini), and therefore, they went in with a self-defeating preconception and attitude, which was mirrored back to them, and through them to the people.

In contrast, the two scouts, Yehoshua and Kalev, understood the inherent benefit of inhabiting the Land and appreciated the gift that it was. They were passionate about Eretz Yisrael and so, even though the Land they observed was the same as the other scouts had seen, what they saw was completely different. The message they came back with was, "We should go up and take possession of the Land, for we can certainly do it" (13:30). They saw the Yesh Amiti, the reality of the Land. They had correct vision.

This way of seeing created a reality in which they were indeed able to conquer it, with Hashem's help. In fact, it was Yehoshua, the one who saw and described the Land in a positive light, who was empowered to finally lead the nation into Eretz Yisrael and conquer the Land.

SHELACH

Energy of the Week:
Positive Vision

This week's Torah reading imbues us with the ability to see correctly and positively. Beyond choosing what we see, we can choose *how* to see the things we see, as well. If we understand that the object or person we are seeing is a reflection of who we are right now, and how we are choosing to perceive; if we know that external appearances are reflections of our internal state, we can then look at things in a way that is positive and uplifting.

When we find ourselves immediately judging an experience as negative, we need to go back to ourselves, where the 'light' is being absorbed from the outside, and change the refraction so that we can view it accurately. If we can look for, or imagine, what is wonderful or favorable in that experience, we can see it that way — and it can certainly become that way for us.

We must be especially careful how we view people, and interpret their words and mannerisms, since our 'seeing' affects not only us but them as well. When we view someone in a positive light, we create positive energy, which changes not only the nature of that person in our experience but also in their experience and view of themselves.

PRACTICE OF THE WEEK:

Choose How You Look at Life

Korach
Genuine Peace

T HE TORAH READING THIS WEEK BEGINS WITH a rebellion against the leadership of Moshe and his brother Aharon. Moshe is the leader of the people, and Aharon is the *Kohen Gadol* / High Priest.

The Torah reading opens with the words, "Korach... together with 250 men, chieftains of the congregation...assembled against Moshe and Aharon...and said, ...The entire congregation are all holy...so why do you raise yourselves above the assembly?" (16:1–3)

It seems this argument makes perfect sense. If the entire congregation is holy, why then would we need to appoint one leader and one High Priest? Why should one person be singled out for distinction? When the Torah says, "You will be to me ממלכת כהנים / a kingdom of priests" (*Shemos*, 19:16), this means that potentially each and every one of us is a Kohen and, in fact, a Kohen Gadol (the Baal HaTurim writes, אלו זכו ישראל היו כולם כהנים גדולים ולע"ל תחזור להם / "If we were meritorious we would have all been High Priests, and indeed, in the future this spiritual status will return to all of us"). Why must Aharon be the one and only Kohen Gadol?

On the surface, Korach is a Levi, not a Kohen, and that is not enough for him; he wants to be a Kohen as well. On a deeper reading, what Korach desires is to manifest a transcendent reality on earth, one that is beyond plurality and distinctions, in which sameness rules. He wants himself, and everyone else as well, to be Kohanim.

In the Mishkan, and later in the Beis HaMikdash, the service of the Kohen was performed in silence, whereas the service of the Levi was performed with a lot of noise. The Levi'im were the singers and musicians who enhanced the ambiance of the Mishkan and Beis HaMikdash. The Kohen's silence represents a transcendence of the world of separation and plurality, and immersion in a world of unity. The Levi represents the hustle and bustle of this world, the cacophony of self-expression and individuality. The Kohen represents the transcendence of this world, while the Levi represents the embodiment — and herein lies the deeper basis of the conflict and contradiction in Korach's assertion.

Korach wanted everyone to serve from a paradigm of 'silence', beyond the world, beyond individuality.

Even though he is a Levi, Korach does belong in some way to the world of silence, a world where everyone is indeed equal, as everyone is the same in silence. In this sense, Korach was connected to the world of the Kohen. The name קרח / *Korach*, in numerical value, is 308 — the same as the word חש / *Chash* / silence. Furthermore, the name *Korach* literally means 'bald'. Hair is an expression of individuality; each blade of hair grows from its own unique follicle, and no two hairs grow from the same place. "I have created many hairs in a man's head, and for every hair, I have created a separate follicle" (*Nidah*, 52b. See also Shaloh, *Sha'ar HaOsyos*, Os Kuf, Kedusha 2. The Zohar views every strand of hair as harboring entire universes: *Zohar* 3, Parshas Naso, Idra Rabbah 129a. Every strand of hair is a distinct conduit of energy and is shaped as a letter Vav: *Sha'ar HaMitzvos*, Parshas Kedoshim). The absence of hair thus represents a lack of distinction and individuality. Indeed, the Kohanim would cut their hair frequently (*Ta'anis*, 17).

In that sense, Korach's instinctual draw to serve as a Kohen had validity. And his intention, at its core, may have been noble — 'Let us all be the same; let all of Klal Yisrael live as equals in the world of silence and sameness.' However, he was missing a fundamental understanding of the workings of the world.

The Zohar, on this week's Torah reading, explains that Shabbos, the sacred day of rest and internal focus, is the quintessential definition of *Shalom* / peace, wholeness, and harmony

(*Zohar*, 3:176b). Yet, Shabbos is separated from the weekdays; it is not the 'same' as the other days. It is precisely the separateness of Shabbos that makes it special. The six days of work and the Seventh Day, which is *Kodesh* / 'set aside from the others', need each other. There is no rest without some form of work, and there is no elevation of work without Shabbos rest. The weekdays and Shabbos make each other 'whole'.

Real Shalom is found in wholeness and harmony, not in *sameness*. A harmonic symphony has many individual notes and voices, many different movements and dynamics, and yet all these distinct elements 'work toward a common goal.' Shalom is defined as 'the unification of opposites'. Yet, even when united as a whole, the opposites are still called 'opposites'.

Shalom includes the elimination of hostile conflict but not the elimination of individuality and uniqueness. To create harmony, a family, community, or society must find shared common interests and goals but not eliminate individuality in the process. True equality requires the recognition and even celebration of individuality.

In response to Korach's rebellion, Moshe replies, *Boker VeYoda Hashem* / "In the morning Hashem will make known who is...." Moshe is telling Korach, 'At night it seems as though all are the same because in the dark we do not see differences, however, come morning, you will see that each of us are individuals and unique. Though we are all holy, we are not all the same. Each of us has our own unique qualities that we need to contribute to ourselves and the world around us. You have a role as a Levi, and Aharon has a role as the Kohen — and these different roles need to be united *in harmony.*'

Moshe is also hinting to Korach that just as Hashem made night different from day, Hashem made people with different gifts and roles. No two people are the same. Each of us is here to fulfill our own personal *Tikun /* soul perfection, and to make our own unique contribution to our family, community, and society.

Furthermore, each of us has divergent 'sub-personalities' and character traits to harmonize within ourselves. Korach was mistaken that he could simply suppress or delete his traits of Levite individualism in favor of the silence of his inner 'Kohen'. His very act of standing apart as an individual to try and enforce anti-individualism proved that he was suffering from an inner conflict. In our own lives as well, we all need to harmonize our inner opposites so that we can have balance and Shalom within, and radiate this wholeness out to others.

KORACH

Energy of the Week:
Eliminating Conflict

This week's Torah reading imbues us with the ability to reach genuine Shalom, to coexist peacefully, inside ourselves and outside, without eliminating our individuality.

When we are in harmony with others, we can celebrate our own uniqueness. We can recognize another person's point of view and let them see ours without descending into conflict. The fact that "no two people have the same opinion" is not necessarily a source of conflict, but rather a source of greater clarity through open discussion and learning.

Ultimately, the differences between all individuals will come together to form a multi-faceted, harmonic symphony of peace, as the prophet says, "All peoples (plural)... will render Divine service with one accord" (*Tzefaniah*, 3:9).

PRACTICE OF THE WEEK:
Reach Out to Others in Peace

Chukas
Life Renewed

IN THIS WEEK'S TORAH READING, THE SISTER AND brother of Moshe, Miriam and Aharon, pass on. The Torah then speaks of the *Tumah* / impurity of death, and the *Parah Adumah* / Red Heifer, the ritual purification for those who have come in contact with death.

"Hashem spoke to Moshe...: Take a perfectly red, unblemished heifer...slaughter it...The heifer shall then be burned... Anyone who touches a human corpse shall become impure... Take for that impure person ashes of the burnt offering (the red heifer), and (they) shall be placed in a vessel with spring water...Take the hyssop and dip it into the water and sprinkle it on him..." (19:1–18).

This, in short, is the ritual of purifying a person who has become impure through contact with a corpse. Sprinkling a solution of the red heifer ashes and spring water on specific days was followed by immersion in a *Mikvah* / ritual pool of water. *Taharah* / 'purity' and *Tumah* / 'impurity' are unrelated to personal hygiene or disease. As previously explored, the term

Tumah relates to 'death' and mortality, both literal and figurative. And *Taharah* is connected with 'life', both literal and figurative. The aliveness of purity is the quality of phenomena such as *Beis Chayeinu* / the House of our Life (the Beis Ha-Mikdash) and *Mayim Chayim* / 'living waters' or natural spring water.

Life is movement and possibility. Death is an 'end' and is subtly present in states of stagnation. In physical death, life ceases, and on a mental and emotional level, hope, progress, movement, and possibility can cease, stagnate, and thus become 'impure'. 'Impurity' can also imply a state of hopelessness or despair, an emotional or mental state of 'death'. 'Purity' is emotional or mental fluidity and newness, and all that stems from a place of possibility and hope.

The Beis HaMikdash as a Place of Renewal and Aliveness
The Beis HaMikdash functioned as a place of *Hischadshus* / renewal, where one could be filled with a sense of awe in Creation and the Creator. To enter the Beis HaMikdash, one had to be ritually pure, alive, and open to new possibilities.

Every moment is, in truth, brand new, a *Yesh* / existence freshly born out of *Ayin* / pure potential. With each inhale, we receive a new Divine breath of life, and we are re-created anew. The Beis HaMikdash, being the epicenter of all space (ושתיה היתה נקראת. תנא: שממנה הושתת העולם. *Yuma*, 54b), is the place in which this spirit of renewal was most tangibly realized. As a demonstration, the *Lechem HaPanim* / 'showbread' in the Beis HaMikdash never grew stale, and it tasted completely fresh even if baked a week before (*Chagigah*, 26b).

The Beis HaMikdash was built upon the site on which Ya'akov once slept and dreamed of the ladder and angels (*Bereishis*, 28:12–18). When he awoke from this dream, he proclaimed, "Surely Hashem is in this place, and I knew it not." If Ya'akov had been aware of the holiness and purity of the place on which he stood, he would not have been able to sleep. Sleep is a minor form of death. Ya'akov was troubled that he had not tapped into the spirit of renewal in that place and was able to enter the subtle paradigm of death.

Parts of the Mystery of the Red Heifer Decoded

Though the ultimate mystery and paradoxical nature of the *Parah Adumah* / Red Heifer is beyond our comprehension (*Medrash Rabbah*, Bamidbar, 19:3), and the way it purifies a person from impurity is super-rational, yet, the specific symbolism is pronounced and some meaning can be gleaned from it.

As a response to the Tumah of death, one needs to 'slaughter and burn the Parah Adumah', the red heifer. Red is the color of *Gevurah* / separation and restriction (*Pardes Rimonim*, Sha'ar 10: 1), which is also the paradigm of death. When something is reduced to ashes, this means that its *Tzurah* / form — in this case, a living cow — has been completely nullified, and now, the original Tzurah is absent. In this way, ashes are the most stark representation of death. The burnt cow makes us confront the very depth of the abyss of Tumah and hopelessness. (*Parah*

/ פרה / cow is the embodiment of the פר /*Par* / 280 fallen sparks, that are created by the 5/ה final letters, the letters that restrict the flow of words and revelation. The final Mem/40, final Nun/50, final Tzadik/90, final Pei/80, final Chof/20 =280. Thus פרה / Parah is פר/ Par that comes from the ה/ Hei.) Yet, precisely at rock bottom, when everything is 'ashes', we mix in *Mayim Chayim* / living waters.

The ashes and water are mixed together and sprinkled upon the person who was defiled. When ashes and water mix, it creates a form of soap, a cleansing of sorts, but there is something deeper occurring. Water is alive, pure, and fresh. Water embodies the primordial fluidity of Creation, as in the beginning when the waters covered the earth. This is when all of Creation still existed in the cosmic 'womb' as pure potential. Ashes represent the extreme opposite: ending, destruction, death, and negativity. By mixing a measure of living waters into the ashes, the ashes begin to be rejuvenated and come to life. They now become like soil in which something new can grow.

Soil, dust, or earth is called עפר / *Afar*, which is nearly identical to אפר / *Eifer* / ash. Whereas Afar gives birth to new life, new *Yesh*, Eifer is existential *Ayin* / no-thingness.

Eifer was once a 'something', but now it 'has no future'; nothing can grow from ashes. Afar may have never been a 'something'; however, it always has the potential to grow new things, and thus, it has a future. And yet, through the mixing of living waters with the Eifer, it becomes Afar — ash becomes soil. As such, the ashes of the burnt heifer are at first called אפר

הפרה / "ashes of the cow" (19:9), yet a few verses later, the Torah calls them עפר / earth (19:17. וכי עפר הוא והלא אפר הוא אפר הוא שינה הכתוב ממשמעו לדון הימנו גזירה שוה / "But is it Afar that is taken? Isn't it really ashes (Eifer)? The verse altered its standard usage and referred to Eifer as *Afar* in order to derive a verbal analogy from it": *Temurah*, 12b. מצינו אפר שקרוי עפר / "We find in the Torah that Eifer is called Afar": *Sotah*, 16a. On a deeper level, from *Parah* / פרה , the פר / *Par* / 208 and Hei, it becomes אפר / *Eifer* / ash, פר with an א / Aleph, i.e. the *Aleph* / 'One' in the Par becomes revealed, and thus it eventually becomes עפר / *Afar* / earth, פר with a letter עין / Ayin / eye, 'looking to the future', and the possibility of new life).

Afar is also a type of אין / 'Ayin'; not an 'existential no-thing-ness', but rather the 'formless pure potential' of all forms. Afar contains the potential of all vegetation, and indeed all life-forms: הכל היה מן העפר / "Everything comes from *Afar*" (*Koheles*, 3:20). Say Chazal, אפלו גלגל חמה / "Even the orbit of the sun!" (*Medrash Rabbah*, Bereishis, 12:11)

With the mixing in of a small amount of life-giving water, hope is born. A new reality can sprout from the earth even when it still appears 'asleep' or lifeless. The living water moistens the sense of dryness, emptiness, or 'impurity' of someone who has been disturbed by death; it irrigates and invigorates their consciousness with new life and potential. Like dew in the desert, it creates for them a tangible sense of *Techiyas Ha-Meisim* / 'revival of the dead'.

With all this symbolism, ritual, and spiritual perception, though, it is imperative that we remember the words of our sages: "The corpse itself does not defile, nor does the water itself purify; rather, it is the Mitzvah of the Holy One (that purifies)" (לא המת מטמא ולא המים מטהרים אלא גזירתו של הקב"ה הוא : *P'sikta D'Rav Kehana*, 4:7). Ultimately, purity comes from our connection to HaKadosh Baruch Hu, the Living Presence and the Ultimate Source of All Life — the One "Who brings death to the living and brings the dead to life." It is the *Mitzvah* / 'Divine connection' that revives us, gives us new hope, purity, and a fresh breath of life.

CHUKAS

Energy of the Week:
Life Renewed

To live in this world is to be touched continuously by both life and death. All people experience some form of death within their lifetimes; unfortunately, one may witness tragedy and heartbreak. Sometimes, there are more subtle, symbolic deaths, such as the unexpected ending of a relationship or job. On either extreme, contact with 'death' can bring feelings of hopelessness, a sense of being cut off from life and movement.

The Ko'ach of this week's Torah reading initiates us into openness and newness, helping us to confront and transform any sense of despair or stagnancy. Just as ashes return to the earth and begin a life cycle anew, the metaphorical ashes of the red heifer will mix with glistening drops of the waters of aliveness, gently beckoning us to come out of our identification with death, and return us to a world of life and hope.

We must first literally immerse in a 'Mikvah', figuratively 'gathering' our entire self into a state of stillness and pure potential, and reconnecting there with the Unity of Hashem, the Source of both life and death. Surfacing from this immersion in Oneness, we can be reborn, find our innate breath, and climb back into the world of movement.

This week, become aware of how a death, real or symbolic, may be holding you back from living fully. When a loved one dies, it can seem as if part of us passes on. It is important to stay still for a time, 'sit in ashes' and mourn. When Miriam and Aharon passed, it was very difficult for the whole community, and everything stopped. And then, gradually, it becomes time to return and stand up, our feet planted firmly on the earth. After a while, we need to check ourselves and see if we are holding on to a perception or way of being that prevents us from fully coming back to life, growth, and living forward.

Let the dew of life touch you when it comes; let it open you to new ideas and new ways of approaching your old ideas. Let your heart open and carry you into relationship, work, hope, and humble joy.

PRACTICE OF THE WEEK:
Allow Yourself to Become Fully Alive

Balak

Transforming Doubt into Wonder

"Balak...saw all that Israel had done...He sent messengers to Bilam... 'Please come and curse this people for me'" (22:2-6).

BALAK IS THE KING OF MOAV, AND HE SUMMONS the prophet Bilam to curse Klal Yisrael / the People of Israel. The Zohar teaches that "Never were two sorcerers greater than Balak and Bilam. Bilam's power was in his mouth and eyes, while Balak's power was in the actions of his hands. Each needed the other for in order to implement a curse, both speech and action are needed."

Who are these two people, and what is this tremendously negative quality that they embody? Clues to their particular brand of diabolical evil can be understood by their names, and the way those names relate to the archenemy of Klal Yisrael, עמלק / Amalek.

The names Bilam, Balak, and Amalek are all phonetically interconnected:

Bilam / בלעם is spelled ב/Beis, ל/Lamed, ע/Ayin, מ/Mem.

Balak / בלק is spelled ב/Beis, ל/Lamed, ק/Kuf.

Amalek / עמלק is spelled ע/Ayin, מ/Mem, ל/Lamed, ק/Kuf.

Notice that the first two letters of the name Bilam and Balak are the same: ב / Beis and ל / Lamed. The last two letters of Balak and Amalek are also the same: ל / Lamed and ק / Kuf.

In addition, the last two letters of the name Bilam (ע/Ayin, מ/Mem) and the last letters of the name Balak (ל/Lamed, ק/Kuf) together spell 'Amalek': ע/Ayin, מ/Mem, ל/Lamed, ק/Kuf:

בלעם

בלק

עמלק

The remaining first two letters of the name Bilam and the name Balak form the word בלבל / *Balbel* — which translates as mixed up, confused and in chaos:

בלעם

בלק

Amalek was the first of the nations that Klal Yisrael contended with in their journey through the desert. Until Amalek attacked Klal Yisrael, they were considered by the nations to be untouchable and miraculously protected. Klal Yisrael's response changed this image of Amalek, casting doubt on their image of invincibility. As such, Amalek came to be associated with the quality of doubt. It is no coincidence that 'Amalek' and the Hebrew word for doubt, *Safek* / ספק, have the same numerical value: 240.

The deepest, most devastating form of *Kelipah* / concealment is doubt. It is a hindrance to all forms of spiritual, intellectual, and psychological life and growth. Doubt leads to chaos and a stagnation of all types of movement. Doubt says, 'You are not capable, it is impossible, it's never going to work'.

When a person suffers from doubt, whether self-doubt, doubting others, or doubting that there is an alternative to the predicament in which they find themselves, they stop moving forward. Doubt cripples through pessimism and cynicism.

Balak and Bilam wield power through their ability to cause doubt and *Bilbul* / confusion and chaos. They were trying to create uncertainty among us regarding our deserving to be a nation that is blessed.

Ayin HaRa / Negative Eye

This is the idea of *Ayin HaRa* / negative eye. Someone looks at your life with jealousy and thinks, 'They do not deserve their life.' This is the projection of the evil eye from the projector to the receiver. And then, if a person does not feel protected, they 'receive' that energy that is projected towards them, within themselves, and they begin to feel undeserving. Eventually, this receiving of negativity can cause actual negativity in one's life.

Indeed, the entire idea of "cursing" Klal Yisrael is to utilize the power of the *Ayin HaRa* / Evil Eye. Notably, Bilam does not have *Einayim Ra'os* / 'evil eyes' in the plural, but rather *Ayin* / 'eye' in the singular. A negative view and power of vision is associated with the left eye. Bilam is blind in one eye (*Sanhedrin*, 105a), and thus his only functional eye was his 'left eye' (*Avos*, 5:19. *Medrash Rabbah*, Bamidbar, 20:10), his Ayin HaRa. Indeed, wherever he looked, he looked with an Ayin haRa (*Zohar* 1, Noach, p. 68b), and this is expressed in the deeper meaning of his name. Bilam is similar to the word *Bal'am* / 'swallow', draw in or absorb (this is related to the name of the first of the eight kings of Edom or Tohu: Bela ben B'or, *Siach Yitzchak*, Likutim, 5). Whatever he looks at, he tries to swallow into negativity by projecting his own inner negativity on everything he sees.

In truth, the negativity of an 'evil eye' really only affects someone who 'swallows', accepts, and absorbs it. This is why, our sages say, Bilam desired to "contaminate" Klal Yisrael using the encouragement and support from the authority of the king Balak. In the words of the Medrash (Rashi, 24:2. *Tanchuma*, Balak, 6), בקש להכניס בהם עין רעה / "He wished to insert within them an Ayin HaRa." He wished to impose the Ayin HaRa upon them with a certain air of authority, but then it should enter *within* them — they should take it in and absorb it to the point that it becomes *their own* way of seeing themselves.

His intention was that Klal Yisrael should begin to doubt their self-worth, destiny, and special mission in this world. This is very similar to Amalek's mission of "cooling off" the spirit of Klal Yisrael, influencing them to undermine their own strength and confidence.

Holy Doubt

Of course, doubt is not always unhealthy. While unhealthy doubt is debilitating, healthy doubt encourages questioning, growth, and progress. Holy, productive 'doubt' is the trusting innocence that opens a person to new possibilities.

Detrimental doubt is a kind of self-rejection, which causes a person to resign themselves and avoid taking risks in the face of uncertainty. This paralyzes a person. Accepting, internalizing, and cultivating a sense of ineptitude leaves one powerless, spawning the belief that no meaning or purpose can be found in one's actions. Nothing can be done, and there is nothing to do.

Crippling, detrimental doubt can, however, be transformed into positive, productive doubt. To do this, one must elevate their doubt to its root in *Keser* / Crown — a state of 'not-knowing' in which everything is possible. Knowing that we don't know everything, we can place our lives in the hands of the Omniscient One, the True King and Authority over the World. This liberates us and gives us a paradoxical stability upon which we can freely choose, make firm commitments, and flourish in this world that the Creator creates for us moment to moment.

When Bilam tried to use King Balak's authority to curse Klal Yisrael, only blessings emanated from his mouth. Due to the indelible essential connection of Klal Yisrael with the crown of the King of all Kings, the energy of crippling doubt was transformed into blessings.

BALAK

Energy of the Week:

Transforming Doubt Into Wonder

This week's Torah reading gives us the ability to connect with our inner certainty and trust. On a deeper level, it infuses us with the power to transform negative, crippling doubt and confusion into a healthy sense of innocence and openness. It will inspire us to live with wonder, open and ready to step into the next adventure Hashem has in store for us, with openness and hope.

If doubt is preventing you from growing or progressing, take the time to recognize this negative impact. This will motivate you to place yourself in the hands of the Creator, and gradually replace confusion with open-eyed, innocent wonderment, positivity and passion.

PRACTICE OF THE WEEK:

Wonderment

Pinchas

Healing Through Aligning Emotions

L AST WEEK, WE WERE TOLD OF BILAAM'S DIABOLI-
CAL plot to destroy Klal Yisrael through an 'evil eye', a
curse (utilizing the 'left side', the attribute of *Gevurah* / contraction). When he was unable to curse them, he then attempted
to entice them through 'love' (utilizing the 'right side', the attribute
of *Chesed* / expansion); he sent the women of Midian and Moav
to seduce Klal Yisrael into idolatry through illicit relations.
"While Yisrael was staying at Shittim, the people profaned
themselves by straying after the women of Moav." Sadly, this
plan worked, a devastating plague broke out among Klal Yisrael and thousands died.

Pinchas, a grandson of Aharon, took matters into his own hands and assassinated a tribal leader who was publicly engaging in intimacy with a Midianite princess. Following the radical action of Pinchas, the plague abruptly ended.

Our Parshah opens with the words, "Hashem spoke to Moshe...: 'Pinchas...the (grand)son of Aharon the *Kohen* / Priest has turned My anger away from the children of Israel... Therefore...I hereby give him My *Bris Shalom* / Covenant of Peace'" (25:10–12). 'Peace' is a power of harmony that creates a synthesis out of diverse elements. It does not necessarily create uniformity or 'sameness', rather an interinclusion of individuals within a greater context.

We might expect that the 'Shalom' came as an *antidote* to Pinchas' zealotry, however, it is described as an *effect* of his action. His violent action paradoxically revealed the blessing of peace — this means that his action was, in fact, an act of Shalom.

A plague had swept through the community due to an excess of *Chesed* / giving or 'love' without proper borders, discipline, or the protective empowerment of Torah law.

'Free love', unbridled by healthy boundaries and a sense of the 'holy otherness' of people, is a negative and destructive expression of *Chesed* / giving. It is paradoxically narcissistic and self-serving 'giving', capable of causing real or metaphorical destruction and plagues.

The zealous act of Pinchas represents *Gevurah* / power or severity, restriction, and strict judgment, beyond the letter of the law. Pinchas himself seems to embody this quality of Gevurah. He understood that the distorted Chesed and widespread licentiousness was not merely a manifestation of frivolity and laxity. He saw that it was indeed a 'spiritual plague', which, if allowed to go on, would ruin the very fabric of the *Kedushah* / sanctity of Klal Yisrael.

The numerical equivalent of the name פינחס / *Pinchas* is ר"ח 208 /, which is the same value as the name *Yitzchak*, the original and archetypal embodiment of Gevurah. Pinchas stepped forward to counter the extreme Chesed with an act of extreme Gevurah, and in an act unsanctioned by the courts, he took a spear and impaled the public offenders.

Yet the Pasuk refers to Pinchas as the grandson of Aharon, the *Kohen Gadol* / High Priest, who was the "lover and seeker of peace", the embodiment of Chesed: "When Pinchas, son of Eleazar son of Aharon the Priest, saw this, he left the assembly, taking a רמח / spear in his hand" (25:7).

רמח / spear has a numerical value of 248, the same value as אברהם / Avraham (*Nedarim*, 32b), the great archetypal embodiment of Chesed. In other words, as 208 / ר"ח / Gevurah, Pinchas takes hold of the רמח / spear, which is Chesed, the attribute of Avraham. In this way, Pinchas strikes a perfect balance between Gevurah / Yitzchak and Chesed / Avraham

370 | AWAKENINGS

(Aharon). This nullifies the extreme, distorted Chesed of the people, and the plague is stopped.

What is more, in deconstructing the name פינחס / *Pinchas*, we find two words: פן / *Pen* / 'turn towards' and חס / *Chas* / mercy, compassion (פן / *Pen*, Pei-Nun, are two of the five 'final letters' symbolizing Gevurah, thus *Pen* is Gevurah. *Chas* / compassion is Tiferes, a middle column Sefirah of balance between Chesed and Gevurah).

Through his act, Pinchas is actually functioning neither as Chesed, 'right column' nor Gevurah, 'left column', rather he is activating the attribute of *Yesod* / foundation, a middle column that unites the diametrically opposite postures, and that is why he is given the *Bris Shalom* / Covenant of Peace.

This Bris is clearly related to the *Bris Milah* / the Covenant of Circumcision, which is imprinted on the Yesod of the male body — the Sefirah of Yesod as manifests in the physical body. This is also the area of the body where the extreme misalignment of Klal Yisrael was manifesting.

Chesed and Gevurah are balanced and synergized through the middle column Sefiros. By funneling Gevurah and Chesed through the middle column of Yesod, Pinchas synergized them in a beneficial way, healing Klal Yisrael and saving thousands of lives. Indeed, any single emotion that is unchecked by another emotion leads to chaotic behavior, and providing a counterbalance to the emotion brings alignment, synergy, and order.

The two middle letters of פינחס / *Pinchas* are נח / Nun-Ches, spelling the word *Chein*, which is commonly translated as 'grace,' but is really more nuanced. Chein is the charm and charisma exuded by a person who is aligned with him- or herself. As such, children have abundant natural Chein; they are totally and always their full self (until they get older and, sadly, people start trying to put them in a box, often triggering alienation). A person who is centered and self-aligned radiates Chein. In contrast, living with internal polarization and conflict within oneself is expressed as a 'tangled' personality without any Chein (Thus the opposite of נח / 'serenity' is ח"נ, which stands for *Chatas Ne'urim* / 'sins of youth', i.e., misaligned and unproductive functioning, especially 'wasting seed', which is a symptom of inner misalignment and leads to even deeper inner misalignment).

Only alignment within oneself can create wholeness, healing, peace and Chein. Through his powerful inner alignment and rectified Yesod, Pinchas was able to create spiritual and physical healing for all of Klal Yisrael both for his time and for all generations.

PINCHAS

Energy of the Week:
Healing Through Alignment

This week's Torah reading brings healing on all levels of our being, and infuses us with Ko'ach to re-balance ourselves and strive towards the inner alignment of rectified Yesod. As a practice, we should see that our self-expression is in harmony with our physical, emotional and spiritual attributes, as well as aligned with the recipient of our self-expression. We should ensure that we give in a way that is healthy for the other and desired by the other, otherwise it is 'Chesed of Kelipah' / distorted, harmful 'kindness'. While not giving at all can be a negative form of *Gevurah* / withholding, we need to balance our Chesed with Gevurah, in order to give exactly what is needed, and what can be properly received by the other.

We should also take note this week of those people in our life whose presence is healing and full of Chein. Recognize that this is an effect of their internal alignment. Find ways to surround yourself with these people.

Also take note of those areas in your own life, both internal and external, which may be off balance, un-focused or mis-aligned. Realize how these currently 'unrectified' areas are creating tension and stress in your system, and perhaps even physical ailments or sickness, G-d forbid.

By correcting and re-aligning these various aspects of your body, mind and heart, you will feel health-ier, lighter and more easily self-expressive. You will find that focusing all of your energies and emotions through Yesod will extend even to physical health.

PRACTICE OF THE WEEK:

Give What Is Needed & What Can Be Received

Matos
Constructive Communication

Astounding as it may seem, spoken words have the power to change the nature of physical things that we speak about.

"Moshe spoke to the leaders...saying.... If a man makes a vow...or makes an oath to prohibit himself (from something otherwise permitted), he shall not violate his word, according to what has emerged from his lips, he shall do" (30:2–3).

This means that through a person's oath, through declaring that a certain permitted *Cheftza* / object is now forbidden for him to use or consume, that object actually becomes a forbidden object. In terms of *Halachah* / Torah law, the nature of the object itself is transformed; if it was a Kosher food, it is now unkosher for the one who made the oath (דתנא נדרים דמיתסר חפצא עליה / "Since it taught the case of vows, whereby an object becomes forbidden to one": *Nedarim*, 2b. The essence of a *Neder* / vow is its power of words to create reality without any other form of action. In the words of the Ran, דנדרים שאני, דחמירי, דאפי' בדבורא בעלמא חיילי, משא"כ בקדושין, שהן צריכין איזה מעשה כסף או שטר או ביאה: Ran, *Ibid*, 6b. This idea is rooted in the concept of a *Korban* / offering according to many Rishonim, such as the Rif, Rashbah, Ritva on the beginning of *Nedarim*, and on *Shavuos* 20a, the main idea of Neder is הדפסה כקרבן / bond like a *Korban* / offering. Although, the Rambam, Ramban, Ran, Tashbatz, for example, argue).

The meta-root of this power of words to transform objects, as it were, is rooted in the first *Luchos* / stone tablets in which the words of the *Aseres HaDibros* / Ten Commandments, the *D'var Hashem* / words of Hashem, were engraved. We recite in the Shabbos morning prayers, ושני לוחות אבנים הוריד בידו / "...The two stone Luchos brought down by his (Moshes') hand." As the *Megaleh Amukos* teaches, this means that Moshe brought the Luchos down into stone, and they were engraved into his hands, as it were' — the words became matter. (בידו / by his hand, literally means "into" his hand).

A human being is defined as a *Medaber* / speaker; we are unique in the world with our ability to communicate and create through spoken language. In this way, we mirror the Unique One, the Creator, Who creates the world through speech.

Human speech is a reflection of Divine Speech.

Creation comes into existence through Divine utterance, and is continually sustained by the Divine utterance (*Tanya, Sha'ar HaYichud,* 1). Prior to creation — before the appearance of space, time, and individual consciousness — there is no division or separation; there is only One. The process of creation begins with a subtle, spiritual radiance and movement within the Infinite One, which gives rise to a physical vibration of energy, which is eventually solidified into matter. Every moment, every place, and every living being is an 'out-picturing' of spiritual light and energetic vibrations.

The process of creation through speech includes four stages: 1) *Atzilus* / subtle differentiation within oneness, 2) *Beriah* / spiritual radiance, 3) *Yetzirah* / energetic and physical vibration, and 4) *Asiyah* / congealing as matter. There is no word for "thing" in Hebrew. Objects are called *Devarim* / words. "Things" are mere externalized manifestations of internal lights and vibrations.

Man below is a reflection of the Creator Above, fashioned in the Divine Image. As Divine speech creates reality, human speech 'qualifies' reality, interpreting it and calling it good or bad. How we language our thoughts is how we 'create' the world as we experience it. Things are, for us, what we call them.

Our speech contextualizes experience, and context is everything.

The most powerful form of creative speech is a vow or oath. A vow is binding, and as such, it creates a very real, and in a sense, 'absolute' or indelible manifestation.

Just as we have the power to create our reality with speech, we have an equivalent ability to destroy through speech. Occasionally, we may stumble and speak ill about others or ourselves. When this happens, we need to recalibrate and undo past negative words through speech. We need to nullify the detriment of our speech by replacing it with sincere, beneficial speech.

We ought to be mindful of how we use our words, whether in communication with others or in communication with our own self. When we desire to change our own life for the better, we should become aware of any inner negative self-talk and nullify it with positive self-talk. We ought to pay attention, especially to any inner monologues that assert that we are not able, not capable, etc. To undo inner negative talk, it can be helpful to repeat positive affirmations as we go through our day. The more we fill our minds with positive, life-affirming words, the emptier the mind becomes of all the inappropriate thoughts. Not only does this create a positive emotional state within us, but it even helps to reveal material blessings.

You may find that your inner voice is pushing you down with negative mental statements. For example, one might detect a subtle inner monologue saying, 'I am not a good person.' One should consciously 'nullify' and reverse such statements.

First, however, it is important to acknowledge, 'I have done such-and-such, which is not in alignment with who I really am.' But this should be followed by positive verbal affirmations such as, "I am essentially a good, sincere, righteous person," and "I have the inner resources to change the direction of my life and align my actions with who I really am." Begin to create a positive reality for yourself through positive speech. Look for the good and speak about it.

MATOS

Energy of the Week:
Constructive Communication

This week's Torah reading infuses us with the Ko'ach of constructive verbal communication, both with others and within ourselves. Whether there are words that you have spoken that need to be amended or words that should have been said and were held back, this is a week to rectify and beautify our speech.

This week's Torah reading will help us have the conversation that we need to have. We will have greater strength to apologize to or compliment others and heal or uplift them. Through an increase in honest and positive self-talk, we can build a better life for ourselves and for those around us.

PRACTICE OF THE WEEK:

Positive Verbal Affirmations

Masei
Short Trips in a Long Journey

"These are the Masei / journeys of the Children of Israel who left the land of Egypt.... They journeyed from... and camped in..." (33:1–5).

This reading completes the Book of Bamidbar, known in English as "Numbers." The literal translation of *Bamidbar* is 'In The Desert'. The Torah reading this week recaps the journeys that Klal Yisrael took, beginning with their Exodus from Egypt and continuing with their forty-year journey in the Desert.

In total, the Torah marks 42 journeys. Each of these 'journeys' includes both the movement of travel and the dwelling in a new encampment. Together, this movement and stillness create a 'journey'. The ultimate destination was the Promised Land, yet the forty-two journeys took them only to the threshold of the Land, not into the Land itself.

Later in this same Parshah, we learn about the 42 cities that were given to the *Levi'im* / Levites, since they did not "inherit" a portion in the Land like the other *Shevatim* / tribes did. The cities of the Levi'im also served as *Arei Miklat* / 'cities of refuge' for those fleeing retribution, seeking immunity, and in need of spiritual and psychological healing.

The 42 journeys of the Desert parallel the 42 cities of the Levi'im (*Kli Yakar*, 35:6). The forty-two cities offered shelter and a home for the wanderers in the Land, nomadic Levi'im, and others. The 42 encampments were places of shelter for the Desert wanderers during their turbulent journeys.

The Baal Shem Tov teaches that the 42 journeys also represent the many 'journeys' or phases through our own lives. Our personal journeys begin with a personal 'exodus from *Mitzrayim* / Egypt'. The etymological root of *Mitzrayim*, is *Metzar* / 'constriction'. In the actual land of Mitzrayim, we were slaves who became free. Internally, we were enslaved to our 'constricted' lower self, our 'Meitzar'. As a nation, before we were able to reach our full freedom from Mitzrayim and enter the Promised Land, we needed to make 42 journeys. As individuals, before we reach our full freedom from our lower self, we need to go through 42 stages of action, movement, and realization.

These 42 stages are also reflected in *Ana B'Ko'ach*, an ancient 42-word prayer that corresponds to the '42 Letter Name of Hashem' (*Kedushin*, 71a. Rosh, *Yuma*, 8:19), which is used to assist us in the transitions that occur during our many journeys in life. Similarly, the Mourner's Kaddish is a bridge that carries us through the life-transition of losing a loved one. This prayer, too, is a structure of 42: there are seven words that begin with the letter Vav, which has a numerical value of 6 (7 x 6 = 42).

To transition from one journey in life to another, we must include a period of rest and shelter. Then, when we are called to move to the next stage, we have the strength to keep climbing toward our life goal.

The great, overarching life goal for which we are constantly striving is to fulfill our purpose and Tikkun. This is our 'Promised Land', as it were. And then there are the smaller achievements we accomplish on the way. These smaller journeys are essential to our overarching destination, and each one is also complete as a journey in its own right.

Another way of understanding the dynamic of the 42 journeys is in the fact that each year, we observe 21 days of Torah-defined *Yomim Tovim* / festive holy days, and also 21 days of *Metzarim* / 'tribulation' and mourning for the destruction of the Beis HaMikdash, the spiritual heart of the world.* These are 21 days of sweet rest and joy, and 21 days of bitterness and efforts to fix our broken world, making up 42 communal spiritual journeys of our holy tradition. This makes it clear that even when we witness destruction or when we seem to be moving backward, we are always traveling with HaKadosh Baruch Hu and moving forward.

* In place of the 21 days of Metzarim, we could also count the 21 days between Rosh Hashanah and Hoshana Rabba, in which we are striving to attain a 'good seal' for the coming year. The 21 days of Torah-defined Yomim Tovim are Rosh Hashanah (2 days, even in Israel), Yom Kippur (1), Sukkos (7), Shemini Atzeres (1), Pesach (7), and Shavuos (1), plus 1 for Shabbos and 1 for Rosh Chodesh = 21. The 21 days of mourning are the "three weeks" from the 17th of Tamuz until Tisha b'Av.

"Vayisu, Vayachanu / And they traveled, and they camped...." Each small journey is a full cycle of movement and rest. Every small step is one step closer to our goal, our Promised Land.

MASEI

Energy of the Week:
Marking Short-Term Goals

During this week, we receive Ko'ach to accomplish our 'smaller' goals.

We must have an overarching life goal, a general purpose statement, and concept of what we wish to accomplish in this life, but we also need five- or ten-year goals, and even smaller goals for the current year, month, or week. All of these smaller journeys should move us towards our ultimate destination in life, yet we must attend to each one individually, with its unique hurdles, celebrations, and plateaus.

While thinking of a long-term life goal, we might become overwhelmed and view that achievement as impossible. For instance, a person who desires to create a warm, loving home and family yet still finds him or herself single may feel that the idea is unattainable. But the road to this destination is paved with many smaller journeys and incremental steps that will take you forward.

For this person, a goal of being open to dating at least once a month might be a small step in the right direction.

When many people look at their life, they experience a malaise, and feel a strong need to make drastic changes. They then set their sights very high without giving themselves concrete, gradual, or attainable milestones to mark their progress along the way. Although their ambitious resolution is genuine, it remains abstract, and in a short time, they return to their old patterns of behavior.

Real change takes real work. Real work requires realistic goals. Realistic goals result from a functional understanding of our inner reality. Grandiose resolutions are not the answer, but rather, consistent, seemingly small actions. A small act can be a goal that we set with regular reminders, such as saying to ourselves, 'Today, when I come home from work, I will give my child fifteen uninterrupted minutes of my time before doing anything else.' Or, 'Next time I go out with my friends or family, I will not look at my text messages at all.'

Eventually, all these 'small journeys' contribute to the bigger vision and greater goal.

This week, take an accounting of your largest life goal, and then set a 'small goal' that is aligned with it yet stands as an achievement on its own. Allow this small goal to be its own journey — complete with active movement and a period of rest.

Mark the accomplishment of the small goal as its own success before moving forward to the next stage.

PRACTICE OF THE WEEK:

Set & Achieve a Short-Term Goal in the Direction of Your Long-Term Goal

BOOK FIVE:
Devarim

Devarim
Connecting to the Ultimate 'I'

DEVARIM, THE TITLE OF THE FIFTH AND FINAL book of the Torah, is literally translated as 'Words': "These are the words that Moshe spoke to all of Klal Yisrael on the east bank of the Jordan."

From Bereishis through Bamidbar, the first four books of the Torah are written in the third person, as in, "Hashem spoke to Moshe...." This book is Moshe's own voice, as in "I said to you...."

Although Moshe wrote the first four books, he was not directly present in them as a speaker or an individual. In the fifth book, however, he is speaking as himself (ומשה מפי עצמו אמרן: *Megilah*, 31b) — even though, of course, his words are spoken through *Ruach HaKodesh* / Divine Inspiration (Tosefos, *ad loc*).

In the Zohar it is written, "The teachings...in the Book of Devarim, were [written by] Moshe himself. Is it possible that even one letter that Moshe spoke came from himself? (Rather), not even one letter that emerged from the mouth of Moshe was self-generated; each letter and sound issued forth was completely precise and calculated. The words that came through the mouth of Moshe were manifestations of the Divine Voice, which possessed him" (*Zohar* 3, 265a).

A statement quoted often over the past several hundred years is שכינה מדברת מתוך גרונו של משה / "The *Shechinah* / Divine Presence spoke through the throat of Moshe" (There is no direct source of this quote in Chazal, although see *Zohar* 3, 232a. *Medrash Rabbah*, Shemos, 3:15. *Mechilta*, Yisro, 18:19).

Devarim is the Divine Wisdom in the way it is channeled through Moshe's perspective and unique personal voice. It is the bridge between the revelation from Above, and the 'oral' dimension of Torah, which includes human innovation and creativity 'from below' (*Zohar* 3, 261a). This is a merging of Heaven and earth, a revelation through the instrument of humanity that is consistent with the Sinaitic revelation from Above.

In contrast to the generation that was miraculously lifted from Egypt, a people who witnessed daily miracles from

Above, the generation addressed in this book was going to enter the physical, natural Holy Land. They were going to see
the face of Hashem, as it were, in nature, in the world 'below'.
Thus, they required a teaching that joined Heaven and earth,
the Formless Creator and created form.

There are two ways by which the Torah was given via Moshe.
One is called מעבר / *Maavar* / passing through, where Moshe
was merely a conduit and the Torah passed through him. This
was like clear water passing through a colored glass; the water
remained unchanged. The other is called התלבשות / *Hislabshus*
/ 'enclothing', where the Torah was 'dressed' within the consciousness and perspective of Moshe. The latter was like water
passing through a painted vessel which gave a tint to the water.

In the first four books of the Torah, the Divine wisdom
simply passed through Moshe. In the final book, the Divine
wisdom was invested within the person of Moshe (*Ohel Ya'akov*,
Devarim).

Either way, through both *Maavar* and *Hislabshus*, the 'I' of
Moshe was not a separate entity. In both modes of revelation,
he had complete *Bitul* / selflessness. Yet, in Devarim, he was
paradoxically also a genuine 'I' with a distinct way of understanding and teaching. Moshe was, in fact, 'the perfect human
being' (Rambam, *Pirush HaMishnayos*, Sanhedrin Chapter 10): he was
tall (*Shabbos*, 92a), strong, wealthy (*Nedarim*, 38a), intelligent, just,
devoted, and compassionate. This means he was fully 'Moshe',
and he even stood out among other people. And yet when

Hashem spoke to him as a *Maavar*, he was selflessly transparent like clear glass; his 'I' was eclipsed.

In the mode of Hislabshus, Moshe's 'I' was not fully eclipsed. He was fully present throughout Devarim, even when not reviewing past experiences but revealing a new Divine teaching. The question is, how could it be that his 'I' was not fully eclipsed in the Book of Devarim? Was he a bit more 'arrogant' in this book? We know that "Moshe was more humble than any other person," but here his 'I' is prominent — he is speaking of himself not in the third person but in the first person.

Once, a Chasid from a different group came and visited the Kotzker Rebbe, and praised his own Rebbe in front of the Kotzker: "My Rebbe is so exceedingly humble!" "Wonderful," answered the Kotzker, "please tell me a story about your Rebbe's great humility." The Chasid said, "Well, our custom for generations is that when the Rebbe has been traveling and is returning to town, all the Chasidim unhinge the carriage from the horses and carry it the rest of the way on our shoulders, with the Rebbe riding inside. Our Rebbe, however, in his great humility, quietly slips out of the carriage and helps us carry the carriage. Just a few days ago, he was sitting in the carriage learning Torah with intense focus and became lost in a trance. His eyes were closed and he was in another world — he didn't even realize that we had unhinged the carriage and were carrying it with him inside it! When he opened his eyes and realized that we were actually carrying him, he was so upset that he actually vomited." The Kotzker tilted his head quizzically and said, "*Oy Nebech*, too bad: he takes his humility so seriously!"

Humility and self-emptying has an opposite: arrogance. In humble Bitul, there is still an ego that is being emptied, and therefore, it is still within the dynamic of Ayin and Yesh; on the spectrum of less or more arrogance. In the Book of Devarim, Moshe has actualized a level that is even deeper than *Ayin* / 'no-self'. He has actualized the fullness of Self.

By being fully Moshe, the 'I' of Hashem became manifest through the 'I' of Moshe. Moshe was one with the Divine 'I', and his words were therefore Hashem's words. This is the greatest level of humility; it is humility without an opposite, for it is being one with the One.

This fifth book of the Torah corresponds to the *Yechidah* / unified one, the fifth level of soul. Yechidah is the 'I' of unity between the *Yesh HaAmiti* / 'True Existence' of HaKadosh Baruch Hu and our *Yesh* / finite existence. Yechidah is our total fullness of self, not merely self-emptiness on the level of Ayin.

Chazal say that when someone is *Moser Nefesh* / self-sacrificing for (teaching) words of Torah, we do not repeat that teaching in his name (*Baba Kama*, 61a: המוסר עצמו למות על דברי תורה אין אומרים דבר הלכה משמו). This means that because he has no ego, we do not attribute his words to his name; it is as if he doesn't have a name. This describes *Bitul* / self-release on the level of Chayah (the fourth and transcendent level of soul; the 'Ayin' within us) but not on the level of Yechidah.

Yechidah is the *re-emergence* of self within the Ultimate Self. Devarim is higher and deeper than the first four books precisely because Moshe, on the level of Yechidah, is the speaker. For this reason, we sometimes refer to the Torah as *Toras Moshe* / "The Teaching of Moshe," attributing Hashem's words to him. If Moshe did not have a 'self' during the unfolding of the Book of Devarim, then Hashem's voice could not become enclothed in him.

This is the highest, deepest level of human existence: being 'no-thing' and 'something' at the same time, in the context of Yesh HaAmiti — being the fullness of who we really are.

Deep within each one of us, there is an aspect of Moshe (*Tanya*, 42. *Kedushas Levi*, Re'eh). When we lay aside our ego, we too can become a conduit of Hashem's Infinite wisdom. However, like Moshe, we also have the ability — and ultimately the responsibility — to be a *Mechadesh* / innovator in Torah, to reveal new 'Divine insight', in a state of profound humility. To do this, we must not only lay aside our ego but paradoxically maintain our transparent individual 'I-ness', including our own unique way of thinking, our own *Seichel* / intellect and understanding of reality. To be a Mechadesh in Torah, we need *Yiras Shamayim* / awe of Hashem. Awe indicates both self-emptiness in front of Divinity and a self-identity — a vessel which can innovate and elucidate ideas.

Ultimately, true humility is expressed in being fully our unique self, while knowing that it is not 'our' self but a vessel of the Only True Self, the One Divine 'I'. Our small i is nothing but an expression of the Ultimate I.

DEVARIM

Energy of the Week:
Connecting to the Tzadik

This week's Torah reading helps us connect with our own inner 'Moshe'. Often, it is connecting with the life and teachings of a Tzadik that allows us to connect with our own inner Tzadik. If there is a certain Tzadik whose teachings have inspired you, or if stories about a particular Tzadik have opened your eyes to what a human being can become, this week is a powerful time to study their words, contemplate their stories, and re-connect yourself to them.

A true Tzadik is someone who is a mirror of your higher self, reflecting your own highest potential. We should not merely put the Tzadik on a pedestal or as-sume that their holiness or humility is infinitely be-yond us. A Tzadik lives to inspire greatness in us, not to distance themselves from us; their deeds and de-votions may be awesome, but they are always in some way models for what we ourselves can achieve.

In fact, as the Rambam writes (*Hilchos Teshuvah*, 5:2), we can all become, in some way, like Moshe himself, the greatest Tzadik. Through observing or contemplating a Tzadik, or learning their teachings, we come in close contact with their light and receive their influence on conscious and subconscious levels.

This week's Torah reading imbues us with the Ko'ach to connect ourselves in particular to the Tzadik's quality of humble fullness, uniqueness, and confidence. This does not have to be a living person, for their teachings and their life of giving leave a legacy and imprint in the world that we can strongly connect with even after their passing.*

This week, study the teachings of a beloved Tzadik or read stories of their life. Note any ways that you can begin to reflect this Tzadik's humbleness, and begin to reveal your own unique inner Tzadik, as well.

PRACTICE OF THE WEEK:
Connect to a Tzadik

---

* *An Additional Quality of This Week: Connecting to the Nine Days of Mourning:* In all of our dealings this week, especially with children, students, or employees, we must be sure to decrease any forms of aggression. We need to be gentle and compassionate in our communication and disciplining methods during this nine-day period between the first day of Av until after Tisha b'Av, the day when we mourn the destruction of the *Beis haMikdash* / the Holy Temple in Jerusalem, and all that it represents.

Va'eschanan
Longing & Reunion

"Va'eschanan / 'I longingly entreated' Hashem at that time, say-
ing, O Hashem, G-d, You have begun to show Your servant Your
greatness and Your strong hand…let me cross over and see the Good
Land that is on the other side of the Jordan" (3:23–25).

OUR SAGES SAY THAT MOSHE IMPLORED *HaKadosh*
Baruch Hu / the Holy Blessed One, with 515 prayers,
as is hinted in the word ואתחנן / *Va'eschanan*, which
has a numerical value of 515. This is also the numerical value
of the classic word for prayer, תפלה / *Tefilah*.

Yet, this multitude of prayers, so deeply felt and expressed,
were only partially answered. Moshe was told, "Go up to the
top of the hill and lift up your eyes…and see with your eyes, for

you shall not cross this Jordan" (3:27). He is permitted to see the Land and observe it from a distance, but not to actually physically enter it with his feet. *Chazal* / our sages say that prayers are עושה מחצה / accepted halfway (*Medrash Rabbah*, Vayikra, 10:5). In other words, while he was not able to enter physically and fully, he *was* able to enter so-to-speak — with his eyes.

Seemingly, the problem with this idea is that being permitted to see the Land without being allowed to physically enter can be seen as a punishment or a tease rather than a response to Moshe's *Tefilos* / prayers. "The heart desires what the eyes see," thus, viewing the Land would have evoked an even stronger sense of lack and separation, creating a perhaps unbearable desire to physically enter the Land which was not fulfilled.

Yet, in our context, seeing a location can create a connection that is even deeper than actually being there. Moshe seeing the Land is just one of many times the Torah repeats the word and idea of 'seeing' in this Parshah: "It is your eyes that have *seen*" (4:3), "*See* I have taught you" (4:5), "You have been made to *see*" (4:35), "Indeed Hashem has allowed us to *see*" (5:24). All of these references are speaking of a full connection and embrace, and thus they reflect upon the way Moshe saw the Land.

On most years, the portion of Va'eschanan is read during the week of *Tisha B'Av* / the Ninth of Av, the day which commemorates the destruction of the First and Second *Beis HaMikdash* / Temples in Jerusalem and our ensuing separation and *Galus* / exile from the Land.

Galus is a painful state of alienation. To be in collective and individual exile is to experience a disconnect and displacement from one's homeland or from one's authentic self. Indeed, the separation of exile creates a fierce longing to reconnect. The greater the sense of missing our home, the greater our longing to reconnect, be redeemed, and be complete. In fact, on a deeper level, longing itself *creates* a reconnection, a type of redemption and reunion.

The connection between what you have or who you are, with what you want and who you desire to become, is forged by longing. The קוה / the hoping for creates the קו / the line, the connection. When Moshe observed the Holy Land, there was a greater longing within him for the Land and, through that, an even closer connection to the Land.

The Grades of Desire

Longing and desire can be divided into four levels, in ascending order:

1. 'Physical desire', a yearning for more stuff, physical objects, and the like.

2. 'Emotional desire', a desire to be loved and to be open to love.

3. 'Intellectual desire', wanting to know more of the world and of one's self.

4. 'Spiritual desire', a yearning to transcend or receive a Divine revelation — or even deeper, a desire to inhabit the 'Holy Land', the unification of Heaven and earth ('Holy' is transcendence, Heaven; 'Land' is immanence, earth).

This is the hierarchy of human desire, each desire enfolded within the next. As we mature, our desires deepen from raw physicality into emotional, intellectual, and spiritual levels of desire. Ultimately, all physical, emotional, and intellectual desires are outer expressions of our inner, essential, and spiritual desire to connect to our Creator and to be whole.

In spiritual desire, our soul experiences an emptiness and yearning to connect with Divine Light, yet we often mistakenly experience this hunger as a desire for materialism. For instance, our soul hungers, yet we think we simply desire another pair of shoes. Of course, if we bypass the deep connection for which we really yearn, and instead acquire those new shoes, we only exacerbate our sense of emptiness and dissatisfaction.

When Klal Yisrael's desires were on a low level, not aligned with HaKadosh Baruch Hu, the two golden *Keruvim* / Cherubim that adorned the *Aron* / Ark of the Covenant miraculously turned and faced away from each other. When our longing was on the highest spiritual level, directed at Hashem, the Keruvim turned to face each other (*Baba Basra*, 99b). Astonishingly, at the moment when the Beis HaMikdash was destroyed and we were driven into exile, the Keruvim were seen not only facing each other but wrapped in an intimate embrace (*Yuma*, 54b,

Rashi and Ritva, ad loc. *Medrash Eichah Rabba*, Pesichta, the Pirush *Yafah Anaf.* See *Likutei Sichos*, 21. p. 157, note 12. These were not the actual Keruvim, however, since during the First Beis HaMikdash period, the Aron was hidden long before the Beis HaMikdash was destroyed (or went into exile). During the Second Beis HaMikdash, there was no Aron, so this refers to the Keruvim that were embroidered on the *Paroches* / partition between the Holy and Holy of Holies: בשעה שנכנסו גוים להיכל ראו כרובים המעורין זה בזה. Says Rashi, קיפלום מן הכותל).

We may deduce that the embrace of the Keruvim took place the moment before the separation, like two lovers who embrace passionately before they part ways. This would be akin to moments of intense emotion expressed in the airport as spouses, friends, or relatives say their tearful goodbyes before embarking on a long trip. Just before destruction, separation, and exile set in, we find the greatest yearning and, in fact, connection and intimacy between the Divine Lover and us, His Beloved.

On a deeper level, this intense embrace can occur at the peak of the state of separation and yearning itself. For example, when your partner or child is with you, their presence may seem routine, and the expressions of affection between you may be less intense. If they need to go away for a week, however, your experience will be very different. The first three days might go by easily, as you have seen your loved one very recently. The last three days could be even easier, as you are then closer to their return than to their departure. The hardest day, the day you would feel the most separation, yearning, and affection, would therefore be the fourth day, the midpoint of the week. It is the day on which you are furthest from both their departure and their return. This very distance has the power to elicit your most passionate longing and desire; you might think of them all day, or certainly much more than when they are constantly with you. Thus, the greater the sense of separation, the greater the inner revelation of unity.

Mutual yearning created by distance reveals a strong, intimate connection. The depths of separation coincide with the heights of togetherness. This is the value of longing. The deeper the separation is felt, the more intense the yearning becomes for reconnection. The deeper we feel our exile, the more we yearn for redemption. "Where your mind is, there you are — *all* of you" (The Baal Shem Tov, *Keser Shem Tov*, Hosafos, 58).

VA'ESCHANAN

Energy of the Week:

Longing & Reunion

This week's empowerment is a difficult one. It is a week of intense, even painful longing. Still, if we have 'eyes to see', we can glimpse the sweet possibility of reunion beneath the surface.

This week of exile, destruction, and spiritual separation is a good time to stay close to home and not travel for pleasure. This is not a good time to seek out the new, to start new projects, a new business, or move into a new house. It is a time to be cautious and stay affectionately close to one's loved ones.

A meditation for this week is to allow yourself to feel the losses in your life. Experience your personal pain as well as the greater pain of the world. Become aware of the unredeemed state of the world, and allow yourself to sit with the sadness that these thoughts call forth.

It is important to contemplate the sadness of exile, separation, imperfection, and lack. However, we engage in this not as a 'punishment', nor even in order to cause pain. The deeper one feels the sting of exile, the more 'spiritual' their desire will become. One's yearning for connection, perfection, and redemption will increase dramatically, and any draw toward superficial emotional and physical comforts will decrease.

Eichah / translated as "Alas" (an expression of mourning), is also the word *Ayekah,* the mournful question, 'Where are you?'" (ורבי נחמיה אומר אין לשון איכה אלא קינה, הדא מה דאת אמר : ויקרא ה' אלהים אל האדם ויאמר לו איכה, אוי לכה *Medrash Eichah Rabbah,* 1).

Sometimes in life we take a wrong turn, and our desires fall to a lower level. At some point, we 'wake up' to the pain of our soul and ask ourselves, "How did I wind up here? Where am I?" This is actually a response to the Divine call, *Ayekah* / 'Where are you? I miss you so much!'

A very deep form of exile is being in the wrong place, and you don't even know how you got there or where to go now.

However, if you allow yourself to mourn your emptiness or 'separation', you will be given a subtle but real vision of your destination, your Promised Land. This itself is *Nechamah* / solace, and will give your life meaning and focus.

Through mourning, we reveal our true underlying longing for personal and collective redemption — and this will allow us to actually "see" redemption and embrace its inevitability. This is what our sages mean when they whisper affectionately to our souls, 'My friend, please know! "Mashiach is born on Tisha B'Av"' (*Yerushalmi*, Berachos, 2:4, *Eichah Rabbah,* 1:51).

May our exiles give birth to redemption immediately, and may we enter the Holy Land all together, with our eyes and also with our feet.

PRACTICE OF THE WEEK:

Allow Yourself to Feel the Losses in Your Life

Ekev

Soul Connections

"And it will be, Ekev / 'because' you will heed these ordinances and keep them and perform, that Hashem, your G-d, will keep for you the covenant and the kindness that He swore to your forefathers" (7:12).

A 'COVENANT' DEMANDS THE UTTER COMMITMENT of all parties, and there are pronounced effects when just one party does not keep it. For this reason, the Torah reading that speaks about the *Bris* / covenant also discusses the concept of 'reward and punishment'. It is important to understand that 'punishment' in Torah does not mean punitive retribution, as in, 'You did that to Me, and I am stronger, so I will do this back to you.' Nor does 'reward' mean 'Because you did something nice, I who hold power will reward you with goodies.' Rather, 'reward and punishment' refers to the spiritual principle of cause and effect; how we experience reality depends on our actions and intentions.

In this dynamic of cause and effect, our external reality mirrors our internal reality more deeply than the eye can see. Not only are all physical creations interrelated and part of a great bio-system, but there is also a deep underlying relationship and interdependence between the material and spiritual worlds. This is the reason that each of us is attracted to specific people, objects, and foods. "Not by bread alone does man live, rather, on all that comes from the mouth of Hashem does man live" (8:3). We assume that it is the nourishment of the bread that we want, when in truth, it's the spark of Divine life force within the bread that draws us and nourishes us.

Likewise, all the objects we own, encounter, use, or consume house sparks of Divine life force that are deeply connected to our soul and our journey of spiritual evolution. Whether animate, vegetative, or inanimate, these objects manifest in our lives in order to help us achieve our maximum spiritual, mental, emotional, and functional potentials. We are drawn to certain things and repelled by others because these things are connected to our soul and our unique *Tikkun* / soul purpose.

The reason that people have distinct tastes in food, clothes, places, objects, and friends is that every individual soul has a unique character. Every soul has distinct sparks of Divine Light, which it is connected to and must elevate during life in a body. These sparks are scattered throughout our environment, beckoning us to find them and raise them back to their Source. Sometimes, the way to return a specific spark to its

Source is through refraining from using or consuming it, and sometimes, the way is to use or consume it with the spiritual empowerment of appropriate *Berachos* / blessings and the protective force of *Halachah* / Torah guidelines. Halachah allows us to truly reunite the spark with its Source, and to do so without any detrimental side effects.

The Torah reading of Ekev is always read close to the 15th of the month of Av, when the moon is full. The meaning of the revealing of the moon represents clarity of vision and soul purpose, and we have the potential to connect with our soulmates. As the Mishnah describes in *Ta'anis*, many centuries ago, the 15th of Av was a day when young men and women found their destined soulmate and became engaged to enter the covenant of marriage.

"Forty days before a child takes form (at the moment of conception), a Divine Voice issues forth and says: 'The daughter of so-and-so is destined to marry so-and-so, such and such a house is destined to be inhabited by so-and-so, such and such a field is destined to be farmed by so-and-so'" (*Sotah*, 2a. The 15th of Av is also 40 days before the 25th of Elul, i.e., the moment of conception of the world). In other words, 'soulmate' synergy is not only found between people but also in all areas of life. While the person we marry is destined for us, so are the homes we live in, the fields, the property, the jobs, and all the experiences and objects in our lives. All are predestined extensions of our soul mission and purpose. We are all connected to particular energetic resonance for a specific reason.

On a deeper level, our 'soulmate' is understood as not a separate soul but actually part of us, sharing with us a single soul
root. Our covenant with them is not only an external 'promise',
but an inherent existential reality. Similarly, says the Baal Shem
Tov, the objects that we own are part of us; our soul extends
into the objects in our possession, so to speak. This reveals a
perspective of *Yichud* / unity, in which objects are not merely
'part' of us, and events don't just happen 'to' us — they *are* us,
for all is essentially one. Our sages also hinted at this by saying:
"Someone who steals from someone, is as if he takes his soul
from him" (כל הגוזל את חבירו שוה פרוטה כאילו נוטל נשמתו: *Baba Kama*, 119a).

In this context, everything that happens to you and everything and everyone that appears in your life, your wife or husband, parents, children, friends, and associates, are all part of
your soul. Just as you have legs, and they are part of you, your
wife or husband, your parents and children, friends and even
possessions, are all part of your inclusive being, your essence.

In another sense, if something is truly 'one' with me, it can
never be 'stolen', lost, or separated from me. It belongs to us
when we need it, and then when it leaves us, it means that our
soul connection is over; we have released the sparks, and it is
no longer a part of us. In any case, since we belong to the Creator of All, we are one with the One in a *Bris Olam* / eternal
covenant — 'soulmates with the Source', forever inseparable.

EKEV

Energy of the Week:
Soul Connections

This week, we receive an extra Ko'ach to sense the connection between our physical actions and spiritual reactions. We also can gain a deeper understanding of our soul's connections with everything and everyone around us.

This Torah reading enhances our clarity to make true soul connections. This applies both to our interpersonal relationships and our relationships with everything around us.

This is a good week to re-evaluate our connections with the people and the things we surround ourselves with, and see that they are properly drawing us toward our soul's purpose in elevating sparks. Sometimes, we feel drawn to a food or experience in order to elevate its spark by reciting a blessing and partaking in it. Other times, a food or experience manifests in our life so that we can elevate its spark by *not* partaking in it.

We also need to ensure that the people surrounding us are helping us in our soul journey, and not dragging us down. Sometimes, a friend or boss is meant to play a temporary part in our journey, and then we are meant to move on. Sometimes, an object can only be elevated by getting rid of it. Sometimes, we need to grow through pleasant experiences, and sometimes through unpleasant ones.

In order to confirm that a person, place, or thing is empowering our journey and not pulling us down, we can focus inwardly and discern: is this interaction, even if annoying, leading to some sense of expansiveness, openness, focus, or wholeness? This week, take advantage of the Torah's supportive guidelines for this type of deep inner work.

PRACTICE OF THE WEEK:

Reevaluate Your Possessions & Ask, 'Does This Object Bring Me Greater Wholeness?'

Re'eh

Seeing Our Unique Circumstance as a Blessing

"Re'eh / behold, I set before you this day a blessing and a curse: a blessing, as you listen to the commandments of Hashem...I command you this day, And a curse, if you do not listen ...turn aside from the path...this day" (11:26 -28).

"I set before you this day a blessing and a curse" can be read as, "Behold I set before you *this day* — a blessing and a curse." In other words, the day itself is a blessing or a curse.

The day, the present moment, the now that is presented to us each day anew, can be viewed as, and made into, a blessing or a curse. "I have set *before you* a blessing and a curse" means the choice is before us. It is up to us whether it is a blessing or, Heaven forbid, a curse. Rather than being mere recipients of life, dealing with whatever is presented to us, we can be co-creators in life, living from the inside out and choosing to interpret reality proactively. We can be the director of our own film.

We have the choice to "see" life and recognize that all of it is in place to help us achieve blessing or the opposite. 'Blessing' means to proliferate, increase, flow, progress, and evolve higher (צאן גורן ויקב מיוחדים שישנן בכלל ברכה: *Kidushin*, 17a. As Rashi explains, blessing means something that increases, צאן פרה ורבה וכן גידולי קרקע. And increases independently: Rambam, *Hilchos Avadim*, 3:14. Indeed, the Even Ezra, writes, נהרא מכיפיה מיבריך: *Devarim*, 11:27. הברכה תוספת טובה והקללה מגרע' והיא מגזרת קלה *Bechoros*, 55b. Rashi: שפרת היו מימיו פרין ורבין). To see life as a blessing means to behold everything as a tool and opportunity to help us flow forward, advance, and grow. All circumstances can be leveraged for living more authentically, being in touch with our deepest nature, and achieving our soul's purpose in the world. Every encounter and experience — even challenges and setbacks — can help us progress spiritually and better our lives. This is how to see blessings everywhere. And indeed, when we live in a way that we see everything as a blessing, we ourselves become a blessing.

"I have set before you *this day*...." What you have is 'this day'; not yesterday and not tomorrow. And every day is a totally new day. Just as no two people are the same, since the beginning of Creation, no two days have ever been the same. Nor, in fact, have two moments been the same. Every day and every moment brings with it new opportunities to create blessings.

Paradoxically, change is the only constant in life. Every prayer is a new prayer, says the Arizal (Arizal, *Pri Eitz Chayim*, Sha'ar HaTefilah 7. *Olas Tamid*, Sha'ar HaTefilah, 11. See also Ramak, *Shiur Koma*, Hakdamah, 13. *Ohr Yaakar*, Kedoshim, 4). And thus, teaches the Baal Shem Tov, every distraction during prayer is a new distraction (*Toldos Ya'akov Yoseph*, Parshas Vayakhel). Every prayer, Mitzvah, distraction, challenge, and *Nisayon* / test is given to us in order to *L'Hisnoseis* / raise us up higher, grow and develop ourselves ("You have given those in awe of You a test by which to be uplifted": *Targum* on *Tehilim*, 60:6. Rebbe Rayatz, *Nasata Li'Yrei'echa*, 5693).

Every detail and, in fact, the entire context of each new day is really placed before us so that we will see it or leverage it as a blessing. Everything in Creation was created by the Infinitely Wise and Compassionate One, for a reason. It is up to us to recognize and harness the present potential for *Avodas Hashem* / service of Hashem, and for bringing life, hope, possibility, and growth, to ourselves and others around us.

From this perspective, everything within and around us is actively conspiring to help us achieve our purpose in existing. Our genetics, parents, upbringing, education, environment, nature, and nurture are all perfectly designed to present us with the choice of creating good from it, or the opposite.

A deliberate activity that we do in order to move toward attaining our soul purpose is called a זהיר טפי / *Zahir T'fei* / 'carefully performed act' (*Shabbos,* 118b). זהיר / *Zahir* / careful can also be translated as 'illumination' or 'shine'. Every aspect of our environment, culture, and history is meant to be a catalyst for attaining our individual soul-illumination in the best possible way. Even the challenges and obstacles that arise are only there to provoke us to martial our deeper strengths and resources, to persevere and to shine.

A blessing is an 'enlargement' of our Divine soul expression, a revelation of more of who we truly are. From our first moments in life, we have been placed in conducive environments for the development and articulation of soul powers. When we "do not listen" to our soul-calling, we deviate from who we really are, and this is the curse. A curse is defined as a concealment or severing of our flow of life and illumination, an alienation of our essential holiness and wholeness.

There never was nor will there ever be another "you," and there never was and never will be again a moment like this one. This means that the most important time is now, and the most valuable person is you, you right now, in this place. The you and the now are coming together in a firm choice to manifest blessing. "And thus it will go well with you and with your descendants after you forever, for you will be doing what is good and right in the sight of Hashem your G-d" (12:28).

RE'EH

Energy of the Week:
Seeing Our Circumstance as a Blessing

This week we receive Ko'ach to more deeply understand our unique journey, and the ever-unfolding blessing in the present moment guiding us along this journey. We receive support in choosing to see our unique circumstances in life as pushing us toward our authentic self, and motivating us to actualize our individual Tikkun on earth.

We are empowered to be more of who we are.

This week, we should view the context of the life we are given as a unique blessing meant just for us. In this way, everything will become illuminated, and we will be a blessing for ourselves and others.

PRACTICE OF THE WEEK:

Choose to See — and Be — Blessing

Shoftim
Filtering Sensory Intake

"You shall set up Shoftim / judges and law enforcement officials for yourself in all your gates...and they shall judge the people with righteous judgment" (16:18).

"JUDGES AND LAW ENFORCEMENT OFFICIALS" ARE IN the plural, suggesting they should be set up in many locations, and yet, "for yourself, in all your gates" is in the singular, as if a single individual is being addressed.

Obviously, this Mitzvah should be read literally as instituting officials at the gates of the many cities we live in; however, because of the singular form, it lends itself to a deeper interpretation as well: "You shall set up judges...in *your* gates," in the multiple 'gates' of your own body (Arizal, *Sefer HaLikutim*, Shoftim. *Shach*, Torah, Devarim, 16:18).

Our body is more than a city. It is our personal *Mishkan /* Temple, as Rebbe Elazar Azikri writes, בתוך לבי משכן אבנה לזיוו / "In my heart I will build a Mishkan for His splendor." This inner Mishkan needs to be protected and guarded from hazardous and potentially destructive outside influences.

In looking at our body, we notice that we have been given natural and biological gates to protect ourselves. Our eyelids can close to protect our vision, our lips and teeth can close to protect our speech and our taste, the soft earlobe (or perhaps more practically, the ridge of cartilage called the tragus) can close off our ear canal, muffling the sounds that reach us, and our nostrils can close against unwanted smells ("Why is the entire ear hard and the earlobe soft? It is so that if a person hears an inappropriate matter, he will fold his earlobe up into his ear to seal it": *Kesuvos*, 5b). It is up to us to devise a system of judgment and law enforcement, to use our naturally provided 'gates' to guard the senses against negative or twisted input that can potentially harm us.

Throughout the day, every day, we are continuously bombarded with sensory input, from visual imagery, words, sounds and tastes, and countless other external influences. Most of these are subliminal and their impressions are absorbed by our subconscious mind. Billions of impressions and messages are fed to us every day.

While we may aspire to turn away when we see or hear something that is destructive in nature, in order to fully protect ourselves from things that can harm us even subliminally, we must consciously put up barriers to protect our senses. For example, one might intend to look away from spiritually harmful imagery on the internet; however, in most instances, the only way to avoid that imagery is to emplace a barrier or filter, or even to not go online at all. Once we put ourselves in a situation in which we *may* be exposed to negatively impactful imagery, it may seep in inadvertently or subliminally.

Even subtle negativity can have a corrosive impact. The eyes, for example, are very delicate and powerful instruments. They have a spiritual quality, as it were, and even the slightest dust of intrusion causes harm (*Ohr HaChayim*, Devarim, 32:10). We therefore need to protect them from even the slightest negative influence.

Sometimes, people walk around angry, or depressed and down, but are uncertain of where it comes from. They do not realize that by simply watching or reading the news, certain negative, disturbing images and suggestions have entered their consciousness and are causing pain to their soul.

To guard ourselves, we need to create or enter into situations which will provide us with controlled positive sensory input. However, insofar as it is too challenging for most people today to control their environment completely and avoid the images displayed on the street, on public transportation, and countless other venues of secular culture, we must learn to *ignore* certain suggestions, images, and narratives.

Furthermore, because we often do not see things the way they are, rather the way *we* are, we actually have a choice in how we see things. This means even when our surrounding culture 'forces' us to see or hear something, we can reinterpret it; we can change the images by changing the way we see them.

Everything in this world has a factual level and an interpretation, a narrative overlay. For example, a narrative suggested by a commercial image may be that a certain beautiful car is desirable. However, the fact is, without that overlay, a beautiful car is simply a beautiful car, and there is no need to desire it, ride it, or buy it. If we allow an external narrative to convince us that we do 'desire' that particular car and that we should imagine owning it, this means we do not have good 'judges' at our gates at that moment. We are allowing our consciousness and mindset to be manipulated and dictated by outside influences and influencers. To have proper inner 'judges' means to turn this tendency inside out. Instead of allowing external agendas to dictate our thoughts, feelings, values, and actions, we should assert sovereignty over our own body, mind, soul, and environment. In this way, we are not mere recipients of life but creative interpreters of life.

Each of us, 'in the singular', needs to stand in our power to judge and define what that car, product, or suggested experience really means to us. We can tell our own story about it, or even see the car without any narrative at all other than 'it is a recently manufactured four-wheeled vehicle, and may even be objectively beautiful.'

We are asked in this week's Torah reading to protect our 'city' that we have been given as a gift. When we do so, we will have correct judgment as a result. When we are careful to absorb only positive and healthy sensory input, and to enforce barriers to prevent spiritual, intellectual, emotional, and physical damage from inhabiting us, we are in a position of 'righteous judgment'. We will have a clear vision and unprejudiced ability to choose a path for ourselves aligned with our deeper purpose. We will not be enslaved to advertising, propaganda, and social agendas; we will rather create our reality from inside out, based on our truth, our pure soul, and our Divine Torah.

A person who has set up good protectors and filters for sensory intake is ultimately even able to rewire their circuit board, so to speak. This means that they have enabled their creative imagination to flow from their mind to the world, rather than passively receiving the world's imagination and letting it replace their creativity. We take hold of the external world, and creatively project our wholesome vision outward, ensuring that we see things how we choose to see them, and hear things how we choose to hear them.

This is free choice in action.

SHOFTIM

Energy of the Week:
Filtering Sensory Intake

By 'living with' the Torah reading this week, we are infused with additional *Ko'ach* / ability to become aware of the subtle suggestions that we receive from all directions, to filter out the detrimental input, and to internalize only the positive and helpful imagery and sensory input.

Notice the different quality of the images and messages that enter your system against your will and conscience, and those that you know are beneficial to absorb. Since imagery, sound, smell, sensation, taste, and cognition are the ways we experience and interact with life, the impressions we internalize can either assist us in getting closer to our purpose, or create a distance from our authentic self.

Use careful judgment and strict policies, to ensure that all input is helpful in your growth and fulfilling your life's purpose.

Sense the clarity of vision and purpose which results from this path. Appreciate the inner strength of being able to decline what is not good for you. You will find that you can make firm decisions without being clouded by bias and emotional sway. You will taste the sweetness of freedom and soulful self-sovereignty.

PRACTICE OF THE WEEK:

Become Aware of What Comes In & Out of Your Sensory Field

Ki Seitzei

Be the Master of Your Challenges

THIS WEEK'S TORAH READING OPENS WITH THE theme of the protocols of battle: "When you (plural) will go out to battle with your enemy, and Hashem will deliver the enemy to your (singular) hands…" (21:10).

While the verse is commonly translated as 'with your enemy', the word the Torah uses is actually עַל / *Al* which literally means, 'upon' or 'over' your enemy.

Additionally, since the verse begins with the plural 'you', and concludes with the singular 'your', it is clear that the verse is speaking about a collective, external enemy and also an internal, personal enemy (Torah often speaks in the singular to the collective, but here the singular actually means the individual, as the laws that follow are addressed to the individual).

What does it mean to go out to battle knowing that you are "over" your enemy? In a literal and external sense, to be above your enemy means that your army is on the high ground, and your enemy is in the plains (*Aderes Eliyahu*, Ki Seitzei, 1). Inwardly and personally, this means that you sense you are above your challenges; you 'have' a problem, maybe, but you are not identified 'as' the problem. You 'have' a struggle, but you are standing 'above' it. In both cases, this means that upon going to battle, we sense that we will be victorious: 'I am already above the enemy and will certainly emerge the victor.'

When we 'do battle' with our inner insecurities, negative habits, and difficult challenges, we have three options. 1) We can approach the challenge or 'adversary' as if it is in control of us, 2) we can approach it as if we are equals on an even battlefield, and 3) we can approach the adversary as if we are already in control of it.

Even when we do battle on an 'even playing field', it is very difficult: "He who wrestles with a filthy person is bound to become soiled himself" (*Tanya*, 28). Complete success is much more likely when we recognize that we are already above our adversary. When we engage in a struggle, we should visualize ourselves as essentially above it, and that we will certainly overcome.

True, a part of us may wrestle with our imperfections, deficiencies, and weaknesses. Yet, another part of us is 'perfect', always whole and strong. There is a 'struggler' within us, and

there is a *Tzadik* / 'righteous one' within us, as well. Our perfection is deeper than our imperfection; perfection is our essence, the pure soul, which is a spark of the Infinite One.

When faced with a deep challenge or temptation, we can either try to meet it head-on, or we can envision ourselves standing above and beyond it, as the master of the situation.

Say a person struggles with time management. He finds
himself frequently pulled down into wasting time and is frus-
trated in attempts to overcome this deficiency. There are two
ways to approach this struggle.

A) He can meditate on the negative effects of wasting time
and how it feels having lost precious opportunities. This is
meeting the problem head-on and working through the issue
on an even playing field. There is a tremendous risk that focusing on negative effects will not bring success, and the person
will only be left with increased frustration.

B) He can recall the occasions when he was tempted to engage in a time-wasting activity but decided against it. There
were times when he was in a state of flow with his work or had
control over his tendency. He can bring up the good feelings
and remind himself that he has the power to master the situation. Instead of contemplating the negative ramifications and
feelings, he can focus on the felt sense of overcoming. He can
recognize and affirm that deep down, he is 'above' this struggle

and is the master of his time. The proof is in the fact that he has mastered this problem in the past.

Overall, it is a healthier and more productive approach to visualize ourselves in our perfection. Rather than identifying as the struggler, see yourself as essentially a 'Tzadik' — and then live up to that image.

We tend to become what we imagine ourselves to be. People who argue for their limitations, powerlessness, or sense of guilt tend to remain within that framework. Entering a struggle in a defensive stance invites an offensive. Start out with an inner battle cry of "I am much bigger than all this," and indeed, you will be.

Argue on behalf of your greatness, and you will be great. Believe that you are 'above' your problems, and you will be. Convince yourself that you are small and identify with smallness, and you will be small. Believe that your problems will overwhelm you, and they will.

KI SEITZEI

Energy of the Week:

Be the Master of Your Challenges

This week's Torah reading gives us the Ko'ach to stand above our imperfections and to identify with the perfection that is at our core, beyond problems and battles. When we assume this stance, we are able to overcome our challenges without a long, drawn-out struggle.

Take time this week to reflect on the times when you mastered specific challenges. Remember the sensations. Understand that if you were able to do it in the past, even briefly, that ability is within you. In fact, that is who you really are, and you can access that mastery whenever you desire.

Ki Seitzei is read during the month of Elul, and this month is connected with the letter Yud (י), as *Sefer Yetzirah* teaches. Yud is the *Nekudah* / point of goodness within everyone and everything. Every Hebrew letter begins with a Yud, a small point of ink at the top of the letter.

This small point descends and extends laterally to form the horizontal line of the letter, and then it extends further into the letter's vertical lines, broadening into an area (*Sefer HaMa'amarim* 5666 [Samach Vav], B'Yom haShemini, p. 490).

Macrocosmically, the letter Yud is the first 'letter of creation' to manifest after the initial *Tzimtzum* / 'contraction' of the Infinite Light.* Yud is thus our primal point of origin, our place of purity, even before Divine Light extends into the dimensions of space and time. During Elul, we recapture that purity, that point 'above' Creation, that perfection beyond the imperfection, that wholeness beyond struggle.

The *Mazal* / constellation of Elul is *Besulah* / Virgo (*Sefer Yetzirah*). This is a metaphor for our pure soul, which soars above all challenges and 'enemies'. You are much greater than you can imagine. You are the Yud 'above' all the dramas and traumas of life, and you are the master of your life.

---

* According to the teachings of the AriZal, as revealed by Rabbi Yisrael Sarug, the first letter to emerge in Creation is the letter Yud, following what is called 'the Tzimtzum of the Square'. Within this 'square' arose an *Avir Kadmon* / a primordial vapor, and this Avir is also the *Ohr* / light of the Yud.

PRACTICE OF THE WEEK:
Stand Above Your Challenges

Ki Savo

Confession & Positive Affirmation

K*i Savo* / 'WHEN YOU COME' INTO THE LAND WHICH Hashem...gives you...and you possess it and settle within it. You shall take the first of all the fruit of the ground...And you shall put [them] into a basket and go to the place where Hashem, your G-d, will choose to have His Name dwell there..." (26:1–2).

When you are settled in your Land, and have already cultivated your space, you then bring the first-ripened fruits, called *Bikurim* (generally meaning 'firsts': *Vayikra*, 2:14. 23:17) of your orchard to the *Beis HaMikdash* / Holy Temple. Once this offering has been brought, then "you shall then recite as follows before Hash-

em, your G-d" (1:5), there is a public declaration that comes with
the offering of the Bikurim that speaks about our history and
the going out of Egypt, which is also called a וידוי / confession
(מצות עשה להתודות במקדש על הבכורים בשעה שמביאם) / "There is a positive Mitzvah
to confess in the Beis HaMikdash, when a person brings them": Rambam,
Hilchos Bikurim, 3:10).

When beginning to reveal the Mitzvah of Bikurim, the Torah says, "When you have set aside in full the tenth part of your
yield — in the third year, the year of the tithe, and have given
it to the Levite, the stranger, the orphan, and the widow, that
they may eat their fill in your settlements...." After this, there
is something called וידוי מעשרות / 'Confession of Tithing', in
which the participant utters a verbal *Viduy* / confession. Rather
than a 'confession of transgressions', however, this is a positive
confession in which one joyfully declares before Hashem that
he has done all that Hashem asked him to do: "I have not eaten
of it while in mourning, I have not cleared any of it out while I
was unclean...I have done just as You commanded me." Then,
he affirms that Klal Yisrael is deserving of the blessings to be
bestowed upon them: "Look down from Your holy abode, from
Heaven, and bless Your people Israel and the soil You have
given us..." (26:13–15).

Why is the above called a "confession"?* By calling this dec-

---

* As the Minchas Chinuch asks, למה יתודה והלא לא חטא כלל ולמה נקרא וידוי מעשר
/ "Why should he 'confess', as he did not sin — why is it called confession:
Minchas Chinuch, Mitzvah 607, 19. As an aside, the Tosefos Yom Tov writes
that it *is* a confession of sin since it is because of our sins that these tithings
are given to the Tribe of Levi and not to the firstborns — הוידוי על שבחטאינו

laration a confession, the Torah is suggesting that just as there are confessions of sin and shame, there are confessions of righteousness, gratitude, and joy.

Bikurim is a 'confession of gratitude', and the text of tithing is a 'confession of greatness', an affirmation of standing proud and exultant before our Creator and declaring that we have done well. We have done our best to do as we were commanded, and thus, we confidently ask for a blessing upon the entire community.

All of this teaches us that when we have "settled" and are cultivating and improving ourselves, it is crucial to acknowledge and affirm our goodness and success.

Our speech is incredibly powerful; angels and cosmic forces are created through our words. We are strongly affected by everything that we say and hear. Language is so primary to our experience that our words determine the very way we think, as in the concept of 'linguistic determinism'. Words create our reality; when we verbalize something, it becomes real to us.

Sometimes, one might make a mistake and tell themselves, 'I am not a *Mentsch* / good person,' 'I am lazy,' 'I am incompetent,' etc. As our words create our perception and reality, ultimately, we will act according to the statements we make of ourselves.

ובעוונות אבותינו הוצרכנו לבער הקודש מן הבית לבלתי תת אותם לבכורות שהיו ראויים לתרומה ומעשרות: Mishnah, *Ma'aser Sheini*, 5:10. See also *Seforno*, Devarim, 26:13.

This week, the Torah is teaching us that just as we need to verbally acknowledge and own our shortcomings, it is vital that we declare our virtues, as well, and make a 'confession of greatness'.

When we do need to acknowledge our shortcomings, we need to learn *not* to make statements such as, 'I am not a good person,' 'I am lazy,' or 'I am incompetent.' We must exchange those statements with accurate confessions of fact, such as 'I have made a mistake,' 'I have been wasting precious time,' or 'I have not been using my abilities and talents,' etc. Then, we need to declare positive affirmations such as, "I am essentially a good person," and "I can and do have the inner resources to change the direction of my life."

Everything that exists in space also exists in time, as these dimensions are part of the same fabric. The Bikurim offering in space is the physical offering of the first grown fruit in the Land of Israel. In time, Bikurim is 'offering' our first waking moment of the day to Hashem, as it were. The *Modeh Ani* prayer that we utter when we open our eyes in the morning is a 'confession of gratitude' like that of Bikurim: "*Modeh ani* / 'I confess gratitude' before You, Living and Eternal King, for You have compassionately returned my soul to me; great is your Faithfulness."

Following the 'confession of thanks-giving', the Torah speaks of a 'confession of greatness'. Likewise, in the morning, following our expression of gratitude for the new day, we follow with a 'confession of greatness' declaring, "Hashem, the soul that you have given within me, is pure…."This is a confession of our greatness (Note that in the evening, before we retire to bed, we recite a 'confession of sin'. First we 'turn away' from the negative at night, and then we emphasize the positive, in the morning).

We need to speak of our accomplishments, at least to ourselves, and continually declare our own innate greatness, being "a part of the One Above, literally."

KI SAVO

Energy of the Week:
Positive Affirmations

This week's Torah reading guides us to view ourselves in a positive light and verbally affirm our achievements and strengths. When you eliminate all negative declarations about yourself, and replace them with positive affirmations and words of gratitude and recognition of your essential greatness, you will believe in yourself more and more. Your actions will align with these positive beliefs.

Ask yourself these questions this week:

What would a person with a high level of confidence do in my situation?

What would a person with a great deal of courage do in my situation?

What would a person with complete self-mastery do in my situation?

Meditate upon the answers, affirm your capacity to put them into practice, and know that you will eventually do so.

PRACTICE OF THE WEEK:
Confession

Nitzavim
Standing Firm

"You are all Nitzavim / standing this day before Hashem, your tribal heads, your elders, your officers; every householder...your children, your wives, even the stranger within your camp, from wood-chopper to water-drawer" (Devarim, 29:9).

THIS IS THE WAY THIS WEEK'S TORAH READING begins. Moshe is joyfully transmitting the Divine affirmation that all of us are נצב / *Nitzav* / 'standing firmly' in our self-mastery before Hashem, the Master of the Universe (נצב / *Nitzav* means 'in charge', ויאמר בעז לנערו הנצב על-הקוצרים / "Boaz said to the servant who was 'standing over' (in charge of) the reapers": *Rus*, 2:5). Standing in this posture itself gives us power, as we are embodying confidence in unity with the Ultimate Source of all Power.

We are "standing this day". What day is "this day"? It is the first day of the year, 'the day', the day of Rosh Hashanah.*

Indeed, we read this Torah reading of Nitzavim every year just before Rosh Hashanah, so these words are meant to infuse us with the *Ko'ach* / strength and *Kavanah* / intentionality that we need to have on Rosh Hashanah. On this day, when we begin again, we should make sure that we are able to stand "firm and confident." To do so, however, often requires a change of perspective.

ראש השנה / Rosh Hashanah is the ראש / *Rosh* / 'head' of the new year, not merely the 'first' day of the year or *Techilas Hashanah* / 'beginning of the year'. Rosh Hashanah is the 'headquarters' or 'brain' of the new year, upon which the template of the coming year is imprinted and from which it is projected into the future. Due to this fact, it is vital that we use our own *Rosh* / head on this day, to create a vision for ourselves. The year that follows is an articulation and unpacking of that original vision.

---

* *Likutei Torah*, Nitzavim: "This day" refers to Rosh Hashanah. See *Zohar* 2, 32b: ויהי היום: דא ראש השנה Generally, our sages teach that היום הזה / 'this day', means 'every single day', as in בכל יום יהיו בעיניך כחדשים / "Every single day, it (the Torah or life) should be like new, a new day" (*Tanchuma*). These two teachings are linked, as Rosh Hashanah is the newness of time, and if we live with the true sense of newness, every day will have a palpable trace of Rosh Hashanah. Every day is a new day, a new Divine manifestation.

שנה / *Shanah* means 'year', and it comes from the same etymological root as the word שינוי / *Shinui* / change (שנה הוא לשון שינוי: See *Zohar* 3, 277b, Ramaz, *ad loc. Shoresh Yesha*, Erech Shanah. *Avodas haKodesh*, 4:19. *Ohr haTorah*, Miketz, 338. *Likutei Sichos*, 4, p. 1323). As such, the term *Rosh Hashanah* also means 'changing your head', shifting and renewing your consciousness and way of thinking. On Rosh Hashanah, we need to change our perspective on ourselves and the people and world around us. On this day, we have to change our consciousness, press the reset button on our life, and begin again with a new mindset of spiritual self-confidence and firmness.

Actually, on Rosh Hashanah, through our *Avodah* / spiritual work, all creatures get to press the reset button on life; it is a new moon, a new season, a new year, and a new world: *HaYom Haras Olam* / "This is the birthday of the world" (*Machzor*).

On this day, we have come from the month of Elul, a month of inner work, reviewing our actions and insufficient actions of the previous year. Having contemplated what we have not yet achieved and formed resolutions to repair our lives, we can now approach the headwaters of the year, confidently remove any blocks or dams, and let a great river of blessings irrigate our lives.

We can stand firm because of the work that we have done in Elul. Once Rosh Hashanah enters, we let go of all accumulated impressions. In the liturgy, there is no mention whatsoever of past misdeeds (*Magen Avraham*, 584:1). Even outside of the liturgy, we should not mention any sin on Rosh Hashanah (*Sha'ar*

HaKavanos, Hakdamah, Derushei Rosh Hashanah). In fact, we should remove our mind from transgressions to the point that we do not even eat foods that could subtly remind us of the concept of sin (The Maharil speaks about not eating nuts on Rosh Hashanah: See Rama, *Shulchan Aruch*, Orach Chayim 583:2. Besides creating extra phlegm, making it harder to sing and Daven, 'nuts' and 'sin' have the same numerical value. Although they are not the exact same value — חט בגימטריא אגוז — yet, since the pronunciation even hints to the value of the word חטא / 'sin', we refrain).

It is the way of the world, says the Medrash (quoted in Tur, *Orach Chayim*, Chap. 581. *Medrash Rabbah*, Vayikra, Parshah 29), for most people to feel uncertainty and humility when they stand to be judged, as they do not know the ultimate verdict. They may show up in court dressed in black (signifying mourning), unkempt, with uncut nails, and looking overwhelmed and weak. Yet, on Rosh Hashanah we act differently. Before Rosh Hashanah we take haircuts, which is a celebrative act. We dress in white garments, white being the color of purity and paradise (*Nidah*, 20a). We enter Rosh Hashanah in our finest attire, and we eat, drink and rejoice, לפי שיודעין שהקב״ה יעשה להם נס / "knowing that the Master of the World will perform a miracle." We stand confidently before Hashem, sensing that the Creator will find favor with us, annul any and all negative decrees, and bless us with a beautiful coming year.

We often need to change our mindset to view ourselves as a vessel worthy of blessings. So long as we cling to our old perceptions of self and world, we are stuck in them and not open to receive anything new and wonderful.

We need to let go of the past, similar to the trees in this season, which let go of their leaves to make room for bright, fresh leaves in the coming year. We need to practice *Havdalah* / separation from the old year, to make ourselves into a vessel to receive the flow of new blessings from Above.

Of course, spiritual confidence should not be confused with hubris or arrogance. True confidence is an awareness that we are 'full' *because* we are standing in front of Hashem.

We stand dependent on the Infinite One for power for our very breath. We are aware of being totally empty and thus ready to receive from on High. In the words of our sages, "A year that begins 'poor' will, in the end, be made 'rich'" (*Rosh Hashanah*, 16b).

רש / *Rash* / 'impoverished' is the state of feeling totally empty. On *Rosh* Hashanah, as we stand before our Creator 'empty' of the past, 'impoverished' of even a hint of negativity, we are actually 'open' vessels. Having nothing of our own, we are open to receive all the light and goodness that is coming to us for the future. We need to picture ourselves as a strong, 'firm' vessel, ready to contain an enormous amount of blessings.

May we open ourselves to the Source of Life, "the King Who desires that we live," and humbly, yet proudly, acknowledge that we are ready to be His "water drawers," ready to draw and carry the waters of life and blessing to all His Creation.

NITZAVIM

Energy of the Week:
Standing Firm & Confident

This week's Torah reading infuses us with the *Ko'ach* / power to stand up, to be inwardly and spiritually confident. This will cause us to increase in mental, emotional, and physical confidence, as well. As spiritual confidence is a power that comes from the Source of All Power and Giving, thus, it is an inner confidence, and it does not need to make another person smaller.

True power, from the Root of All Power, gives life; it gives power to others rather than assuming power over others. Our posture of standing tall comes from standing before Hashem, our Source, the Source of All Power.

Before one learns how to walk, one must first learn how to stand. Before we can walk into the next year, we need to be able to stand up for what we believe in, but from a place of real power, not force. On this birthday of humanity, we need to stand up for others, not over others; our only power comes from the One who is creating and recreating every human being.

PRACTICE OF THE WEEK:

Picture Yourself as a Strong, 'Firm' Vessel, Ready to Contain an Enormous Amount of Blessing

Vayelech

The Circle Within the Line

THIS WEEK'S TORAH READING BEGINS: "And Moshe 'went' (walked) and spoke these things to all of Klal Yisrael" (*Devarim*, 31:1).

"Moshe went" — where did Moshe go? Where was he coming from, and where was he going? On a simple level, the verse means that he walked, on his own initiative, to each and every *Sheivet* / tribe to inform them that he was about to die, to take leave of them, tell them that they should not fear, and offer them comfort (*Even Ezra, Ramban, Seforno, Malbim, HaEmek Davar*, ad loc. Alternatively, he 'went' to tell the *Avos* / Patriarchs that Hashem was keeping the promise and bringing their descendants back to the Land: *Baal HaTurim*, ad loc).

A further clarification comes from the Zohar: "Where did Moshe go? Rather, it means he walked feebly כגופא בלא דרועא / like with a body without an arm…. Since Aharon (his brother) had passed away, and he was like (Moshe's) right arm" (*Zohar* 3, 283b). Indeed, "*Moshe* went" implies he went alone, without Aharon; he was 'incomplete', missing his 'right arm' and the right arm of all of Klal Yisrael.

The Zohar explains: "Three holy siblings walked among Klal Yisrael — Moshe, Aharon, and Miriam." In this way, if Aharon was Moshe's right hand, then Miriam was his left hand, and Moshe was the body. This Torah reading takes place at the end of Moshe's life, and Aharon and Miriam are no longer alive. After the death of Aharon and Miriam, Moshe was like a body without arms. He was only able to "walk" upright, as a 'line' without arms.

Symbolically, this means that Moshe was 'upright', the man of law, of Torah, of unwavering and unchanging balance and *Emes* / truth.* In walking, one's arms give the body balance. The

---

* חותמו של הקדוש ברוך הוא אמת / "The Seal of Hashem is *Emes* / Truth" (*Shabbos*, 55a). *Emes* / truth means something that never changes; it is absolute. Thus, the three letters in the word *Emes* are the first letter of the Aleph-Beis (Aleph), the middle letter (Mem), and the final letter Tav. Emes never changes, in the beginning, middle, or end. As the Seal of Hashem, the word *Emes* appears in the Torah in the first three words. The final letters of the first three words of the Torah, בראשית ברא אלקים, contain the three letters that spell אמת / *Emes* / truth. Furthermore, the first letter of the Ten *Dibros* / Commandments is א / Aleph, the first letter in the Mishnah מאימתי, beginning with a מ / Mem, and the first letter in Gemara is תנא, beginning with the letter ת / Tav, spelling the word *Emes*. Indeed, in Rashi, the greatest Torah commentator, we find a similar pattern. In his commentary on

man of truth was taking his 'last walk' as it were, without arms, and saying goodbye to Klal Yisrael as his life was ending.

In simple terms, the difference between a *Guf* / body without arms and one with arms is that the arms can create a circle, and without arms, the body is only a line. And the primary difference between a line and a circle is that while a line has a beginning and an end, the circle is continuous, having no place of beginning and no definite ending.

Later on, in this Torah reading, it says, "And now, write down this *Shirah* / 'song' and teach it to the Children of Israel" (31:19). This is the Mitzvah, the positive command to write the entire Torah (Rambam, *Hilchos Tefillin, Mezuzah, v'Sefer Torah*, 7:1. *Sanhedrin*, 21b). The Mitzvah is not just to write the particular poem or song that is described in these Torah readings (Rashi), but actually to write the entire Torah (זו, שירה בה שיש תורה לכם כתבו, לפי שאין כותבין את התורה פרשיות פרשיות: Rambam, *Ibid*, see *Tzafnas Paneach*, ad loc. ע"כ כונת התורה דצריך לכתוב התורה כולה ונ"מ אם בלתה התורה ונשתיירה השירה אם יצא: *Sha'agas Aryeh*, Siman 34). As such, the entire Torah is called a *Shir*, even though the main body of the Torah is not poetry but law and instruction. In fact, the Torah is actually called *Torah*

the Torah, Rashi begins with the letter Aleph, אמר. In the middle point of the Torah, the word גחון / '(You shall not eat, among all things that) "swarm" upon the earth' (*Vayikra*, 11:42) says Rashi, the expression גחון denotes bending low, alluding to, "That which walks bent down and fallen upon its מעיו / belly," and מעיו starts with the letter מ / Mem. The final letter of Rashi's commentary on the Torah is ששברת / "which you broke," ending with the letter ת / Tav, hence the word אמת / Emes / truth.

from the word meaning 'teaching' through direction, guidance, and law.

Law and song, prose and poetry, seem to be opposite sides of a spectrum. Law is absolute, true, rigid, objective, and 'linear', whereas song and poetry are flowing, subjective, fluid, and cyclical or 'circular'. In fact, the word *Shir* itself alludes to a circle (כשיר מהו: *Baba Metziya*, 25a. The word *Shir* in Hebrew and Aramaic means 'a piece of round jewelry', like a bracelet: *Yeshayahu*, 3:19. *Targum*, Bereishis, 24:22. Mishnah, *Shabbos*, 51b. וסוס בשיה. וכל בעלי השיר יוצאין בשיר ונמשכין בשיר).

Moshe, the lawgiver, embodied the quality of subjective 'truth' whereas Aharon, the man of the people, embodied the quality of 'peace'. Truth is absolute and unbending, while peace seeks compromise. *Miriam / Mir-Yam* means 'a sea of bitterness', pointing to her deeply emotional rejection of exile and enslavement. She also hoped and dreamed of the rebirth of Klal Yisrael, and later expressed herself through a Shir at the *Yam / sea*, and a circle dance. Truth unemotionally establishes justice, while spiritual yearning dreams of resolution and celebration.

Law is linear, and song is circular.

Speaking about the Mitzvah of writing "this Song," Torah, the Torah says ועתה / "And now, write down this song...." Our sages tell us elsewhere that the words "and now" refer to *Teshuvah / return* (אין ועתה אלא תשובה: *Tanchuma*, Beshalach, 15). Law is an unchanging line, whereas Teshuvah, the ability to change and start anew at any moment, comes from the world of circles.

A *Kav* / line symbolizes the absoluteness of cause and effect. In this paradigm, once something is set in motion by a person's action, there will be a consequence. In this linear reality, there is no possibility for real change nor the option to go back 'before' the action and start anew. In contrast, circle reality affords us the possibility to change our course in life, to do a complete about-face, as it were. With Teshuvah, one can circle back to a point where an action occurred and recreate the action in a different way. If you break the law, there will be an effect, but with Teshuvah, you can return to a place 'before' the cause, create a new effect, and start again.

The Torah itself, the Law, is called a "song." It is written 'line by line', but then all the lines are rolled together as a scroll, a circle. Torah law also leaves room for Teshuvah; it contains the Mitzvah of Teshuvah. Torah includes both paradigms; it is the combination of lines and circles.

When he has 'arms', Moshe, the embodiment of law, has balance and the qualities of a circle. When 'law' no longer has arms, when it is not flanked by 'peace' and 'yearning', it is no longer a 'poem', or 'song'. Thus, Moshe can no longer lead the people, as he is now embodying the *Guf* / body, alone, the linearity of law.

This is why it says Moshe "walked" to all the camps without strength — his time for leadership was over, his song was complete; he was just a line without a circle.

Originally, before he had Aharon and Miriam at his side, Moshe also demonstrated qualities of harsh judgment, unbending truth, and strict justice. For example, when Hashem asked Moshe to take Klal Yisrael out of Egypt, Moshe responded: "הן / *Hein* / and indeed, they will not believe me" (*Shemos*, 4:1). He spoke harshly about Klal Yisrael. As a consequence, when Hashem tells Moshe in this week's Parshah, that he is about to pass on from this world, the Torah says, "הן / *Hein* / indeed the days of your death are nearing" (*Devarim*, 31:14). Moshe was bothered by the harsh, blunt language, yet Hashem informed him that this went back to the way he originally spoke about Klal Yisrael (*Medrash Rabbah*, Devarim, 9:6). It seems that justice, without the balances of peace and yearning, is too harsh for Klal Yisrael, and Moshe needs to pass on so that a new leader can arise (now that Aharon and Miriam have passed away, Moshe has returned to functioning through direct Emes and strict justice, and Hashem is telling him that he can no longer lead Klal Yisrael).

VAYELECH

Energy of the Week:
Going Beyond the Linear

This week's Torah reading injects us with the Ko'ach to connect with the circle world, a reality that goes beyond linear logic and where radical newness is a real possibility. The things that you feel are impossible, based on the reality of the line, are completely logical and possible in this circle reality.

To tap into this transcendent reality, we need to open ourselves up to being fully in the present moment, and set our ego aside. In this humble place, we are an open vessel, a circle, ready to receive the Divine blessing that is not reliant solely on past deeds and causes.

In these times, this Torah reading is always read in close proximity to Rosh Hashanah. On Rosh Hashanah, we celebrate not only the 'beginning' of the year, but the *Rosh* / 'head' of the year, the 'brain' of the year, the nucleus from which the whole circle of the year emerges.

With this new year, a new Light that was never revealed in Creation will flow down, giving us the ability to tap into the amazing quality of newness.

Rosh Hashanah contains the entire year in seed
form. Everything physical and spiritual blessing we
will attain in the coming year is drawn down into us
in its potential state on Rosh Hashanah.

When we stand, balanced before Hashem on Rosh
Hashanah, we are saying, 'Give us blessings via the
circle paradigm, in which cause and effect are not absolutely set in stone. Rather, let us receive blessings
purely on the basis of our standing before You right
here and now, in the posture of Teshuvah, acknowledging Your Infinite Kindness.'

PRACTICE OF THE WEEK:

See Yourself as an Open Vessel,
Ready to Receive Blessings,
Regardless of the Past

Ha'azinu

The Song of Opposites

THIS WEEK'S TORAH READING IS PRIMARILY A SONG, composed by Moshe and delivered to Klal Yisrael before his passing. Ha'azinu is often referred to as "the *Shirah* / Song of Ha'azinu." It is a song of prophecy foretelling Klal Yisrael's future.

As explored earlier, the entire Torah is called a *Shir* / song (the masculine form of *Shirah*). In fact, the first word of the Torah, בראשית / *Bereishis*, contains the three letters that form the word שיר / *Shir* (*Tikkunci Zohar*, 24b), and the last word of the Torah, ישראל / Yisrael, can create the words שיר א-ל / *Shir E-l* / a song to Hashem (*Tikkunei Zohar*, 3a). In this way, both the beginning and the end of the Torah remind us that it is one great circular song repeated each year.

Ha'azinu is a shorter song within the great song of Torah —
a poem, as it were, which Hashem asked Moshe to write. But
it seems to be a strange song. A Shirah is usually an outburst of
emotions or an epiphany in response to an extraordinary vic-
tory or miracle, such as the songs of Moshe and Miriam after
the splitting of the sea. What is Ha'azinu in response to? Here,
Moshe is given instructions for his death, and informed that
he will not be able to enter *Eretz Yisrael* / the Land of Israel,
and the generation he led out of Egypt is gone — what is there
to sing about?

What's more, the content of this song is peculiar: it basically
details the harsh reality to befall the nation when they stray
from the path. In this way, it is like a 'warning poem' meant to
arouse further generations, something they should continually
recite to ensure that they do not go astray. But hasn't this message already been transmitted in the *Tochechah* / rebuke in the
previous Torah reading?

Lastly, the Parshah emphasizes the importance of witness:
"Therefore, write down this song and teach it to the People
of Israel, put it in their mouths, in order that it may be My
witness against the People of Israel" (31:19). Indeed, it opens
with Moshe calling heaven and earth as witnesses: האזינו השמים
אמרי־פי ואדברה ותשמע הארץ / "Give ear, O heavens, let me speak;
let the earth hear the words I utter" (32:1). Moshe is saying,
'Let heaven and earth be my witness that I have warned them'
(Rashi).

Between Prose and Poetry

One hint we should notice is that the Tochechah, the earlier rebuke, is written as prose, while the warnings in Ha'azinu are written as poetry. If we can understand the deeper difference between prose and poetry or song, then we will be able to appreciate the nature of the 'testimony' or 'witness' revealed in this week's Torah reading.

Prose operates within formal linguistic rules; it is a very clear and defined form of communication, replete with logical structure, sequential steps, and correct syntax and grammar. Poetry and song function primarily to portray a feeling, and feelings sometimes defy perfect logical structures and even words. Poetry allows for a free flow of ideas.

Prose functions in a linear universe, while poetry is in a unified, circular universe.

The previous rebuke speaks of a Bris, a covenant, a promise established in which one who abandons Hashem will eventually be exiled. For us, this is also a metaphor, meaning that we will eventually become alienated from our authentic self. This is pure prose, setting forth a 'linear', causal relationship (A *Bris Milah* / circumcision occurs on an organ shaped like a line, and in the Torah, the *Bris Bein HaBesarim* / 'Covenant Between the Parts' occurs through walking in a line, between the halves of the slaughtered animals). In a linear covenant, if one breaks one's promises, there are definite consequences.

Here, the rebuke is poetic, and speaks of *Hastir Panim* / hiding the face: "I will hide My Face from them" (32:20). This image is a paradox. A face is by definition 'seen' (the face of something is that which is revealed to us), but here it is hidden. It is revealed and concealed, tangible and ephemeral, close and distant. Only poetry can express such paradoxical perceptions. Only poetry can convey the feeling that Hashem is both present and 'absent' at the same time, and the knowledge that we are never abandoned, although we may feel alone. Hashem loves us unconditionally, and yet we don't take this for granted.

Witnesses Reveal the Concealed

The objective of 'witnesses' is to reveal a deeper truth, even one that is hiding in plain sight. They demonstrate that there is revelation in concealment itself; in other words, witnesses reveal what is concealed. If everything was plainly revealed, there would be no need for witnesses. The Shirah of Ha'azinu reveals a revolutionary insight: Hashem is intimately present with us within the very perception of distance and absence. In our national state of exile, we are paradoxically in redemptive unity with our Creator. We can simultaneously mourn our separation and 'sing' with gratitude.

Ha'azinu Is the Ultimate Song, Containing All Emotions & All of History

This is why Ha'azinu is the ultimate 'song', and it is not an expression of one emotion only. Moshe's death is referred to as "life," and it was even experienced as a 'kiss'. The Shirah includes all of life and, in fact, all of our collective and personal

history. As our sages tell us, גדולה שירה שיש בה עכשיו ויש בה לשעבר,
ויש בה לעתיד לבוא, ויש בה לעולם הזה ויש בה לעולם הבא / "Great is this
song, for it contains the present, the past, and the future, this
world and the next" (Sifri, 333:5). The Ramban writes that this
song contains all of Jewish history: היא כוללת כל העתידות למו /
"The Song contains everything that is to come upon them —
to Klal Yisrael" (Ramban, Devarim, 32:40).

The Rambam had a student named Avner who left his
teacher and lived a very 'un-Jewish' life. Once, the Ramban
met up with Avner and asked him, "Why did you leave me,
and why did you leave Yiddishkeit / Judaism in general?" Avner
told him, "My dear teacher, you are a great man, but I realized
the things you teach are simply not true. Look, for example,
you said that everything in the universe, all of history, all of
humanity is encoded within the song of Ha'azinu."

"Yes, that's true," said the Ramban.

"Well, if so," said Avner, "tell me where I appear in the Torah." Upon reflection, the Ramban quoted the verse in Ha'azinu, אמרתי אפאיהם אשביתה מאנוש זכרם — "I said I would make
an end of them. I would cause their memory to vanish from
among mankind" (Devarim, 32, 26). The third letter of each of
these words spell the name R' (Reb) Avner (Emek HaMelech,
Sha'ashu'ei HaMelech, Sha'ar 1, 4).

Ha'azinu is a circle that includes all of life and all emotions.
And each part on a circle can be a new beginning. And so,

no matter how difficult or alienating our life experiences have been, we can start now to see with fresh eyes, and even 'sing Shirah'.

Rebbe Shimon and the Peculiar Blessing

Rebbe Shimon once sent his son Reb Eliezer to receive blessings for certain sages…They said to him, "May it be [Heaven's] pleasure that you plant and do not reap, that what you bring in does not go out, that what goes out you do not bring in, that your house be destroyed, and that your guests live in it, that your table be disorderly and that you do not see a new year." When he came home to his father, he said to him, "These were so far from blessings; they even distressed me very much!"

"What did the sages say?" asked Rebbe Shimon. He told him. Said his father, "Actually, all of those *are* blessings. 'Planting and not reaping' means your wife will have children and their lives will not be cut short. 'That what you bring in should not go out' means your sons will take in wives and their lives together will be long and happy so their wives will never leave. 'That which goes out you do not bring in' means your daughters will marry and will never have to return home for support.

"'That your house be destroyed and your guests live in it' means your grave will not see your presence for a long time but rather your guests, namely your earthly desires, will be buried. 'Your table will be disorderly' means you will have disorder with many children and grandchildren. And 'You won't see a new year,' means your wife will have a long life and you won't have to marry another" (*Moed Katan*, 9b).

This story begs a question. If the sages wanted to bless Reb Eliezer, why did they not bless him openly, with clear, factual prose? Why did they poetically couch the blessings in curses? The answer is that they were trying to teach him how to look at life, and how to reframe and re-contextualize his experiences; how to see redemption in exile.

Reframing

If the sages had simply blessed Reb Eliezer with healthy children, long life, and ample sustenance, Reb Eliezer might have felt that the blessings of life were only manifest when they were fully and clearly revealed as blessings. But they wanted to teach Rebbe Eliezer something deeper: how to look at life not only as linear prose but also as circular *poetry*; how to see blessings in every experience.

For us, as well. If our house is in chaos and is a tremendous mess, perhaps that is because we have been blessed with children. And if our apartment is too small for our family, perhaps that is because Hashem has given us many children. In any case, look at your blessings; many people yearn to have children but do not have them.

If you don't yet have children, perhaps you have been blessed to teach or influence someone for the good. Perhaps you have been given this time for study, contemplative self-development, service to others, and other great achievements. Perhaps Hashem has plans for you that you simply cannot imagine.

This way of thinking is not about whitewashing the real challenges of life nor claiming that the bad is really good. Still, this Parshah calls us to reframe our story by stepping back and viewing the entire picture. This will eventually allow us to sing to Hashem for all our ups and downs, our revelations and concealments. This is the deeper message of the Shirah.

When faced with the devastating news of the loss of his sons, Aharon "remained silent" (*Vayikra*, 10:3), and was rewarded for this silence. Yet, King Dovid declares, "In order that my soul may sing praise to You, and *not* be silent" (*Tehilim*, 30:13). As the Kotzker Rebbe once observed, here are three ways to deal with hardship. Some do it with tears and cries of pain, others are able to remain stoic and silent, yet the highest level is to transform the tears or stoicism into song.

HA'AZINU

Energy of the Week:
Reframing Life Challenges

Ha'azinu, the 'Song of Life', gives you the wisdom to see 'Hashem's Face' in the ups and downs. This week, experiment with placing your painful experiences or 'rebukes' within the circular context of a 'Shirah'. In this circle, every point is an opportunity to reframe the nature of the experience and understand it in a new, positive interpretation. You will begin to see how your life story is a beautiful, sometimes poignant ballad, often revealing hidden achievements, moments of courageous self-sacrifice, and always glowing with *Ohr Ganuz* / hidden light.

"Hashem nourishes the world with Hidden Light" (*Zohar* 2, 149a).

PRACTICE OF THE WEEK:

Reinterpret Your Challenges in Positive Terms

VeZos HaBerachah
The Destination Is Within the Journey

W E HAVE NOW ARRIVED AT THE FINAL TORAH reading of the Torah: *V'Zos HaBerachah* / "'This is the blessing' which Moshe…bade the children of Israel before he died." Following the blessings, the Torah concludes with the death of Moshe, and the Torah comes to a close — without Moshe or Klal Yisrael actually entering into Eretz Yisrael.

The bulk of the Torah narrative occurs between the Exodus and the journey of Klal Yisrael through the Desert toward Eretz Yisrael, our national destination and promised homeland. However, the Torah ends with what appears to be an anti-climax. Moshe dies, and Klal Yisrael does not yet reach its destination.

Last week's Parshah concludes: "And Hashem spoke to Moshe, on the essence of that day, saying, ascend...to Mount נבו / Nevo, and view the Land...which I am giving the Children of Israel...You may view the Land from a distance, but you shall not enter it" (32:48–52).

After offering a blessing, the Torah says, "Moshe went up from the steppes of מואב / Moav to Mount נבו / Nevo" (34:1). This is a steep movement upwards.

Everything and everyone can be observed by means of its external, physical dimension as a *Kli* / vessel, and by means of its deep, internal, spiritual dimension as an *Ohr* / light. In his more external dimension of Kli, Moshe is 'punished' and does not enter Eretz Yisrael; he only gets to see it. But in his deep internal dimension of Ohr, the 'punishment' is actually a revelation drawing him closer to the Divine essence of Eretz Yisrael (כי א'ל נקמות הופיע, ר"ל שהנקמה הוא במה שהופיע לו מגדולתו: *Keser Shem Tov*, Part 1, 108). If one assimilates such a revelation properly, it allows them to attain an even higher level of spirituality and closeness to HaKadosh Baruch Hu than would be possible on a Kli level.

Hitting the Rock

From the external level, Moshe only has the Ko'ach to see Eretz Yisrael from outside of it, but does not in actuality get in; he is missing the *Po'el* / actualization of his dream. Moshe dies in the process of the journey and seemingly doesn't reach his destination. This is due to his 'shortcoming' of hitting the rock to bring forth water for the people instead of speaking to the rock, as he was instructed to do.

Speaking to the rock to miraculously bring forth water would be a great miracle, but hitting the rock seems to be a significant miracle as well. Why is Hashem so 'upset' with Moshe? There are multiple reasons offered as to what Moshe's transgression really is. Perhaps it was his becoming angry and venting his frustration with Klal Yisrael. Before we explore these questions, let's return to the simple narrative: Moshe hit the rock instead of speaking to it.

Potential and Actual

Again, in our world of separation, there is a difference between Kli and Ohr, and between כוח / *Ko'ach* / potentiality and פועל / *Poel* / actuality. Such dualities, including those of up and down, right and left, past and future, etc., are inherent to the worldview of *Pirud* / separation.

From the perspective of *Achdus* / Unity — which is the Creator's perspective, as it were — אין כוח חסר פועל / "a potential does not lack actuality" (*Pardes Rimonim*, Sha'ar 11, 3. *Derech Mitzvosecha*, HaAmanos Elokus, 11). Here, there is no separate past and future; if something exists in potential, it exists already in actuality. There is no divide between process and product, journey and destination, conception and realization.

In our dual perspective, first we have an idea in mind, then we might formulate the idea in speech or write it down, and only later actualize the idea. The garments of our soul are *Machshavah* / thought, *Dibbur* / speech, and *Ma'aseh* / action. Through these stages, we can transform intuition into fruition.

When the Torah describes Hashem creating the world, manifesting actuality, it simply says, "And Elokim said, 'Let there be light,' and there was light." There was no division between speaking and creating. *Dibbur* / speech was one with *Ma'aseh* / action. In the language of *Chazal* / our sages, "From where do we know that speech is like action? As it is stated: "By the word of Hashem the heavens were made" (מניין שהדיבור שמים נעשו / כמעשה שנאמר: בדבר ה' / *Shabbos*, 119b). This is the immediate, 'process-less' creative power of the world of Unity.

By speaking to the rock, Hashem wanted Moshe to 're-enact' His Unitive Creative power as displayed in the beginning of the Creation. This generation, which was about to enter Eretz Yisrael, did not personally experience *Yetziyas Mitzrayim* / the Exodus from Egypt, nor the shattering of the natural order with the plagues and the Splitting of the Sea. Hashem, therefore, wanted Moshe to show them the *Ko'ach HaBoreh* / the Power of the Creator *within* Creation.

At the beginning of Klal Yisrael's journey into the 'natural' world of Eretz Yisrael, where they would need to work the land, they needed to see and experience the unitive Ko'ach HaBoreh within Creation. Unlike the Desert, in which their parents and grandparents witnessed open miracles such as the

Mon / Manna from Heaven and the protective Clouds of Glory, Eretz Yisrael was a land that would need to be physically conquered and settled. They needed something more than miracles of 'cause and effect' and distance. They needed to see that the natural world is being sustained and recreated every moment by the Ko'ach HaBoreh *without separation.*

As this generation did not physically stand at Mount Sinai and hear the miraculous Divine speech of *Matan Torah* / Revelation of Torah, they needed to hear miraculous revelatory speech from Moshe. Then they would experience the perspective in which a potential does not lack its actualization and the Ko'ach HaBoreh is one with the Creation. As they would soon be entering the intense physicality of Eretz Yisrael, they needed to experience firsthand the *Devar Hashem* / 'Divine creative speech' *within* creation, and not get lost in *Olam HaZeh* / 'this world'.

Thus, Hashem asked Moshe to speak to the rock so that it would release water; Hashem asked him to be the instrument to demonstrate the Ko'ach HaBoreh in Creation, revealing the Transcendent power from the world of Unity, the principle of אין כח חסר פועל / "a potentiality does not lack the actuality" within this world. Instead, 'just another' miracle occurred, and a physical action released water from the rock. This was like the miracle of Mon from Heaven, which they were already experiencing. But that is not what they needed in order to enter the Land.

Hitting the rock to bring forth water was a miracle; however, it was a demonstration of כח חסר פועל / "A potential *lacking* actuality." Moshe performed a 'separate' action that caused water to emerge, showing a kind of 'potential' for unifying spirituality and physicality, but not in a way that could be 'actualized' in the Land. He was still functioning in the paradigm of duality — of cause versus effect, spirituality versus materiality, and miraculous versus mundane. He was coming from the paradigm of the Desert rather than the paradigm of *Eretz HaKodesh* / the Holy Land, which is a paradoxical unification of 'Land' and 'holiness'.

Buried on the 50th Level

As Moshe did not show readiness to enter Eretz Yisrael, he was told to go up to the peak of Mount נבו / Nevo, and there he would be able to see the Land and then pass on (32:29–50).

Moshe ascended this mountain from the steppes of Moav. נבו / *Nevo* is נ-בו / *Nun-Bo*, meaning 'Fifty Within It'. מואב / *Moav* is numerically 49. Moshe had attained the 49 'steps' of awareness and understanding during his lifetime. However, his 'punishment' was rising beyond that to the 50th level of consciousness (Moshe attained the 49ᵗʰ level during life: *Rosh Hashanah*, 21b. *Nedarim*, 38a. On that level, he was unable to cross the Jordan River, which had a width of 50 cubits: Tosefos, *Sotah* 34b. See also Devarim, 3:25, *Ba'al HaTurim*).

Forty-nine symbolizes the world of opposites and dualities. Hence, there are 49 ways that an act can legally be an *Isur*

/ prohibition and 49 ways that an act can legally be a *Heter* / allowance (*Medrash Tehilim*, 12); there are 49 ways of purity and 49 ways of impurity (*Yerushalmi*, Sanhedrin, 4:2. See also *Eiruvin*, 13b, Ritva, *ad loc*). The number 50 symbolizes the level of Unity, where there is no 'left side', no opposite, and thus it is above, as it were, the level of duality, where אין כח חסר פועל / "A potential *does not* lack actuality."

This is why, when Moshe goes up the mountain to pass on, he does so in the middle of the day, when all can see (Rashi, 32:48). They are now witnessing the revelation that Moshe is finally reaching the deepest point of unity, the 50th level. He is entering a state in which there is no separation between Ko'ach and Poel, and between seeing something from a distance and actually being there.

From this deeper perspective of *Ohr* / light, Moshe does enter the essential reality of Eretz Yisrael since he ascended to *Nun-Bo* / 'Fifty Within Him', and אין כח חסר פועל / the 'potential' entry into the Land did not lack the 'actual' entry into the Land. When he sees it, he is actually there, not merely 'potentially' there. Seeing is not just 'believing'; seeing is *being*.

In this way, the end was revealed in the means, the destination was revealed in the journey, Eretz Yisrael was revealed outside the literal borders of Eretz Yisrael. The revealing of 'presence' within apparent 'absence'.*

---

* One opinion in Gemara is that Moshe himself wrote the last eight verses of the Torah, and did so with *Dimah* / tears: *Baba Basra*, 15a. The

VEZOS HABERACHAH

Energy of the Week:

The Peace of the Destination
Within the Journey

After the journey of an entire year of Torah, this week's reading gives us the Ko'ach not to get disheartened or spiritually weary from our long spiritual journey.

Our relationships, occupation, and activities in this world are all part of this great journey. Perhaps we are working on building up enough credit or funds to buy a home, laboring on a text in *Gemara* / Talmud for years until we are able to master it, learning to play a musical instrument on a higher level of skill, or working diligently on our marriage.

Gra asks, "If so, does it not appear as if Moshe is telling a lie? Did he write that he died?" Therefore, the Gra continues, the word *Dimah* comes from the word for 'mixed up' or 'scrambled' (see *Shemos*, 22:28), and this means Moshe wrote all the letters but not in a way that was then understandable to those who read it. The letters were all there, but they were scrambled. Only later on did they become crystallized into comprehensive words. The Baal Shem Tov says that *Dimah* comes from the word *Damua* / silent (as in *Dom*), and that is why no one knows where he is buried; *Chassidus L'Shas*, Sotah, 386. This, perhaps, alludes to the level of Atik, which is transcendent silence

Every small act of self-refinement within any such activity is a step forward, bringing us closer to our destination, our ultimate wholeness and state of Unity.

On the one hand, completing our reading of the Torah without Moshe entering the Land tells us that life is all about the journey, the process. As long as we are moving incrementally toward our 'Promised Land', we are doing very well. In general, we can find joy in journeying itself and not focus exclusively on destinations.

On a deeper level, this final Parshah draws Ko'ach to us from Moshe, the *Rayah Mehemnah* / "Faithful Shepherd." This Ko'ach helps us tap into the destination within the journey; to come and see, and even 'touch', the Divine Presence within the mundane, and to come to know the peace and stillness of *Olam HaBa* / the World to Come while still in this world.

Indeed, our ultimate freedom, joy, and inner peace is not just in the 'distant' future, it is, on a deeper level, here and now and always available. May we merit to experience this truth as we cycle back to Bereishis and begin a new level of our journey of self-refinement and blessing.

PRACTICE OF THE WEEK:
Finding Peace Within the Journey

Other Books by Rav Pinson

RECLAIMING THE SELF
The Way of Teshuvah

Teshuvah is one of the great gifts of life. It speaks of a hope for a better today and empowers us to choose a brighter tomorrow. But what exactly is Teshuvah? How does it work? How can we undo our past and how do we deal with guilt? And what is healthy regret without eroding our self-esteem? In this fascinating and empowering book, the path for genuine transformation and a way to include all of our past in the powerful moment of the now, is explored and demonstrated.

THE MYSTERY OF KADDISH
Understanding the Mourner's Kaddish

The Mystery of Kaddish is an in-depth exploration into the Mourner's Prayer. Throughout Jewish history, there have been many rites and rituals associated with loss and mourning, yet none have prevailed quite like the Mourner's Kaddish Prayer, which has become the definitive ritual of mourning. The book explores the source of this prayer and deconstructs the meaning to better understand the grieving process and how the Kaddish prayer supports and uplifts the bereaved through their own personal journey to healing.

UPSIIERNISH: The First Haircut
Exploring the Laws, Customs & Meanings of a Boy's First Haircut

What is the meaning of Upsherin, the traditional celebration of a boy's first haircut at the age of three? Why is a boy's hair allowed to grow freely for his first three years? What is the deeper import of hair in all its lengths and varieties? What is the meaning of hair coverings? Includes a guide to conducting an Upsherin ceremony.

A BOND FOR ETERNITY
Understanding the Bris Milah

What is the Bris Milah – the covenant of circumcision? What does it represent, symbolize and signify? This book provides an in depth and sensitive review of this fundamental Mitzvah. In this little masterpiece of wisdom – profound yet accessible —the deeper meaning of this essential rite of passage and its eternal link to the Jewish people, is revealed and explored.

REINCARNATION AND JUDAISM
The Journey of the Soul

A fascinating analysis of the concept of Gilgul / Reincarnation. Dipping into the fountain of ancient wisdom and modern understanding, this book addresses and answers such basic questions as: What is reincarnation? Why does it occur? And how does it affect us personally?

INNER RHYTHMS
The Kabbalah of MUSIC

Exploring the inner dimension of sound and music, and particularly, how music permeates all aspects of life. The topics range from Deveikus/ Unity and Yichudim/Unifications, to the more personal issues, such as Simcha/Happiness and Marirus/ sadness.

MEDITATION AND JUDAISM
Exploring the Jewish Meditative Paths

A comprehensive work encompassing the entire spectrum of Jewish thought, from the sages of the Talmud and the early Kabbalists to the modern philosophers and Chassidic masters. This book is both a scholarly, in-depth study of meditative practices, and a practical, easy to follow guide for any person interested in meditating the Jewish way.

TOWARD THE INFINITE

A book focusing exclusively on the Chassidic approach to meditation known as Hisbonenus. Encompassing the entire meditative experience, it takes the reader on a comprehensive and engaging journey through this unique practice. The book explores the various states of consciousness that a person encounters in the course of the meditation, beginning at a level of extreme self-awareness and concluding with a state of total non-awareness.

THIRTY - TWO GATES OF WISDOM
into the Heart of Kabbalah & Chassidus

What is Kabbalah? And what are the differences between the theoretical, meditative, magical and personal Kabbalistic teachings? What are the four paths of interpreting the teachings of the ARIzal? What did Chassidus teach? These are some of the fundamental issues expanded upon in this text. And then, more specifically, why are there so many names of G-d and what do they represent? What are the key concepts of these deeper teachings?

The book explores the grand narrative of the great chain of reality, how there was and is a movement from the Infinite Oneness of Hashem to a world of (apparent) duality and multiplicity.

———————

THE PURIM READER

The Holiday of Purim Explored

———————

With a Persian name, a masquerade dress code and a woman as the heroine, Purim is certainly unusual amongst the Jewish holidays. Most people are very familiar with the costumes, Megilah and revelry, but are mystified by their significance. This book offers a glimpse into the hidden world of Purim, uncovering these mysteries and offering a deeper understanding of this unique holiday.

———————

EIGHT LIGHTS
8 Meditations for Chanukah

What is the meaning and message of Chanukah? What is the spiritual significance of the Lights of the Menorah? What are the Lights telling us? What is the deeper dimension of the Dreidel? Rav Pinson, with his trademark deep learning and spiritual sensitivity guides us through eight meditations relating to the Lights of the Menorah, the eight days of Chanukah, and a fascinating exploration of the symbolism and structure of the Dreidel. Includes a detailed how-to guide for lighting the Chanukah Menorah.

PASSPORT TO KABBALAH
A Journey of Inner Transformation

Life is a journey full of ups and downs, inside-outs, and unexpected detours. There are times when we think we know exactly where we want to be headed, and other times when we are so lost we don't even know where we are. This slim book provides readers with a passport of sorts to help them through any obstacles along their path of self-refinement, reflection, and self-transformation.

—————

THE FOUR SPECIES
The Symbolism of the Lulav & Esrog

The Four Species have inspired countless commentaries and traditions and intrigued scholars and mystics alike. In this little masterpiece of wisdom both profound and practical - the deep symbolic roots and nature of the Four Species are explored. The Na'anuim, or ritual of the Lulav movement, is meticulously detailed and Kavanos,, are offered for use with the practice. Includes an illustrated guide to the Lulav Movements.

—————

THE BOOK OF LIFE AFTER LIFE

What is a soul? What happens to us after we physically die?

What is consciousness, and can it survive without a physical brain?

Can we remember our past lives?

Do near-death experiences prove immortality?

What is Gan Eden? Resurrection?

Exploring the possibility of surviving death, the near-death experience and a glimpse into what awaits us after this life.

(This book is an updated and expanded version of the book; Jewish Wisdom of the Afterlife)

THE GARDEN OF PARADOX:

The Essence of Non - Dual Kabbalah

This book is a Primer on the Essential Philosophy of Kabbalah presented as a series of 3 conversations, revealing the mysteries of Creator, Creation and Consciousness. With three representational students, embodying respectively, the philosopher, the activist and the mystic, the book, tackles the larger questions of life. Who is G-d? Who am I? Why do I exist? What is my purpose in this life? Written in clear and concise prose, the text, gently guides the reader towards making sense of life's paradoxes and living meaningfully.

BREATHING & QUIETING THE MIND

Achieving a sense of self-mastery and inner freedom demands that we gain a measure of hegemony over our thoughts. We learn to choose out thoughts so that we are not at the mercy of whatever belches up to the mind. Through quieting the mind and conscious breathing we can slow the onrush of anxious, scattered thinking and come to a deeper awareness of the interconnectedness of all of life.

Source texts are included in translation, with how-to-guides for the various practices.

SEVEN PATHS TO LOVE, LIFE, PURPOSE & SERENITY:
A Book on the Sheva Mitzvos

SOUND AND VIBRATION:
Tuning into the Echoes of Creation

Through our perception of sound and vibration we internalize the world around us. What we hear, and how we process that hearing, has a profound impact on how we experience life. What we hear can empower us or harm us. A defining human capacity is to harness the power sound -- through speech, dialogue, and song, and through listening to others. Hearing is primary dimension of our existence. In fact, as a fetus our ears were the first fully operating sensory organs to develop.

This book will guide you in methods of utilizing the power of sound and vibration to heal and maintain mental, emotional and spiritual health, to fine-tune your Midos and even to guide you into deeper levels of Deveikus / conscious unity with Hashem. The vibratory patterns of the Aleph-Beis are particularly useful portals into our deeper conscious selves. Through chanting and deep listening, we can use the letters and sounds to shift our very mindset, to induce us into a state of presence and spiritual elevation.

THE POWER OF CHOICE:
A Practical Guide to Conscious Living

It is the essential premise of this book that we hold the key to unlock many of the gates that seem closed to us and keep us from living our fullest life. That key we all hold is the power to choose. The Power of Choice is the primary tool that we have at our disposal to impact the world and effect change within our own lives. We often give up this power to outside forces such as the market, media, politicians or peer pressure; or to internal forces that often function beyond our conscious control such as ego, anger, lust, greed or jealousy. Making conscious, compassionate and creative decisions is the cornerstone of living a mature and meaningful life.

MYSTIC TALES FROM THE EMEK HAMELECH

Mystic Tales of the Emek HaMelech, is a wondrous and inspiring collection of stories culled from the Emek HaMelech. Emek HaMelech, from which these stories have been taken, (as well as its author) is a bit of a mystery. But like all good mysteries, it is one worth investigating. In this spirit the present volume is being offered to the general public in the merit and memory of its saintly author, as well as in the hopes of introducing a vital voice of deeper Torah teaching and tradition to a contemporary English speaking audience

---

INNER WORLDS OF JEWISH PRAYER
A Guide to Develop and Deepen the Prayer Experience

While much attention has been paid to the poetry, history, theology and contextual meaning of the prayers, the intention of this work is to provide a guide to finding meaning and effecting transformation through the prayer experience itself.

Explore: *What happens when we pray? *How do we enter the mind-state of prayer? *Learning to incorporate the body into the prayers. *Discover techniques to enhance and deepen prayer and make it a transformative experience.

This empowering and inspiring text, demonstrates how through proper mindset, preparation and dedication, the experience of prayer can be deeply transformative and ultimately, life-altering.

WRAPPED IN MAJESTY
Tefillin - Exploring the Mystery

Tefillin, the black boxes and leather straps that are worn during prayer, are curiously powerful and mysterious. Within the inky black boxes lie untold secrets. In this profound, passionate and thought-provoking text, the multi-dimensional perspectives of Tefillin are explored and revealed. Magically weaving together all levels of Torah including the Peshat (literal observation), to Remez (allegorical), to Derush, (homiletic), to Sod (hidden) into one beautiful tapestry. Inspirational and instructive, Wrapped in Majesty: Tefillin, will make putting on the Tefillin more meaningful and inspiring.

SECRETS OF THE MIKVAH:
Waters of Transformation

A Mikvah is a pool of water used for the purpose of ritual immersion; a place where one moves from a state of Tumah; impurity, blockage and death— to a place of Teharah; purity, fluidity and life.

In SECRETS OF THE MIKVAH, Rav Pinson delves into the transformative powers of the Mikvah with his trademark all-encompassing perspective that ranges from the literal, Pshat observation and Halachic implications of the texts, to the allegorical, the philosophical, and finally, to the deep secrets of the Mikvah as revealed by Kabbalah and Chassidus.

This insightful and inspirational text demonstrates how immersion in a Mikvah can be a transformative and life-altering practice, and includes various Kavanos—deep intentions—for all people, through various stages of life, that empower and enrich the immersion experience.

THE MYSTERY OF SHABBOS
Shabbat Rediscovered

Delving into the transformative power of Shabbos. With an all-encompassing perspective that ranges from the literal, Pshat observation and Halachic implications of the texts, to the allegorical, the philosophical, and finally, to the deeper secrets as revealed by Kabbalah and Chassidus, creating an elegant tapestry of thought and experience. THE MYSTERY OF SHABBOS is a profound meditation on the meaning of Shabbos and demonstrates the physical, emotional, mental and spiritual possibilities available and given to us with the gift of Shabbos. Studying and contemplating this inspired text on the depths of Shabbos will unveil a redemptive light in your experience of the Seventh Day -- and by extension, every day of your life.

THE SPIRAL OF TIME:
A 12 Part Series on the Months of the Year

VOL 1: THE SPIRAL OF TIME:
Unraveling the Yearly Cycle

Many centuries ago, the Sages of Israel were the foremost authority in the fields of both astronomical calculation and astrological wisdom, including the deeper interpretations of the cycles and seasons. Over time, this wisdom became hidden within the esoteric teachings of the Torah, and as a result was known only to students and scholars of the deepest depths of the tradition. More recently, the great teachers, from R.Yitzchak Luria (the Arizal) to the Baal Shem Tov, taught that as the world approaches the Era of Redemption, it is a Mitzvah / spiritual obligation to broadly reveal this wisdom.

"The Spiral of Time" is volume 1 is a series of 12 books, and serves as an introductory book to the basic concepts and nature of the Hebrew calendar and explores the special day of Rosh Chodesh.

———

VOL 2: THE MONTH OF NISAN:
Miraculous Awakenings from Above

The month of NISAN is the first month of the lunar cycle of the year, a month that brings in the spring and a month of redemption. Spring represents a time of plenty, abundance, sunshine, hope, and possibility. Redemption, on whatever level, feels palpable and accessible. In spring, the world is redeemed from the cold winter, the flower is redeemed from the tree, the grass from the earth, and we too feel that redemption is possible. A whole complex of ideas, including newness, redemption, going out of Egypt, and being freed from slavery, is intricately bound with the idea of Aviv / spring and the powerful month of Nisan.

———

VOL 3: THE MONTH OF IYYAR: EVOLVING THE SELF
& The Holiday of LAG B'OMER

The month of IYYAR is the second month of the spring, a month that connects the Redemption from Egypt in Nissan with the Revelation of Torah in Sivan. The Chai/ Eighteenth day of the Month is the day we celebrate the Rashbi (Rabbi Shimon Bar Yochai) and the revealing of the hidden aspects of the Torah. This is the 'Holiday' of Lag b'Omer. The book explores the unique quality of this special month, a month that has a Mitzvah of counting the Omer every day. In addition, the book explores the roots and significance of the mystical 'holiday' of Lag b'Omer. Including the customs & Practices of Lag b'Omer, such as, bonfires, bows & arrows, parades, Upsherin, and more.

VOL 4: THE MONTH OF SIVAN:
The Art of Receiving: Shavuos and Matan Torah

Sivan is the third month of the lunar cycle. One is a singularity. Two is division. Three is harmony, a unity that synthesizes individuality and multiplicity, Heaven and Earth, Spirituality and Physicality. During this month we celebrate Shavuos and the giving of the Torah, the ultimate expression of the unity of the Above and Below and we aspire to connect with the Keser/Crown of Torah that Transcends and yet includes all Worlds. Learning how to truly receive Higher wisdom in our Lower faculties is the mental, emotional, and spiritual exercise of the month.

VOL 5: THE MONTHS OF TAMUZ AND AV:
Embracing Brokenness –
17th of Tamuz, Tisha B'Av, & Tu B'Av

Each month and season of the year, radiates with distinct Divine qualities and unique opportunities for growth and Tikkun.

The summer month of Tamuz and Av contain the longest and hottest days of the year. The raised temperature is indicative of a corresponding spiritual heat, a time of harsher judgement and potential destruction, such as the destructions of the first and second Beis HaMikdash, which began on the 17th of Tamuz and culminated on the 9th and 10th of Av.

A few days later, on Tu b'Av, the darkness is transformed and reveals the greatest light and possibility for new life. During these summer months of Tamuz and Av we embrace our brokenness so that we can heal and transform darkness into light.

VOL 6: THE MONTH OF ELUL:
Days of Introspection and Transformation

Each month of the year radiates with a distinct quality and provides unique opportunities for growth and personal transformation. Elul, as the final month of the spring/summer season is connected to endings. Elul gives us the strength to be able to finish strong, to end well. Elul also serves as a month of preparation for the New Year/Rosh Hashanah.

We inhale our past year, ending with wisdom and then we also gain the wisdom to begin anew and exhale a positive year into being. The mental, emotional, and spiritual objective of this month is introspection and the reclaiming of our inner purity and wholeness.

VOL 7: THE MONTH OF TISHREI:
A Time of Rebirth & Upward Movement

Each month of the year radiates with distinct Divine qualities and unique opportunities for growth and spiritual illumination. As Tishrei begins the new yearly cycle, it is an appropriate month to introspect, reflect and resolve to move forward and preserve moving forward into the more inward months of the winter. This month creates the space to unburden ourselves from our negativities, and enter a more sacred, grounded sacred space. In Tishrei we are given the gift of forgiveness and then the ability to truly regain our space and inner joy.

VOL 8: THE MONTH OF CHESHVAN:
Navigating Transitions, Elevating the Fall

Directly on the heels of the inspiring and holiday-filled month of Tishrei, Cheshvan is a month that is quiet and devoid of holidays. In the month of Cheshvan we use the stored up energies of the previous months to self-generate our inspiration and creativity and provide ourselves with the strength to rise up after a fall. In Cheshvan we are entering into a stormier, wetter and colder season. It is a month of transition. The mental, emotional and spiritual objective of this month is to weather the transitions, learn to self-generate and stand tall. And if we do fall, we use the quality of this month to get back up and do so with more conviction, strength, wisdom and clarity.

VOL 9: THE MONTH OF KISLEV:
Rekindling Hope, Dreams and Trust

Kislev is the final month of the fall. Throughout this month, daylight progressively shortens, and the temperatures drop. Towards the end of the month, at the darkest hour, the winter solstice arrives and we begin the celebration of Chanukah. We commemorate the miracle of a small jug of oil that burned for eight nights, and as we celebrate, daylight expands. In the month of Kislev-despite the darkness, or perhaps because of it-we have the ability to tap into the Ohr HaGanuz, the hidden light of hope that rekindles our dreams and aspirations.

VOL 10: THE MONTH OF TEVES:
Refining Relationships, Elevating the Body

The quality of Teves is generally harsh—much like its counterpart Tamuz in the summer, thus the tendency for many is to hunker down, retract, curl up and wait for the month to pass by, only to reemerge when the harshness has dissipated. Think for a moment about the 'easier' months of the year, which, like gentle waves in the ocean, carry us where we want to go. We can ride these energies easily and they can propel us forward effortlessly, we just need to go with the overall flow, so to speak. The harsher months, on the other hand, can be compared to the more powerful waves that emanate from the belly of the ocean, which come forcefully crashing down and can easily drown a person before they even realize what has happened. However, those who want to utilize the momentum of the powerful energy that is available during such times can, with caution and creativity, harness these intense waves and ride them higher and farther than other, more gentle circumstances may allow. However, harnessing the power of Tohu, the raw energy of the body, does in fact need to be approached with great care and attention.

VOL 11: THE MONTH OF SHEVAT: ELEVATING EATING
& The Holiday of Tu b'Shevat

Each month of the year radiates with a distinct Divine energy and thus unique opportunities for growth, *Tikkun* and illumination. According to the deeper teachings of the Torah, all of these distinct qualities, opportunities and natural phenomena correspond to a certain data set. That is, the nature of each month is elucidated by a specific letter of the Aleph Beis, a tribe, verse, human sense, and so forth. The month of Shevat is particularly connected to food and our relationship to bodily intake. During this month we celebrate Tu b'Shevat, the New Year of the Tree, and aspire to create a proper and physically/emotionally/spiritually healthy relationship with food.

VOL 12: THE MONTH OF ADAR:
Transformation Through Laughter & Holy Doubt

Each month of the year radiates with distinct Divine qualities and unique opportunities for growth and spiritual illumination. As Adar concludes the monthly cycle of the year, as well as the solar phenomena of the winter, it is an appropriate month to think about our essential identity, before moving out to meet the world come spring. This month we strive to create a healthy relationship with holy humor, unbounded joy, and a general sense of lightness of being. Through the work of Adar we transform negative, crippling doubt and uncertainties into radical wonderment and openness.

ILLUMINATED SOUND:
The Baal Shem Tov on Prayer

In the year 1698 a great light was revealed to the world with the descent of the holy soul of the Baal Shem Tov. In time, the Baal Shem Tov became one of the most important and influential teachers of Torah in all of history, and the founder of Chassidus.

Amongst the vast repository of profound and revolutionary teachings of the holy Baal Shem Tov, the teachings on the path of Tefilah / Prayer are the most elaborate. The teachings of the Baal Shem Tov on Tefilah include some of his most innovative expressions, or Chidushim. Tefilah is the essential and central tenet from which all other teachings flow.

In this masterful and practical text, Rav Pinson revives the awe-inspiring and transformational teachings of the Baal Shem Tov, and illuminates his unique path to Tefilah.

The High Holiday Series:

A CALL TO MAJESTY:
The Mysteries of Shofar & Rosh Hashanah

The Shofar is the preeminent symbol of Rosh Hashanah, waking us up to a time of deep introspection and celebration. But why do we blow the Shofar on this most special of days? While the Torah decrees that the Shofar must be blown, it does not provide a reason. On the deepest level, the Shofar is of course beyond reason altogether, and yet, from within its shape, sound and story, a constellation of "reasons" emerge. Rebirth. Responsibility. Radical Amazement. On a primal vibrational level, the Shofar calls each of us to a place of deeper consciousness and community as we crown the King of All Creation.

A CALL TO MAJESTY delves deeply into the world of Rosh Hashanah and its primary Mitzvah, the sound of the Shofar. Weaving together a multi-dimensional tapestry of practical, allegorical, philosophical, and mystical ideas and implications, the teachings collected herein empower us all to answer the higher calling of the Shofar.

———————

A LIGHTNESS OF BEING:
Your Guide to Yom Kippur

Yom Kippur is unabashedly transformative; the power of the day beckons us to work toward fundamental transformation and Teshuvah / return to who we really are. Often, the word Teshuvah is unfortunately translated as 'repentance'. It is more accurately rendered as 'return', meaning both a return 'from' our states of spiritual alienation and exile, as well as a 'turning to' experiencing our deepest selves. Yom Kippur empowers us to return to our essence, reclaim who we truly are, and live from that place.

A LIGHTNESS OF BEING delves into the powerful and transformative day of Yom Kippur. Weaving together a multi-dimensional tapestry of practical, allegorical, philosophical and mystical ideas and implications, the teachings gathered herein empower us all to enter Yom Kippur and truly feel enlightened, elevated, lighter and transformed.

———————

THE HAGGADAH:
Pathways to Pesach and the Haggadah

"In every generation a person must regard oneself as having gone out of Mitzrayim / Egypt." This means that when recalling the Exodus, which occurred thousands of years ago, we also need to envision ourselves as being taken out of Mitzrayim and freed from enslavement.

Introducing the Haggadah and the themes of Pesach, this book delves into the greater context of the Festival and the Seder, allowing us to tap into the profound inspiration and Koach / power that Pesach and Seder Night offers.

www.ingramcontent.com/pod-product-compliance
Lightning Source LLC
Chambersburg PA
CBHW041922160426

42812CB00101B/2511